D1664979

IT'S *NOT* ABOUT
YOU

*Ancient Wisdom,
New Leadership*

-THE PARADISE SHAPER METHOD-

PAUL SMILDE

BALBOA.PRESS

A DIVISION OF HAY HOUSE

Balboa Press books may be ordered through booksellers or by contacting:

Balboa Press
A Division of Hay House
1663 Liberty Drive
Bloomington, IN 47403
www.balboapress.com
844-682-1282

Because of the dynamic nature of the Internet, any web addresses or links contained in this book may have changed since publication and may no longer be valid. The views expressed in this work are solely those of the author and do not necessarily reflect the views of the publisher, and the publisher hereby disclaims any responsibility for them.

The author of this book does not dispense medical advice or prescribe the use of any technique as a form of treatment for physical, emotional, or medical problems without the advice of a physician, either directly or indirectly. The intent of the author is only to offer information of a general nature to help you in your quest for emotional and spiritual well-being. In the event you use any of the information in this book for yourself, which is your constitutional right, the author and the publisher assume no responsibility for your actions.

Any people depicted in stock imagery provided by Getty Images are models, and such images are being used for illustrative purposes only. Certain stock imagery © Getty Images.

Print information available on the last page.

ISBN: 978-1-9822-6314-0 (sc)
ISBN: 978-1-9822-6316-4 (hc)
ISBN: 978-1-9822-6315-7 (e)

Library of Congress Control Number: 2021901935

Balboa Press rev. date: 04/23/2021

To Dorine. You're Once, Twice, Three Times a Lady.

*"When the best leader's work is done,
the people say, 'We did it ourselves.'"*
—Lao Tzu

CONTENTS

INTRODUCTION

The Paradise Shaper Method

*"We're taking this amazing group of young, fantastic kids
and put them in corporate environments that care more
about the numbers than they do about these kids. They
care more about the short-term gains than the long-term
life of these young human beings. It's the total lack of good
leadership that's making millennials feel the way they do."*
—Simon Sinek[1]

"Go tell that philosophical crap to some social worker. You clearly have no clue how companies are run!" my parents' friend sneered.

It was the joyful occasion of my mother's fiftieth birthday. My parents had invited their closest friends and family to celebrate at an exclusive restaurant. Upon arrival I bumped into one of their friends who was a seasoned businessman with a strong reputation as a leader who got things done. I had just started my career in corporate finance and was excited about a recent presentation I had attended at my postgraduate course.

The presentation was about a company that had successfully experimented with decision making in circular teams of employees based on "sociocratic" principles. Policy decisions were based on consent, even those involving the selection of individuals for leadership roles in the company. The results were truly encouraging—employees felt engaged in decision making, clear about their priorities, and responsible for the organization's performance.

But I must have hit a red button when talking to my parents' friend. To me, his agitated response felt like a slap in the face. Here I was, a young, ambitious professional with great hopes to contribute to a business environment where every person was valued for their input. At the brink of a new millennium I was certain we needed a different leadership style. The first signs of a dot-com epidemic were evident. Our generation clearly sensed the internet, fueled by dazzling innovation in communication technology, would disrupt entire industries.

As the economy had shifted to the services era, new times called for a different leadership paradigm. How could modern leaders hold on to management structures designed for Adam Smith's industrial revolution of the 1850s? Employees could no longer be considered production assets, performing standardized, repetitive work that had to be supervised in a hierarchical control system. Instead, the traits that really mattered were conceptual capabilities. Their creativity to fulfill customer requirements. Their eagerness to think out of the box and find smarter ways to get the job done. Their ability to see the bigger picture.

That encounter with my parents' friend was exemplary of winter freezing over one last time after the first days of spring. Right upon the millennium change, the internet bubble burst in 2000. Dot-coms as well as information and communication technology firms went bust or lost up to 80 percent of their stock value, leaving the corporate community with the impression it was back to business as usual.

But the tectonic plates on which the global economic foundations were built were definitely shifting. Reckless expansion by the banking industry was the prelude to a massive earthquake in the global financial system in 2008. But through the cracks in the old structures, the green leaves of the 2.0 economy emerged.

This time, the internet firms did gain momentum. As all of us got hooked on smartphones, online shopping, Netflix, Spotify, Airbnb, Uber, and a zillion apps to keep us informed, healthy and amused, incumbent organizations got a clear message. Adapt or become irrelevant.

Yes, most companies and other organizations did adjust their strategies—often successfully. In the past decade, they wrote inspiring mission statements, launched digital platforms, invested heavily in technological advancements, fostered partnerships with the new kids on the block, pruned their organization layers, and shaped open office spaces.

The struggle for relevance triggered one more effect—a laser beam focus on short-term financial results. *Make the month, make the quarter, make the year.* There was increasing top-down pressure to deliver on commitments, igniting endless forecasting and review cycles, budget cuts, hiring freezes, and travel bans. There was hardly any time left for employees to take a moment to relax, reflect on actions taken, and learn and do things in a smarter way next time. People were thrust into a rat race to serve the 24/7 economy. They were made to believe that their golden handcuffs came closest to experiencing a purpose in their earthly existence.

And then the Corona Crisis Struck ...

In early January 2020, the evening news in many countries devoted just a brief segment to the outbreak of this new virus in the Chinese city of Wuhan. The devastating impact of the outbreak of Coronavirus Disease-2019 (COVID-19) initially barely registered on people's radar outside of the Far East. China, and then South Korea, took draconian measures to protect their populations. Wuhan was hermetically sealed. People were ordered to stay in their homes. Hundreds of millions of workers were told not to return from their Chinese New Year's holiday. Temperature measurements, virus detection tests, and even the mandatory use of a health check app were all part of a policy cocktail to curb the trend.

In February 2020, just as China appeared to be controlling the spread, the virus jumped to other nations. European countries rapidly were affected, followed by the United States and eventually almost every other country in the world. Within days, democratic governments took measures that were unthinkable just weeks before—curfews, the complete shutdown of schools and universities, hibernation of nonvital industries, restrictions on grocery shopping, and even military presence on the streets in some countries. Economies that were on the verge of overheating plunged into deep recessions overnight. Millions were sentenced to unemployment and having to worry about their most basic needs such as paying the rent and feeding their families. Dramatic pictures of overcrowded intensive care units and the daily rise in death rates became burned into our retinas forever.

While many were merely trying to weather the storm, a new reality began to dawn—life as we knew it will never be the same again. We entered the Transformation Age. Social media bombarded us with well-intentioned advice and clarifications. Most of the advice failed to explain the very reason this virus struck and in which direction it pointed us. On my first bike ride in the early spring of 2020, I passed a farm. The owner had decorated his trees along the road with words that formed a powerful saying: "Distance is just a test of how far love can travel."

It was a sentiment that wouldn't have looked out of place on a Hallmark card, yet it was one with multiple layers. In a time of social distancing, we are being challenged to find ways to connect on a more meaningful level. We have been given a timeout—a gracious kick in the butt. Is the gold rush we had been pursuing worthwhile if our perceived gains can slip through our fingers in the blink of an eye? What lessons should we learn about creating a sustainable society now that Mother Nature is striking back? How can we rebuild our business environments to adopt the values that inspire our young generations to shape their future?

While the past decades took their toll on my Generation X contemporaries—born between 1965 and 1980—we just hung in there. Concerns about earning a living, supporting the family, and taking care of the mortgage induced us to endure our stress and lack of motivation for our jobs. We denied our ideals for the sake of making money. We sold our soul merely to survive. An utter mistake, as this crisis brutally shows us. At this crossroads in our human development we cannot afford to waste the impeccable talents of the next generations.

The Millennial Delusion

As they embark on their promising business careers, millennials— Generation Y, born between 1981 and 2000—often find themselves confronted by a heartbreaking deception. In many ways they have much more to offer today's companies than previous generations. They are the most educated generation ever. Raised in the digital age, many have magnificent data processing capabilities. They can find simple solutions for complex problems at mind-boggling speed. They are masters of online communication and understand how to touch consumers in their personal space. They have a genuine desire to make an impact on society and to grow quickly in a successful career.

Lured by an inspiring mission statement and wonderful development perspectives, millennials accept jobs and have sky-high expectations. But as soon as the honeymoon is over, reality kicks in. They are instructed to be at the office by 8:00 or 9:00 a.m. and work all day long, sitting still and producing analyses and reports for hours at a time. Their team leads provide task-related instructions and check whether things are done. They are expected to reach out to colleagues, build relationships, and solve issues. They receive feedback only once a year in the form of a performance appraisal, emphasizing "areas for improvement." As for impact, they feel they are at the bottom of the pyramid, with no opportunity to leave their mark on anything meaningful. Up to 17% of millennials in the United States are experiencing depression and 14% suffer from anxiety.[2] And the situation isn't much different in many other Western societies.

What is the cause of the cold shower many millennials experience upon entering the workforce? If we look at the way they were raised, we see the stark contrast with the top-down, financial result-driven systems most organizations have become. Millennials receive lots of attention during their upbringing in the form of praise from their parents and loved ones. Even if they decide not to have children of their own, they tend to put family values above corporate values. They view their manager as *primus inter pares*—first among equals—and expect a lot of recognition and affirmation. Work-life balance and flexible hours are considered high priority, which managers may mistake for lack of commitment. They work hard and efficiently and get things done at a much faster pace than their older colleagues. Owning a house or a car is of lesser importance to them, although that does not imply lesser interest in making money. Millennials like to spend it on other interests, such as events, travel, and gadgets. There is so much more to life than work alone.

On social media, millennials have crafted an illusory image of their marvelously successful, mega-eventful and unimaginably joyful lives. They are married to their smartphone, looking for constant entertainment and confirmation of their relevance in the groups of which they are part. Their core strength of teamwork and inclusiveness has a hidden downside, however, as many millennials have a constant fear of being left out. The contrast of their superstar image on social media and the harsh reality of daily life may give rise to feelings of insecurity or even depression. Many are not used to sitting down and having a heart-to-heart conversation about how they really feel inside. They often avoid conflict and vote with their feet by hopping to the next exciting opportunity to make a difference.

You Can Make a Difference

You may hold a leadership position for a team or an entire organization. Or perhaps you wish to grow your personal leadership. In either case, I have written this book with you in mind. To me, it means you feel a responsibility to connect with other people in a meaningful way. By the end of this book you will realize that this desire to bond, by human design, includes everyone.

We are facing a magnificent leadership challenge as we enter the Transformation Age. I am counting on you. I am offering you a comprehensive pathway to a new leadership era that meets the demands of our confusing times. A self-evident approach that perfectly fits the zeitgeist of today's digital, service-driven economy. A paradigm shift that builds on the premise that people themselves are in the best position to decide how to organize their work. Your employees perfectly know how to improve the processes and quality of their work to deliver an unrivaled customer experience. All you need to do is facilitate the process and be available to them.

Recently millennials have become the largest generation in the workforce. In the years to come, Generation Z—born after the year 2000—will complete their education and start their first jobs. Amazing kids with even more stunning digital processing skills than their millennial predecessors. Yet their upbringing and education have, to an even lesser extent, built their perseverance, social skills, and self-esteem. And these traits will not be built by exercising more top-down pressure and control. As a father of four fantastic children, I feel a deep and personal responsibility to shape work environments where their generation will flourish and be full of joy.

The coronavirus crisis has made it painfully clear that we cannot continue to sanctify the economy by sacrificing ecology. Our world today is facing major perils—including pollution, global warming, rising sea levels, deforestation, extinction of species, floods, droughts, hurricanes, hunger, migration, and terrorism. These challenges are a direct or indirect result of our top-down, short-term-focused, materialistic leadership exercised in companies, governments, and other organizations worldwide. To curb these adverse trends, we need to reinvent ourselves and the way we lead others. This implies a more inclusive leadership style, tapping into the mighty ingenuity of all talent in our organizations.

As leaders, we need to learn how to become transformational coaches and mentors. To feel comfortable not hiding behind our status, our prerogatives, and the dictates of the financial markets. To put it simply, we need to build bridges between our heads and our hearts. Wise new leaders who are prepared to make this transformation are whom I call Paradise Shapers. They learn how to balance their nearsighted thinking with deep intuitive feeling. They make a brave and deliberate transition from our current fear-based systems to sparkling communities of trust. They foster caring environments with a clear sense of direction, in which millennials and all other generations will thrive to provide the answers to the test of our time.

The time has come to shift gear. There's a sweeping solution for grabs if you are courageous enough to make an inward journey in order to become a Paradise Shaper. It's a personal transformation that, granted, will be confrontational at times. But all it takes is a fundamental insight into the development of our human consciousness. Some guidance on proven ways to unleash the resolve, resilience, and resourcefulness of your people. It's my calling to work with you in this direction.

My Personal Journey

What makes me a credible guide to take you on this odyssey? For sure I am no all-knowing guru who will take you home across the ocean of ambiguity. Like everyone else, I stumble from failure to victory. Just when I am certain I have reached a next level of understanding, I find myself taken aback by sudden twists of life. At last, it has dawned on me that I'd rather put the journey above the destination. I have collected some valuable experiences in my backpack that I would love to share with you.

If there's one characteristic that has served me well, it is this—I am eager to learn. As I have turned my hobby into my work, I have coached and guided thousands of people. Most of them may not realize that I am learning just as much as they are. Every day I am having dozens of conversations with anyone prepared to squander their two cents of wisdom. I read thought-provoking books and articles, attend a host of courses, and enjoy watching succinct and surprising TED talks (what a format!). Yet I protect my system against a short circuit of conflicting views with a simple fuse. I won't take the beliefs or opinions of others at face value. I'll only accept a concept as the truth if I can personally experience it. In other words, I have developed an inquisitive attitude. Whatever I hear or read, I check if it really works for me. Trial and error. If I see and feel the benefits, I keep it. If I don't, I dismiss it for now and may explore with additional questions in the future.

Another personal quality, which I can't help really, is my fascination with people. Their colorful versatility, belly-shaking sense of humor, and uncurbed creativity to find solutions in most unlikely circumstances. Their tenacity to pursue long-cherished dreams, flexibility to cope with setbacks, and ability to love unconditionally. Time and again I have been flabbergasted by the hobbies and hidden talents of people who, I'm ashamed to admit, I initially perceived as rather boring. Slowly I found that the more I abandon my judgment and simply observe and listen, the deeper life's lessons unfold. With every acquaintance, I am silently asking, "Why did you cross my path? What is it I can learn from you?"

In my twenty-five-year business career, I have been blessed with many opportunities to lead global organizations through existential transformations. In each of these we changed the game. We boosted customer satisfaction and business growth while achieving significant cost savings. One of these turnarounds is central to the last part of this book. I was faced with a crisis situation in a logistics organization handling billions of dollars in customer deliveries. In just nine months, we managed to curb unfavorable trends in absenteeism and performance. And the best news is—our people did it themselves.

What was the secret to our success? In each of these transformations, my view of organizations differed from those of most of the leaders I met. A company is not a machine that we operate efficiently. We don't just convert input into output to maximize profit. An organization is built on interactions between human beings. It is a living organism. It has its own sense of purpose, energy, and dynamics. We can draw some illuminating parallels with the field of biology. It has taken nature billions of years to organize life from the lowest level up. What lessons can we learn to enhance our organizations?

Another area that fascinated me was the study of anthropology. Looking at human history, it's been only twelve thousand years since our ancestors roamed the forests as hunter-gatherers. I found it hugely interesting to read about studies of native tribes in Middle America who still live in a similar way. To get a feel for the size of their communities, the hierarchy, and the task divisions they applied. It wasn't until people developed farming methods that their communities began to increase in number. Since that time, less than three hundred fifty to five hundred generations have passed. Our physiology has had no chance to carry out major mutations. Our biology has certainly not adapted to our current digital society with all its stimuli. Isn't that a remarkable paradox? We want to understand how people can thrive in today's fast-paced organizations. Still, we'd better look for clues in how our greater-than-great grandparents must have lived.

As I progressed through my career, I adopted all kinds of insights from different angles and disciplines. The ancient wisdom traditions proved to be an invaluable guide. I was in the fortunate position to explore how to truly engage people and let business prosper—insights I am eager to share with you to try out yourself. I really want you and your team members to experience the miracle of enjoying work to the fullest while achieving magnificent results.

How to Become a Paradise Shaper

In this book you'll get lots of ammunition to become a Paradise Shaper yourself. This implies accepting full ownership to transform yourself. You then learn to shape the conditions under which your people will thrive. Thus, you will turn your organization into a paradise for all stakeholders—customers, employees, and partners alike.

To become a Paradise Shaper is a metamorphosis that mirrors the process of a caterpillar transforming into a butterfly. A caterpillar is in a pretty pathetic state. It hardly senses its environment. Its eyes and antennae are immature and its legs won't go far. The caterpillar takes in lots of food as its sole desire is to grow. It will shed its skin up to five times if the old ones become too tight. Once the caterpillar is fully grown, it will enter the cocooning phase as a pupa. On the outside, nothing appears to be happening, yet on the inside a major transition is taking place. The pupa is rapidly growing its talents. The protection of the cocoon is needed for the pupa to gain strength and practice. Once fully grown, the pupa breaks free and leaves the cocoon as a marvelous butterfly. It is showing its true colors, moving freely from flower to flower. Its long antennae and advanced eyes enable the butterfly to be in full contact with its environment. It acts as a catalyst of nature by pollinating plants and flowers. Where butterflies appear, the environment is healthy. Is it any wonder that throughout history, people have been infatuated with butterflies? Almost every language has a unique word to honor these divine creatures.

I have developed the Paradise Shaper method to guide you in your metamorphosis. Over the years I have compiled the core steps and refined them to a natural flow. The Paradise Shaper method provides the essential steps. They are strongly rooted in my twenty-five years of experience in leading successful organizations through impactful transformations. They form a bridge between modern science and ancient teachings of wisdom. A Paradise Shaper combines them into an astute business acumen.

We will cover the complete cycle of your transformation in this book. I will describe to you my personal leadership journey and guide you on yours through eighteen transformation exercises. How do you dissolve stress from your life? How do you uncover the hidden powers of your body? What does it take to gain mastery over your mind? What does a real connection with others imply? How will you surpass your goals without being result-oriented? What is the secret to ceaseless creativity? Stay tuned for answers to all these questions—and more!

What's the Structure?

Here's a summary of what you may expect to learn:

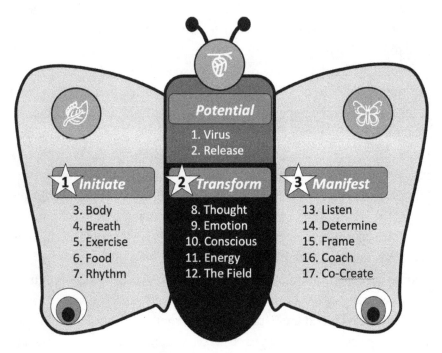

Exhibit 1—The Paradise Shaper Method.

Prelude—A Blessing in Disguise
Potential (... the Egg)

This prelude provides new perspectives to trigger your thinking. It is evident that the impact of the coronavirus crisis goes well beyond a nasty inconvenience. Measures instituted to prevent a healthcare collapse have ignited an economic recession. Six-foot social distancing transmuted our culture and deprived us of our liberties to travel, work, and socialize. What is the deeper trend that has come to surface and how can you grasp the opportunities that are emerging?

Part I—You Too Are a Caveman
Initiate (... the Caterpillar)

In this Part, we will kick off with the carrier of your existence—your body. Our physiology has developed over millions of years to function optimally in our environment. Only in recent times have we altered our surroundings to our convenience. What is the impact on your breathing, eating, exercising, and sleeping habits? How do you best manage your energy level throughout the day?

Part II—Consciousness? Awesome!
Transform (... the Pupa)

This Part dives deep into the stunning insight that our outer world is merely a playground of what really matters in life— our inner development. Our experience is 100 percent a creation of our own thoughts. As we become conscious of the design of life, our notion of inclusiveness is bound to grow. How does the mind really work? How can you choose the thoughts you wish to pursue? What does it mean to be a conscious leader? How can you connect with the source of unlimited creativity and wisdom?

Part III—Paradise Shaper Leadership
Manifest (... the Butterfly)

In this Part, we will explore how to plant the seed of genuine engagement by fulfilling a silent yet heartfelt cry that your people subconsciously utter: "Notice me!" How do you tune your antennae to their real questions and views? How do you co-create a path to the future that they fully endorse? What does it take to activate your change agents to gain experience with the proposed direction? In other words, how do you groom your team to unlock boundless opportunities and Shape Your Paradise?

SHAPE YOUR PARADISE *ONLINE*

The Paradise Shaper method is at the heart of all our online transformational coaching, in-company programs, and leadership expeditions. At Paradise Shaper Academy, we believe in blended learning. Some people love to read. Others like to listen or watch videos. The one thing that matters is you will only transform if you practice your new insights. We have therefore created an online self-coaching series called Shape Your Paradise. The program follows the structure of this book. We have put together three modules, each comprising five weekly lessons—one for each chapter of this book (starting at Chapter 3). A total of ninety insights and transformation exercises are presented in the form of videos and podcasts. Each week you apply this powerful material directly in your life and work. I really want you to have this unique experience. Visit www.paradiseshaper.com to deepen your transformation!

Do you want to become a Paradise Shaper Coach yourself? Pursue a life-changing career switch or enrich your current practice? Do you really wish to master our proven Paradise Shaper method and take leaders and their teams into the Transformation Age? We offer the unique opportunity for a limited number of candidates to be trained and certified as a Paradise Shaper Coach. Our intensive training program not only deepens your expertise in human design, you also extensively train your transformational coaching skills in a safe environment. As we want your coaching practice to thrive, business development is an integral part of our Paradise Shaper Coach program. Find out what's possible for you at www.paradiseshaper.com!

The Leadership Paradox

Your personal transformation is at the heart of the organizational change you wish to accomplish. The buck stops with you to Shape Your Paradise. And at the same time, it is crucial to realize one thing:

It's *NOT* about *YOU*

How are you to comprehend this paradox? It will all become clear as each chapter builds on the previous one in a powerful sequence. You are about to embark on a discovery expedition that will take you to the core of your being as an individual and a leader.

I feel honored that you're making the effort to become a Paradise Shaper. You are willing to move inward, face your inhibitions, and find your inner treasures. That is what Paradise Shaper Leadership demands of us. On behalf of your team, I would like to thank you in advance. I am convinced you will find our journey most rewarding!

Let's get started. Sit back, relax, and enjoy the ride!

—PRELUDE—

A BLESSING IN DISGUISE

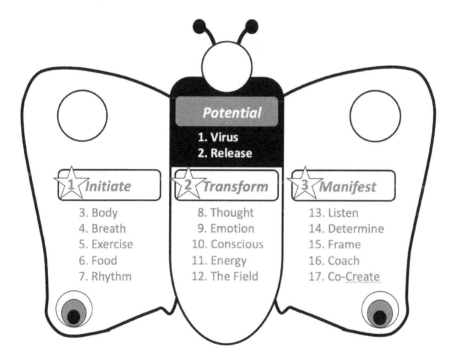

The virus is Nature's way to restore balance.
You're invited to become aware of what really matters
and learn to connect on a much deeper level.

POTENTIAL

Hatch the Lessons of the Corona Crisis

... the Egg

*"It [the coronavirus] is reminding us that we are all
equal, regardless of our culture, religion, occupation,
financial situation, or how famous we are. This disease
treats us all equally, perhaps we should, too."*
—Bill Gates

This Prelude paints the context of the transformational process
we will explore in Parts I to III. It contains two chapters in which
we'll take a deeper look at the coronavirus crisis. Is this virus just a
nuisance, a hiccup after which we'll resume our busy lives as Homo
consumens—people whose main purpose is to consume in pursuit
of pleasure? Or could there be a deeper cause?

- ❖ In Chapter 1 we'll briefly look at the role of viruses in our
  evolution. Then we'll take a closer look at the message that
  the coronavirus is giving us based on ancient wisdom.
- ❖ In Chapter 2 we'll explore the cyclical nature of the systems
  we're part of, such as economic relations and warfare. We'll
  discover the perfect timing of the virus outbreak and our
  unique task as leaders to take full advantage of this crisis
  and shift gear.

Never Waste a Good Crisis

While parking my car in the lot, I take a half-minute break before
getting out. It's early March 2020, the coronavirus is in the country,
and I am heading to conduct an interview for an article. I notice how

awkward it all feels. There is no talk of a lockdown yet, but we're requested to replace the handshake with an elbow salute and wash our hands regularly. I enter the premises, use the disinfectant, and as I turn around my interviewee walks up to me with an outstretched hand. "You must be Ellen," I say, extending my elbow toward her with an uneasy smile. "Ah, that's right. We're not supposed to shake hands," Ellen smirks.

As we sit down to start our small talk, I inquire about the measures Ellen is taking in his company. "Yeah, we'll need to weather the storm," she says. "We'll try to keep the business going and get back to normal as soon as possible. I guess it will take a month or so, maybe until summer. We're going on a cruise in the Caribbean in June, so I really hope this is over soon."

Evidently, the cruise didn't happen, and the company took more stringent measures just a few weeks later. Temporary workers were dismissed and office workers were asked to work from home and accept a salary cut. The factory continued to be operational until suppliers were unable to meet their delivery obligations. Before long, the company depended on government support to survive. And all of this in less than five weeks.

In these surreal times, our lives have been turned completely upside down. Everything that seemed certain to us has rapidly changed in unprecedented ways. We have seen the images on social media and TV of crowded intensive care units, funerals with hardly any attendees, and seniors greeted from outside the window by their children. Our hearts go out to the large number of those who have died and their families. It is weird how we long to bond emotionally yet serve each other best by keeping a physical distance. Fear for our health and financial future occupies our minds. We're thrown to the lowest level of Maslow's Pyramid as we're "looting" the stores for canned food and toilet paper.

But something dawned on me recently. This is merely the end of our days as we know them. This crisis forces us to quit being focused on our outer expansion and personal wealth for a while. To accept the cyclical nature of every creative process and make an inward journey. To take a break from all external stimuli and reconnect with ourselves.

As I reflect and explore what is really happening, I find a treasure hidden beneath the drama. This crisis was not accidental. It did not happen just because someone might have eaten a sick bat from a market in Wuhan. That's merely the form in which the drama manifested itself. In reality it's a seemingly rude yet effective way for nature to give us an unmistakable message. As humanity, we have reached the end of our "caterpillar" era. We've consumed our environment by creating a footprint that goes far beyond the level our planet can carry sustainably. We haven't understood how to share. Half the world's population owns only 1 percent of wealth, while the richest 1 percent knows exactly how to play the capitalist system—and the gap is widening. Concurrently, the vast majority of employees worldwide aren't happy, with growing numbers suffering burnout and depression.

This crisis may be a blessing in disguise. The teacher kicked us out of the classroom to reflect on our behavior. We've been sent home to enter our cocooning phase. To understand what really matters in life and at work. To develop our hidden talents. To find ways to truly connect with each other. To learn how to become a lighter version of ourselves. It's a complete shift in our thinking to become more inclusive, joyful, and much more effective. Only then will we be ready to spread our wings as colorful butterflies.

1

VIRUS OR VACCINE?

"We long to return to normal, but normal led to this."
—Ed Yong

Viruses Boosted Our Evolution

Where there is life, there are viruses. They have been around for billions of years. Life on Earth started some 3.5 billion years ago with bacteria. These single-celled organisms took 1.8 billion years— almost half the time between their origin and today—to learn how to collaborate and become multicellular organisms. By specialization and ever-increasing division of tasks, these organisms evolved. They developed into a wide diversity of increasingly complex life forms. Our body contains fifty to seventy-five trillion cells, all interacting and aligning their activities in spectacular ways.

So why have viruses been around throughout evolution? Some researchers even suggest they might have come first. They have possibly been the steppingstone from protein molecules to cellular life. Others argue that viruses have a common ancestor with bacteria. They found ways to become increasingly lighter, while bacteria grew more complex. In any case, viruses are extremely efficient. They are, in essence, a tiny protein bag carrying genetic material (such as DNA). They are experts in attaching themselves to exactly those cells they aim to attack. A virus needs a host, a living cell, in order

5

to multiply as it instructs the cell's genes to do so. And then it kills the host cell, or it becomes latent to take its chance for a later time when the host cell is in stress.

Viruses are feared for the diseases they cause, such as the flu, herpes, measles, or AIDS—and COVID-19. What most people don't know is that we have well over a hundred trillion virus particles in our body. Some of these viruses are fully integrated into our cells' DNA! In other words, the virus DNA has enriched our human genetic material. In fact, many jumps in evolution have been ignited by viruses. Even coronaviruses have been around for millions of years throughout mammalian evolution. It's just that COVID-19 is novel—a new variant.

Viruses are particularly geared to impacting proteins. Proteins provide structure to cells. They are responsible for key functions in a cell, such as chemical reactions (think of hormones), communication, and transport. Certain proteins act as receptors to which the virus binds. To evade the binding of a new virus, a cell will try to alter the protein composition of its receptor. Recent scientific research by Stanford University suggest that "30 percent of all protein adaptations since humans' divergence with chimpanzees have been driven by viruses."[3]

While 98.5 percent of our human DNA equals that of chimpanzees, what really sets us apart is our more advanced brain, our neocortex. And within the neocortex, the far more developed prefrontal lobe is what makes us truly unique. It enables us to be self-aware, to not be solely ruled by our instincts and patterns. It allows us to rethink the past and learn from it. It helps us to visualize the future and plan ahead so we can prevent trouble and improve ourselves. As such, we have the capacity to be boundlessly creative and Shape Our Paradise.

Until recently, it was quite a mystery how evolution was triggered to endow Homo sapiens with this spectacular prefrontal lobe. The reason for this giant leap from our ancestors (Homo erectus) could not be explained by any environmental changes. What induced our appearance on Earth some two hundred thousand years ago? If we put these first modern human beings on the operating table to study their anatomy and physiology, we would find that they were virtually identical to our bodies today.

Yes, there had been spectacular changes in temperature, but these appear to follow a cyclical pattern. And the control of fire some three hundred thousand years ago allowed primeval humans to extract more nutrients from their food by cooking it. At best, this has caused some modest mutations. This cannot explain how we were already equipped to drive all of our technological innovations of the past centuries at a time when we were still roaming nature as hunter-gatherers. We were hugely overdeveloped to survive in our environment at the time. What accelerated the expansion of our brain capacity? We now have a plausible explanation—virus infections caused our sudden cognitive enhancement. But *why* did they do that?

The Art of Vaccination

Throughout history, people depended completely on their immune system to defuse viruses. It was the survival of the most adaptable—if the immune system found ways to overcome or neutralize the virus, the person would live. If the immune system couldn't handle the attack, the person would die. If an entire species were defenseless against a virus, it became extinct.

A virus that tormented human societies for more than two thousand years was smallpox. It is estimated to have killed more than five hundred million people in the last hundred years until its eradication in 1980. Smallpox was a highly contagious disease. It would start with high fever, muscle pain, and fatigue. Those symptoms were followed by lesions in the mouth and then the skin, causing pimples all over the face and body. The most common form of the disease, *variola major*, had a death rate of around 30 percent.

During the Ming dynasty in sixteenth-century China, an inoculation technique was developed to make smart use of the body's own immune system. Rather than waiting for the virus to attack, it was proactively embraced in a controlled way. Crusts were removed

7

from the skin of patients who had caught *variola minor*, a milder form of smallpox with a mortality rate of 1–2 percent. These crusts were ground to powder and blown into the nostrils of healthy people. In this controlled manner, they would usually contract only a mild form of the disease. Their immune system would develop enough antibodies to withstand a smallpox attack when they came into contact with an infected patient. In eighteenth-century Europe, the technique was further refined by rubbing *variola minor* virus material into a small wound on the hand of a healthy person. The disease was usually only visible on the arm and left limited scar tissue.

A revolution in the fight against smallpox occurred when Edward Jenner developed the first vaccine in 1796. Jenner discovered that inoculation with cowpox virus material, rather than smallpox material, was much safer and more effective, while symptoms were greatly reduced. The word vaccine actually stems from the Latin word for cow—*vacca*. Over time, the knowledge and application of vaccines has been further enhanced. Worldwide vaccination programs eventually led to the official end of smallpox. Other diseases that are effectively prevented or treated with vaccines include polio, measles, tetanus, rubella, rabies, and diphtheria.

The use of vaccines prevents millions of deaths every year. However, a new trend is gaining momentum in industrialized countries. The number of parents who are against their children's vaccination is increasing. They may have religious or other objections that have a certain validity. These reasons aside, people may have simply forgotten about the devastating impact of infectious diseases on entire populations. The potential danger of a virus had become inconceivable in our modern society. Until the coronavirus struck.

Ancient Wisdom

It is remarkable how the coronavirus brought the whole world to its knees within a matter of months, if not weeks. It struck our hectic existence like thunder from a clear sky. The vulnerability of our health and of the society and economy we created became painfully clear. Our gold-rush and entertainment bubble proved meaningless.

Is it just bad luck we had to overcome to get back to where we left off before this crisis? Could this pandemic really be reduced to the incessant talk-show discussions of precautions to flatten the curve, absorbing the economic damage, and the race to vaccinate people? How about you? Confined to your home, have you had a chance to make an inward journey? Or have you simply transferred your action mode to an online environment, working day and night to replan and set new goals?

Advances in life sciences continue to amaze us. Within a year a handful of vaccines have been developed and approved to protect our population. But it would be imprudent to resume our normal life as if nothing happened. There are lessons to be learned. Deep insights we must grasp if we want human life on Earth to have a future. The real answers to our contemporary problems are found in an unexpected source—the ancient wisdom traditions from all across the globe. They will open our eyes and provide us with clear direction amid uncertain times. We will unveil the undeniable task and magnificent opportunity that awaits us as leaders.

Here are five insights the ancient wisdom traditions share:

1) Nature operates as one integrated system that is constantly seeking balance.
2) As human beings, we live in the illusion that we are separate individuals. We're not!
3) We're part of a bigger purpose—nature wants to raise our consciousness.
4) The secret to shaping our own future lies in learning to navigate our inner world.
5) We are carried by a Field of Intelligence that's in our direct awareness.

One Integrated System

The whole planet is one body that is constantly seeking balance. There is an implicate order in all of nature. A balance between receiving and giving is observed at every level. This equilibrium is visible even at the atomic level, where negatively charged electrons circle a nucleus of neutrons and positively charged protons. Photosynthesis, the process by which plants and trees convert water and carbon dioxide into oxygen and organic food, is a next-level example. In the animal kingdom, as beautifully depicted in Disney's *The Lion King*, a balance of species is maintained; instinct will keep even predators from consuming more than they need.

Everything is interconnected. If the balance is distorted, nature will find ways to restore its equilibrium. Scientific support for this ancient insight was first provided by James Lovelock in the 1970s. Working as a consultant for NASA, he developed the Gaia hypothesis, which suggests that all living organisms provide feedback to Earth. Thus, a self-regulating system is enacted in order to maintain the conditions for life on Earth.[4] Global warming, the rise in ocean levels, and extreme weather events of the past decade with hurricanes, floods, and droughts should all be viewed as corrective actions by our planet to end excessive human exploitation. While initially received with skepticism, the hypothesis has meanwhile been adopted and substantiated by thousands of scientists.

Viruses are an important means for nature to restore balance. As viruses have played a key role in our evolution, it shouldn't come as a surprise that nature released the coronavirus in order to achieve exactly what happened—a temporary standstill of human activity. Air traffic and commuting shut down, factories closed, streets emptied, and people were sent home for reflection. Since we didn't take previous messages seriously, it took a more effective tool from nature's arsenal to slow us down and contemplate our future.

Piercing the Illusion of Separation

As human beings, we are equipped with the most incredible technology in the form of our brain and body. We have instant access to the ingenuity of billions of years of evolution. The problem is that the user manual got lost in translation. We have developed only a fraction of our capabilities. We focused our attention outward in pursuit of safety, convenience, and entertainment. Our progress has been impressive, especially in the post-World War II era. Never in human history has there been more peace, health, and prosperity.

If there is one thing this pandemic clearly demonstrates, it is that we are all connected. Within weeks after its international outbreak, the virus had spread to nearly every country in the world. Without realizing it, in the past decade, we have become one global society. Our technological innovation has connected everyone in the world through travel and, of course, the internet. Our economies are fully intertwined, our financial crises are just as contagious as the virus itself, and our environmental problems affect us all. Regardless of the walls we build, refugees will cross borders in search of a better life.

And yet we live in the illusion that we are separate individuals. Unlike all other life on Earth, we do not know how to receive in order to share. We don't just take what we need, we take what we can. We lack mastery of our inner technology and believe we must survive in a world of scarcity. Thus we've become extremely competitive and are driven by an internal program that's constantly controlling our thoughts—what's in it for me? But it will never fulfill us. The pleasure of new toys and accomplishments fades within days, and then we chase the next thing. We're yearning for freedom, fulfillment, and connection but don't know how to change the game. Our discontent stems from a complete fallacy in our thinking. It's our individual egoism that, on a collective scale, is at the root of every crisis we are facing—whether it is environmental, financial, work motivation, terrorism, inequality, or hunger. It's time to see through the illusion and study our user manual, which the ancient wisdom traditions now openly share, to find inner peace and true connection.

A Bigger Purpose

Our life is not arbitrary. We did not come to this world by a series of random turns in evolution. We are neither sinful nor expected to endure the miseries of life to earn a better afterlife. We're not punished for bad behavior. We're simply reminded that our time has come to take a crucial step in our evolution as human beings.

There is a clear purpose to our existence. As humanity we are at the summit of 13.8 billion years of evolution since the Big Bang. A long history of increasingly complex collaboration at an ever-faster pace has made us who we are today. Electrons and protons took ages to become atoms. Atoms slowly figured out how to construct molecules. Molecules found an ingenious way to form a living cell. These three steps alone took ten billion years. Then cells slowly joined forces to develop increasingly complex organisms such as plants and animals. And in the past five million years since prehistoric man evolved from apes, our brain capacity has expanded remarkably.

We're in every sense unique. We're the only species that is fully aware of its existence. We have gradually developed that consciousness since the first Homo sapiens (modern human being) saw the light about two hundred thousand years ago. The society that we're part of has expanded from about thirty-five people in our early days as hunter-gatherers to virtually all people in the world today. With each subsequent generation, our notion of what's important in life has changed. And the speed of change is exponential. Every time we got in over our heads, we entered a crisis in which a new perspective emerged. A solution from a higher intelligence. A new view that has brought us closer to the truth of life.

Our purpose is to attain the power of creation. To experience life in its purest form. Our gateway there is to connect in a meaningful way to all life on our planet. The journey of our evolution isn't the survival of the fittest. It's a discovery of what it takes to move from egoism to altruism. To learn to receive in order to share.

Our individual egoism has come to an all-time high. Our current value systems aren't up to the task of solving our many challenges.

We need to break through and become a lighter version of ourselves. The coronavirus invites us to form a new mindset and raise our level of consciousness.

Shape Your Paradise

To expand our consciousness is first and foremost an inward journey. For most people this is unknown territory. Western culture is focused almost entirely on the external world. The education we enjoy from our parents, teachers, and employers is geared to maneuvering safely and successfully in this outer world. We learn where to go and not go, what situations to avoid, what actions to take to yield results, and what is supposed to matter in life. It's rational thinking that counts along with pursuit of status and financial success.

In our material world, emotions and feelings are often considered a nuisance. To soothe our busy mind and numb our worries we pursue all sorts of kicks—vacations across the globe, drugs, alcohol overconsumption, excessive junk food, Netflixing, YouTubing, gaming, porn, social media, and shop-until-you-drop, just to mention some. But when the fun is over, the pain is still there and growing. Of every six employees worldwide, five are not engaged at work. Half of the American population is overweight or obese. One in five millennials in industrialized nations experience burnout symptoms. One in three people in Western societies use antidepressives. On a global basis, more people die from suicide than war. School shootings, especially in America, hit the news regularly.

What we haven't learned is to navigate our inner world. Our mainstream societies lack the complete wisdom of the realm of our emotions and feelings. We aren't taught any energy techniques that enable us to manage our health. We don't have a clue how the mind really works and how we can effectively focus it to find clarity. We don't know how to balance our emotions and free our confidence and attain innate bliss. It's a world that goes way beyond the weekly yoga class or basic mindfulness course that have become popular in

13

recent years. Our inner world is as vast as the outer world. With some practice, we'll learn to explore it safely and effectively.

Life's best kept secret is that mastery of our inner world defines our success in the outer world. Everything in the world originated in a thought. Our inner world is where every thought first appears. The quality of our thinking completely depends on inner mastery. If our thinking is conditioned by our fears, as it is for most people, our limiting beliefs will limit the outcomes we create for ourselves. As we learn to liberate ourselves from these habits in our inner world, we open our creative potential.

Paradise Shapers confidently navigate their inner world and set the conditions for their people to liberate their motivation. In deep connection, they create the solutions that are valuable for their customers and for society in the Transformation Age. Thus, they Shape Their Paradise.

The Field of Intelligence

As we've lost touch with our inner world, we have also been completely alienated from a source that's readily available. There's a Field of Intelligence, a world of infinite possibility, into which we can tap for instant inspiration. As "woo-woo" as this may sound, it actually is obvious. It's the force that entices trees to grow, birds to migrate across continents, and babies to learn to stand. Although you're not aware of it, it perfectly tunes the functioning of your organs, the growth of your hair, and your rejuvenation while you sleep at night. Every cell of every living being is directly connected with the Field and operates optimally through its guidance.

As human beings, we have been endowed with a special gift— our self-awareness. But we're using it poorly. We're concerned about ourselves and try to control our circumstances. Our negative thinking is reflected in negative emotions that drain our energy and distort our well-being. If we do this long enough, we unknowingly train our mind and body to adopt self-destructive habits. As a result, we suffer, develop disease, and don't live the life we desire.

Yet we're designed to excel. If we learn to focus our attention, we can directly experience the Field. You can actually do this right now. Just sit still, close your eyes, and notice you're alive. Go ahead, I'll wait ...

... Have you done it? How was it? Did you find it hard or was it easy? Did your mind get carried away by thoughts? That's exactly what I mean. We're so used to feeding our habitual thoughts with our attention that we lose touch with who we truly are. We don't see the sun anymore as it's covered by the thick cloud cover of our thoughts. But the sun is shining. Always has. Always will. If we learn to tune our awareness to our aliveness and integrate it in our daily activities, miracles will happen. The more we get out of the way, the easier it becomes. We'll get the brightest ideas, find it easy to make decisions, experience unity with others, and feel lifted in our performance.

But the moment we entertain a thought of concern for ourselves, the magic ends. It's as if our Wi-Fi connection is interrupted and we no longer have access to the internet. We feel left to our own devices and have only our own hard disk of memory from which to retrieve data. We become nearsighted and develop even more negative thoughts that are triggered by past experiences. Our body responds and expresses emotions of agitation, frustration, dejection, or anger. This again feeds our thoughts, and before long, we're in a vicious circle.

It isn't the situation that's causing this. It's us. Our own thoughts trigger this chain of events. And what's even worse, these thoughts and feelings get hardwired in our brain and body. We are more likely to respond to outer events in similar ways time and again. In this book we'll explore how this mechanism works and what you can learn—or rather unlearn—to stabilize your Wi-Fi connection and experience a state of flow more often. And thus you will learn to tap from the Field of Intelligence!

A Lighter Me

COVID-19 is certainly a dangerous virus. Most efforts in the months following the outbreak were geared to the quest for an effective vaccine by which we regain our freedom. But looking through a different lens, the coronavirus might be nature's vaccine against humanity's ego virus, which threatens our collective well-being and the planet on which we live. The longer we allow our fear of survival to rule our behavior, the more creative nature will become to make us jump off the diving board. Once we do, we'll plunge into an ocean of abundance and prove to be excellent swimmers.

It's not as hard as it seems, and it's more real than ever before. The essence of what's needed is to stop worrying about yourself.

Will my boss consider me a strong leader? Will I be able to get a promotion? What happens if I don't meet my targets? How will my team think about me? Will my partner respect me if I fail? How about my friends and family?

These very thoughts are the barriers that keep you from being yourself. It's not about you! You're a channel to radiate energy to your team, your customers, your managers, your family, your friends, and everybody else. Allow it to flow and you'll literally be "in flow." You'll also learn to train your team to be in flow more often. It's a wonderful paradox—a true cosmic joke. The less you are concerned about the result of your actions, the better you perform. As human beings we are endowed with a magical capacity to visualize our future. If done correctly, it prompts our mind to realize our vision while surrendering its active control to make it happen. Thus, we'll learn to become a lighter version of ourselves.

TOP THREE TAKEAWAYS

1) Viral infections have been around for billions of years and played a crucial part in our evolution. Recent research suggests that the sudden cognitive boost that sets Homo sapiens apart from our ancestors can be attributed to viruses.

2) Nature operates as one integrated system that is constantly seeking balance. What if nature released the coronavirus in order to achieve exactly what happened—a temporary standstill of human activity? It was time to reflect on our behavior and reset our priorities.

3) The secret to shaping our own future lies in learning to navigate our inner world. In deep connection, Paradise Shapers create the solutions that are valuable for their customers and for society in the Transformation Age.

THE GREAT RELEASE

"Yesterday I was clever,
so I wanted to change the world.
Today I am wise,
so I am changing myself."
—Rumi

Everything Moves in Cycles

The universe has a cyclical nature. We're quite aware that the Earth revolves around the sun, which we use to determine the length of our year. And since the Earth is tilted at 23.5 degrees, we go through the different seasons because of the varying amounts of sunlight per day and changes in weather that result. The moon's orbits around the Earth form the basis for our months, although we have slightly adapted their length to fit our calendar. Because the Earth rotates on its own axis, we have the measure of a day. As the Earth spins round, the moon's gravitational pull on the oceans varies, which is why we have the tides of ebb and flow.

As our societies have become increasingly detached from nature, we tend to think of time as a straight line. This is especially true for Western cultures. We plan for uninterrupted growth, and if a crisis hits, we immediately recalculate and define an updated growth plan. But companies and other organizations are formed by people and, therefore, are also living organisms. They must abide by the rules of nature, which means that their development is cyclical. Or spiral when taking next-level cycles into account. This development is studied by complexity theory. Let's first get introduced to this field and then revisit how two global arenas of human interaction have both shaped complex systems of a cyclical nature—economic relations and military conflict.

In the last fifty years, complexity theory has emerged as a new field of science that studies the collective behavior of complex systems. This discipline aims to help us understand both the interactions between the elements that constitute systems as well as the exchange of systems with their external environment. The Adaptive Cycle (see exhibit 2) provides a simple framework to understand the dynamics of complex ecosystems.[5] These dynamics can be found everywhere in nature, be it living cells, organisms, entire forests, or the climate. Likewise they apply to all forms of collaboration between people, such as transportation or communication systems, or a city or country.

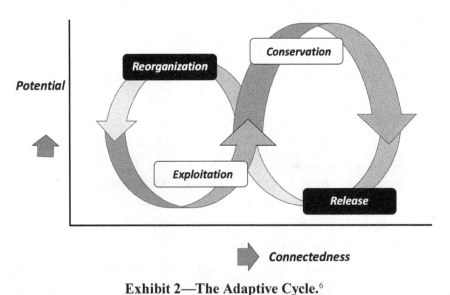

Exhibit 2—The Adaptive Cycle.[6]

When a system is first formed—meaning its elements are sufficiently connected and there is a purpose to their collaboration—the system experiences a phase of **exploitation**. As the elements connect more tightly, the potential—the benefits of the collaboration—is rapidly growing. This is the entrepreneurial phase in companies. At some point, however, the system begins to experience a slowdown in its growth potential. The system has entered the **conservation** phase, in which it becomes increasingly inflexible to adapting to changes in its environment. In companies, this is the bureaucracy phase, when central functions are formed that create rules and exercise control. In due course, the changing environment (external) and the collaborating elements (internal) begin to destabilize the system.

At a certain point, the tension that has been building up causes an implosion of the system. It's a phase of creative destruction, which in complexity theory is called a **release**. The ties that hold the elements together are cut loose and the system experiences a freefall. It's a time of great disturbance for the elements as all certainties vanish overnight. Yet this phase is badly needed to create the necessary space to build a new future. Much energy that was stored in the system is set free and is now used to find improved ways of collaboration. The system enters the **reorganization** phase, in which the elements are placed in an advanced new order. Some upcoming elements that weren't given the oxygen to grow in the incumbent lineup now take advantage of the newly created order. Former dominant elements are relegated to playing second fiddle. It's the restructuring phase in companies that sets the stage for the next cycle of expansion.

The system then embarks on a new exploitation phase at a higher level of potential than the previous cycle. Of course, certain systems may be shattered altogether during the release phase. The underlying elements may be heading in different directions and join alternative systems. This is the force of evolution, which constantly adjusts and improves different forms of collaboration as it reaches a more advanced level. Both the exploitation and conservation phases tend to take a vast amount of time, while the release and reorganization phases are likely to be much faster.

Economic Relations

Robb Smith, CEO of the digital platform Integral Life, wrote a most insightful essay that explains the imminent economic breakdown called "The Great Release." At the time of its publication in 2017, amid a glorious economic boom, it was hard to fathom that this economic doom scenario would indeed be unfolding in just a few years' time.

The past eight hundred years represent the capitalist era, which can be divided into four evolutionary cycles of economic accumulation.[7] In each of these cycles, one economic power dominated global economic relations. This power is called the hegemon. The hegemon initially leads a period of rapid economic expansion (the exploitation phase) by focusing on trade. Its example is followed by other powers, leading to a signal crisis, which marks the end of this first phase. Consequently, the hegemon shifts gear from trade to finance (the conservation phase). It uses its excess cash to fund and invest in political entities that help to preserve its power. Over time, the capital accumulation of the happy few undermines social cohesion with the masses. As the system loses its resilience, it is unable to respond to changing dynamics—both external and internal.

Eventually, the hegemon's reign ends in a terminal crisis (the release phase). This is a period of significant disruption and economic depression that shakes the existing order on its foundations. In this period, the prevailing economic paradigms start to shift. Existing monopolies falter and capital is released for new entrepreneurs to market innovations. A new hegemon gets the chance to manifest its leadership and shape a new economic order (the reorganization phase). The system is now resilient to deal with higher complexity, and a new cycle of capital growth commences driven by trade expansion (see exhibit 3).

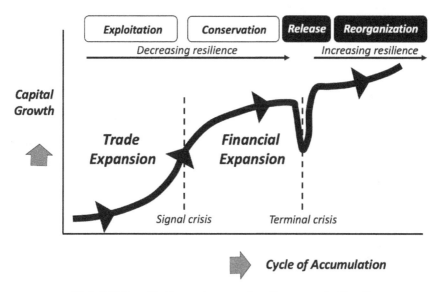

Exhibit 3— Patterns in a cycle of accumulation.[8]

In the fifteenth and sixteenth century, the city of Genoa (in today's Italy) was the dominant player in the first economic cycle. Initially focusing on trade, it had to switch to financial innovations (such as bills of exchange) upon the bankruptcy of Spain in 1557 (the signal crisis). It became the financier of the major powers in Europe. Spain needed to fund its war against Dutch rebels, who tried to liberate their country from Spanish rule. Spain's second bankruptcy in 1627 marked the terminal crisis of the prevailing economic order. This was a decisive event in the first decade of the Thirty Years' War—the first systemic war in which virtually all European powers were involved.

When this deadly war finally ended with the Treaty of Westphalia in 1648, the Republic of the Seven United Netherlands emerged as the next economic hegemon to lead the way in trade expansion. Leveraging their naval supremacy—which today we would consider piracy—the Dutch turned Amsterdam into a commercial powerhouse. When other nations followed the Dutch mercantilist strategy, the Netherlands switched to financial innovation around 1740, establishing the world's first stock market. The Dutch funded wars between France and Britain, as well the fight for freedom by the thirteen colonies in the New World, to which the Dutch could relate. Again, the cycle ended in a war, as Britain retaliated by attacking and defeating the Dutch fleet in 1784. It proved only a prelude to another systemic war that tormented the European people when France's Napoleon waged war across the continent. The bloodshed of the Napoleonic era ended at the Vienna peace conference in 1814.

Now Great Britain had become the leading commercial nation. Trade expansion was spurred by the industrial revolution, particularly the production of railways, ships, and textiles. It took several decades for other nations to catch up, which eventually resulted in a price war in the early 1870s. The signal crisis that forced Great Britain to change course to *haute finance* was the Great Depression of 1873, which lasted until 1896. Britain financed a serious buildup of military force across Europe as populism and nationalism were on the rise. For the third time, a cruel systemic war was fought in Europe, heralding the release phase. While Britain was one of the victors, it was the United States that reluctantly made its entry as the likely new hegemon. The Roaring Twenties merely turned out to be a temporary extension of the status quo. After the stock market crash of 1929, Britain renounced the British pound's gold standard in 1931, marking the end of British dominance.

We are all educated about the Great Depression of the 1930s and the atrocities of World War II, which was truly fought on a global scale. In fact, we can regard the entire period from the start of World War I to the end of World War II as one release phase, which for the third time spanned three decades. The United States took the initiative in the reorganization phase. It outlined the Bretton-Woods currency standard by virtue of which the U.S. dollar became the world's reserve currency. It orchestrated the founding of the United Nations and set the terms for global trade. It launched the Marshall Plan to get war-ridden nations back on their feet and enforced the end of colonialism. In the footsteps of America, the world economy experienced rapid annual growth of 5 percent between 1950 and 1970. Yet a new signal crisis emerged. The Bretton-Woods currency system collapsed in 1971, followed by a global oil crisis in 1973 and an ensuing stock market crash and economic recession. And what did the United States do? As we've seen in the previous three cycles, the hegemon shifted its focus from trading to financial leadership.

Neoliberalism became the new adage. President Reagan unleashed all ties for multinational capital to flow and flourish. An unrivaled belief in private markets and shareholder value led to a retreat of government from typical public sector domains such as education, healthcare, culture, infrastructure, and even prisons. Just as in the three previous cycles, financialization disguised the fact that the hegemon's leadership position was dwindling away. Smith depicts a host of statistics that demonstrate how irresilience has extended to virtually every aspect of society:

➢ Entrepreneurship is replaced by cash-rich multinational powerhouses.
➢ Federal regulation has grown fivefold since 1960.
➢ With sugar intake, the percentage of obese Americans has tripled from 12 percent in 1974 to 36 percent in 2010.
➢ The money spent on healthcare has risen from 7 percent to nearly 17 percent of GDP in the same timeframe.
➢ Education spending per pupil has exploded while results are stagnant.
➢ Political polarization is at an all-time peak.

Now that the world is connected as one global economy, the trend of financialization is visible everywhere. Smith argues that we're already in the release phase of the present cycle, which we entered with the financial crisis of 2008. While the consequences of the irresponsible and unethical fundamentals on which the financial system is built became painfully clear, we have not really learned our lesson. Banks and incumbent industrial giants were bailed out and the party continued as if nothing really happened. Government debt of the G7 (the world's largest trading nations) has quadrupled since 1973. Central banks of the United States, Europe, and Japan created an unprecedented money supply that has already led to significant inflation. It's not visible in our grocery spending, but as a bubble in stock and real estate prices. This pre-coronavirus period may be likened to the Roaring Twenties, a final chord of the old economic order, because a profound reorganization phase after World War I had not yet come about.

People aren't stupid. They feel the system has become irresilient. They face the consequences of the closed factories, the unjust distribution of profit between capital and labor, the disparity between the haves and have nots. It's exactly this irresilience of the economic-political system that caused people to vote for Donald Trump, Brexit, and populist parties all over the world. The social divide awakens a desire to return to the good old days when economic growth benefited everyone. It's easy to point to globalization as the main cause for inequality in the world. But there's no way back. It is simply a fact that we're all globally connected—the coronavirus global outbreak is a clear demonstration.

The longer we linger looking in the rearview mirror, the longer this period of confusion will last. In that respect, President Trump did the progression of the economic cycle a great favor. He accelerated the release of current constraining structures. He withdrew from international treaties, such as the Trans-Pacific Partnership and the Paris Climate Agreement. And he also put NATO under pressure. Yes, this led to more chaos and disruption. It also gave newcomers the necessary air to pick up the pieces and reorganize the system. This is only possible by moving forward rather than backward. China is the apparent candidate to become the new hegemon. Yet it remains to be seen if it has the answers to the challenges of our time. In all three previous cycles, the release phase took a total of thirty years. Smith therefore notes that this chaotic period, which he aptly labels The Great Release, may last until 2038.

Military Conflict

Former marine Ingo Piepers wrote a prescient book in 2017, giving a "WARning" that the tensions that have built up in the last decade are prone to be released around 2020 by means of a world war.[9] The astonishing thing is that his predictions are not the somber contemplation of one expert. They are the outcome of years of sound academic research. A powerful simulation model was used, fed with the characteristics of the 134 wars that have taken place over the past 500 years.

The research shows that our global community has become seriously unstable—anarchistic, in system theory terms. The combination of our fear of survival and this anarchistic system makes the outcome predictable. Armed conflict seems inevitable, as it will release the tension and free up the energy that has been charging. The severity will be devastating and lead to tremendous human suffering, which may last up to 2036, according to the model. The released energy will eventually be applied to bring the system to a higher order and introduce a new period of relative stability. A new international order will be created that adjusts for the shifts in power between nations. This new order will be able to handle the type of tensions that led to the war.

These are the exact dynamics that were at play in the Thirty Years' War (1618–1648), the Napoleonic Wars (1792–1815), World War I (1914–1918) and World War II (1939–1945). As we've become more globally connected than ever before, we have formed one system that is subject to physical laws—thermodynamics, in particular—that are highly deterministic. We do have a chance, however, to evade war if we are able to adjust one input variable—our fear of survival. A negotiated reorganization of the United Nations is an urgent and viable option to establish a new international order without war. A unique deviation from the doomsday scenario is possible if we are able to collectively step over our shadow.

A New Perspective on Leadership

While the implications of the coronavirus are immense and a serious setback for all of us, it may actually be a blessing in disguise. Its outbreak may be admired for its impeccable timing, providing an intervention that has given us a timeout to consider what really matters in life—valuable time to think over our behaviors (in the outer world) and our intentions (in our inner world) that are the cause of the tragic collective outcomes we create. The complete lack of international coordination in response to the outbreak is a clear example of the fact that the fear of survival still conditions our thoughts and our actions. Governments and central banks have opened all monetary floodgates and are creating more debt. But these funds are only a reprieve. They barely support the real economy. Since the cost of money is virtually nil, company valuations are going through the roof. While economies experience a historic downturn, stock prices are rising. It is evidently the final phase of an economic cycle in which the old establishment is anxiously trying to prevent a paradigm shift, a final twitch before reshuffling the cards to foster the emergence of a new order.

I believe that leadership cannot be left to the likes of career politicians and top managers. Most of their thinking is colored by the cultural systems in which they grew up. The collective dynamics of their individual tradeoffs will only lead to outcomes no one desires. History will inevitably repeat itself and we will be facing the ultra-black scenarios of economic depression, or even armed conflict, for the next fifteen years. Fear-based, egoistic motives will entice protectionist measures that will destroy the existing order and turn this decade into what may well become the Harrowing Twenties.

Unless ... we pick up the gauntlet and gracefully embrace our fate. The Transformation Age is knocking on the door. The next fifteen years will determine what the next long cycle will look like. We are collectively being challenged to be the best version of ourselves. The time has come for organizations to be led just like nature organizes itself. That implies a bottom-up, voluntary collaboration

28

of individuals who have come to understand that relinquishing part of their autonomy in favor of the whole brings prosperity to all. Autocratic leadership does not awaken this awareness in employees. It keeps them in a lethargic victim role, feeling sorry for themselves. Even a common term like delegation does not convey what I mean. It is still based on the assumption that power rests with management and is allocated downward. In nature it's the other way around. The power is with the individual. Miracles happen when they come to an agreed process by which they voluntarily align their activities.

Then what's the role of the leader? Do organizations even need leaders if employees are meant to organize themselves? I've found that they certainly do. We cannot expect employees to get organized without any guidance. I have seen many organizations that converted to a self-steering team composition and failed miserably. Middle management layers were removed before the teams themselves functioned properly. Is it any wonder? It took single-celled organisms 1.8 billion years to figure out how to collaborate and we may want to do it a little faster this time. That's why we need leaders to be the guides. They serve as process facilitators to achieve a level of active participation throughout the organization. This requires excellent coaching and process management skills based on a deep understanding of what genuinely motivates people.

The challenge for us as leaders is to make a personal transformation. To learn how we can facilitate such a guided process. An arduous task because it does not only require skill. What we're seeking is nothing short of a leap in our consciousness. To do what was adumbrated by sages and mystics throughout history—to release the compulsive control of our ego and become a beacon of wisdom and energy. It doesn't take much study. And I do not propose a philosophical treatise. This isn't about knowledge. It's about gaining an insight about our true nature as human beings. An insight that has been out there for ages but requires fertile soil to take root. The coronavirus crisis may well be the fertilizer for our soil (or soul?) to adopt a whole new paradigm.

TOP THREE TAKEAWAYS

1) Companies and other organizations are formed by people and therefore are living organisms. Like everything in nature, their development is cyclical. After phases of fast growth and conservation, there is a creative destruction and reorganization phase.

2) We are living at the end of the fourth cycle of capitalist expansion. The coronavirus crisis heralds the creative destruction phase as the global economic system has become irresilient. The power of capital and international institutions will crumble to make way for entrepreneurship and more flexible forms of collaboration.

3) A new perspective on leadership is needed to prevent long-term depression or even warfare. As leaders, it is time to make a personal transformation. A leap in our consciousness. To overcome our ego-based fears and become the facilitators of a guided process to help our people organize themselves from the bottom up.

Ready to Grow?

Now that you have read the introductory sections of this book, you may be open to the suggestion that the coronavirus is not just bad luck. Nature can be admired for its perfect timing. For the first time in eight hundred years of capitalist history, we have the unique opportunity to prevent a systemic war at the end of an economic cycle. Each of us is personally challenged to raise our level of consciousness and address the perils in our direct environment.

As a first step, let's explore our human nature. Our body is an accumulation of 3.5 billion years of high-tech innovation. On a physical level, we are identical to our forebears who lived as nomads on the African savanna. Nature designed our body to function optimally in the circumstances that they faced. How do we use our innate technology to push us forward in the Transformation Age? Are you ready to lay the foundation for your transformation? Let's enter Part I!

—PART I—

YOU TOO ARE A CAVEMAN

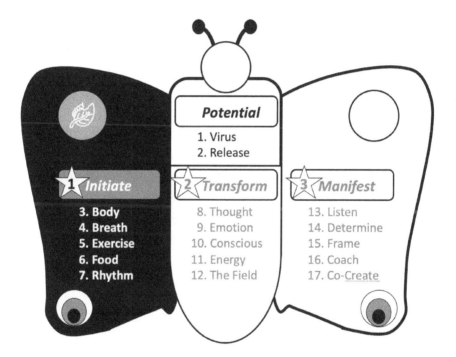

Potential

1. Virus
2. Release

1 Initiate

3. Body
4. Breath
5. Exercise
6. Food
7. Rhythm

2 Transform

8. Thought
9. Emotion
10. Conscious
11. Energy
12. The Field

3 Manifest

13. Listen
14. Determine
15. Frame
16. Coach
17. Co-Create

In its essence, your body never left the Stone Age.
Transform the way you breathe, exercise, eat and sleep
to function optimally in the Transformation Age.

INITIATE

Strengthen Your Body and Build Your Foundation

... the Caterpillar

"We exist in a bizarre combination of Stone Age
emotions, medieval beliefs and god-like technology."
—Edward O. Wilson

This Part lays the foundation for your transformation to become a Paradise Shaper. We will focus on our physical presence—our body. Since rational thinking has become so dominant in business and society today, we have lost touch with our body and its tremendous power. We use the wrong tools in our attempts to make decisions, connect with others, and realize our dreams. In doing so, we have overruled our factory settings and forgotten how to breathe, eat, exercise, and sleep as intended by nature. This Part contains five chapters that provide us with the user manual of our temple of life—our body.

- ❖ Chapter 3 explores how we carry the whole of evolution within us. We'll discover that we don't have just one brain, but three! And we'll learn a powerful practice to reconnect our three brains to enjoy a state of balanced power.
- ❖ In Chapter 4 we'll dive into the art of breathing. We'll experience how we waste energy by not enjoying a natural breathing cadence. We'll revisit the impact on our well-being and apply some powerful techniques.
- ❖ Chapter 5 explains why it is so hard for us to adopt an active lifestyle, and what makes it so crucial that we do. We'll learn an amazing ten-minute practice developed by Tibetan monks to boost their energy level on a daily basis.

❖ In Chapter 6 we will focus on our eating patterns. How do we get most energy from our food? We'll find that how often we eat has major implications for our digestive system. And we'll review healthy (and tasty) choices when selecting what food to eat.

❖ Chapter 7 recounts the natural rhythm of the day. How well we sleep at night depends entirely on the way we organize our day. We will divide the day into five blocks and discover how to best plan activities to optimize our energy level.

My Wakeup Call

"How do I get this budget right?" My head was racing for answers as we were in the middle of a challenging workshop. I had just started my new role as a regional CFO. I was convinced our emerging markets region was an unpolished diamond, with growth opportunities just around the corner. But how could I weave in the inevitable investments when costs were already under scrutiny? My colleagues didn't seem to get it. I needed to draw a line in the sand!

I was getting up to intervene when I suddenly started trembling. I had quivers up and down my spine, with sweat bursting out. My heart was pounding a hip-hop beat. And then I had an aching pain, as if a crusader had just pierced his sword straight through my chest.

I dropped back in my chair. Alarmed faces were staring at me. "Are you OK, Paul?" my colleagues were asking. "Should we drive you home?" my assistant suggested as I excused myself from the meeting. Even now I was keeping up appearances. "I'll manage, let me go home and see the doctor," I replied. I embarked on the longest twenty-minute drive in my life. As I stumbled through the door, my wife Dorine came running to support me. She arranged for a neighbor to take care of the kids and took me to the hospital.

"I have a pneumonia, right here," I told the doctor, pointing at the exact spot next to my heart. "Well, sir, you're a young man, let's first see for ourselves," the doctor responded as he pressed his stethoscope on my chest to listen. Ten seconds of deep breathing were enough for him to change his mind. "Pneumonia, indeed. And a heavy one!" he exclaimed. "You must have ignored all signs. We'll get you an amoxicillin cure. You stay in bed."

And there I was, thirty-two years old, sentenced to stay in bed, with oceans of time to ponder on the very question: "How could this have happened?" The doctor was right. I had ruined my own body. For years I had taken pride in always going the extra mile. I wasn't necessarily smarter than others. I simply worked harder, pushed beyond all limits, and, hence, felt that I outperformed everyone.

We had just returned from a two-year expatriation to Seoul, South Korea. I'd been leading the valuation team for a major initial public offering of our joint venture with a prominent *chaebol* (a family-owned business conglomerate) in the wildly expanding LCD industry. I literally skipped sleep for nights in a row as we raced to make the deadlines. The prospectus had to be submitted and road-show decks were due. We were writing history—the first dual listing of a multi-billion-dollar venture at the stock exchanges of both Seoul and New York.

And then there was this other "project" at the same time—a personal one. Just a few days after the road show began, Dorine was due to deliver our fourth child. As was local custom in Korea, the delivery date was planned, which at the time I actually found rather practical. Of course I was running late again, having to speed to make it home in time and onward with Dorine to the Samsung Cheil hospital. As we arrived, I thought we would move straight to the delivery room. But that wasn't the case. These doctors understood the key things in life you simply do not rush. They served us a nice dinner and made us (especially me!) wind down and get some sleep. Our son Benjamin was not born until two o'clock the next afternoon. He was a burly ten-pound kid—quite a funny sight amid all the smaller, cuddly Korean kids in the maternity ward.

Yet nearly missing my son's birth still hadn't taught me a lesson. Headquarters called to ask if I was ready for a next assignment as the CFO for an emerging markets region. Of course! Count me in! So we emptied the house and boarded a plane just a few weeks later.

And now I had collapsed, not even two months into the new role. I went to visit my father, an internist at another hospital, who had my chest X-ray taken. I will never forget his words: "Not even sixty years ago you would certainly have died. It is about time you start to listen to your body." Indeed, while penicillin had accidentally been discovered by Alexander Fleming in 1928, it wasn't until World War II that people were treated for bacterial infections with this miracle fungus.

Learn to listen to my body. Where to start? The first few days, I just laid in bed coping with headaches, stinging chest pain, and shivers. But the tricky thing with penicillin is that as soon as it gets a grip on the infection, you start feeling a whole lot better. My mind cleared and I had this wonderful idea how to fix our company budget by simplifying the organizational setup. So I took the next week to work from home on the proposal and resumed my shake-rattle-and-roll rhythm as soon as I returned to the office.

Short of two years later, I had a nasty cough again. I was about to attend this executive leadership program at the Wharton School in Philadelphia for which I was selected to participate. I called my dad, who checked me over. "You're this close to scoring your second pneumonia," he said, with his thumb and index finger less than a quarter of an inch apart. He didn't need to say more. Armed with more amoxicillin, I was on my way to the "City of Brotherly Love" that Sunday, determined to make some fundamental changes.

The solution dropped right out of the sky. Part of the program was an evening session with Phil Nuernberger, a pioneer in self-mastery, and the integration of mind, body, and spirit within a corporate setting. Phil didn't share any theories, strategies, or business cases. He simply let us ... breathe.[10]

A few exercises and meditations were all it took to introduce us to a different dimension. A realm I had not experienced before. My inner world. A place of serenity, calmness, and perfection. A land of boundless opportunities.

No beta blockers, no tropical drink, no theme park would ever provide me with the balance and ease I experienced by what's available to all of us, day and night—breathing properly.

It meant the first step on my journey to truly getting to know myself, what I really want in life, and how to collaborate with others to get there. It dawned on me that leading people is a momentous endeavor that involves taking full ownership. Yet how could I be responsible for others if I did not even take a serious interest in my own health? Transforming myself implied fully understanding how I tick. Our human physiology became the logical first subject of my deep dive.

SHAPE YOUR PARADISE *ONLINE*

Anchor your transformation with the Shape Your Paradise online self-coaching program. Module 1, "You Too Are a Caveman," follows this first Part of the book. In five weeks you will work intensively with the topics presented.

You carry the entire evolution within you. An insane potential! How do you function optimally in your daily activities? In this module you will experience:

➢ why stress is an illusion and how to eliminate it
➢ how to develop your intuition and make better decisions
➢ how nature teaches you to use your time optimally
➢ how you manage your energy perfectly throughout the day

You will learn how to breathe, eat, exercise, and sleep naturally. You will find out how you open the gateway to the hidden powers in your body.

Go to www.paradiseshaper.com and accelerate your learning!

3

YOUR BODY'S INTELLIGENCE

"I try to change my physical appearance for every role."
—Robert Z'Dar

You Carry the Whole Evolution Within You!

All living creatures have a physiology that is optimized to function in their direct environment. Millions of years of evolution slowly but steadily adjusted the structure of their bodies, oxygen uptake, the way they obtain and process food, sleeping patterns, hormone management, and social engagements. The whale is perfectly attuned to the ocean, the lion to the savannah, and the eagle to the air.

How do you see your body? Are you your body? Or do you have a body? To what extent do you notice that your body is changing? You will remember from a biology class that our body is made up of cells. As I mentioned in Chapter 1, we have 50–75 trillion of them, that is, 50–75 million times a million. It's insane if you think about it! Every minute, cells die, and new ones are added. Within a year your body almost completely renews itself!

Groups of cells specialize in performing certain functions. That wasn't always the case. The first cells—the first appearance of life—were created about 3.5 billion years ago in the primordial soup that formed the surface of our planet. Those first cells did what all life forms still do—collect information about their environment and take appropriate action. They actually have two modes of operation—growth and protection. In the growth state, they are in flow and do what they are meant to do. In protection mode, they have what we call "stress." They stop their normal functioning and focus all their attention on one thing—survival. This makes sense in times of acute danger, but that shouldn't encompass long periods of time. They will cease to function properly and deform—which, in fact, is cancer—or die.

Those cells took half the time since their first appearance to convert from single-celled to multicellular organisms—a stunning 1.8 billion years to learn that working together is better than doing everything alone. These cells surrendered part of their autonomy to become stronger as a whole. And they all benefited in the end! That's a theme in nature that repeats itself on an advanced scale—atoms sync with each other and form molecules. Molecules learn to collaborate and become cells. Cells find intelligent ways to integrate into organs and complete bodies. And now we as humans are also in the midst of a process to embrace the art of unification. Once we figure out how to do this, we will benefit not only collectively, but also individually.

How can you take good care of yourself and others? Evolution has equipped our body with some magnificent tools. We are simply unaware how to use them optimally. Let's continue our journey through evolution to understand how our body was constructed. We'll find that our body truly is the result of increasingly savvy innovations that were literally placed on top of one another.

Neuroscience is unveiling sensational details about the intricate design of our nervous system. We do not just have a brain in our head. It turns out our heart and gut also have neural networks—brain cells—with an intelligence of their own. Modern research is confirming what ancient esoteric wisdom has expounded for thousands of years—each of our three "brains" represents a specific function of our intelligence. If we learn to access and use each for the right purposes, we balance our system and become progressively more powerful. Once all three brains are in alignment, each neural network can function in its highest expression.[11] If we understand the evolutionary background of each of the three brains, we'll find it much easier to make proper use of them.

Brain 1—No Guts, No Glory!

If we put the entire evolution of 3.5 billion years since life began on Earth on a twenty-four-hour timeline, the first twelve hours were spent shifting from single-celled bacteria to multicellular organisms. Over time, these organisms expanded in complexity and developed into jellyfish and—this is super interesting!—worms. Worms were the first mobile animals, as they slithered across the bottom of the sea about 560 million years ago—less than four hours ago on our twenty-four-hour timeline. Just think about their functioning for a second. They need to ensure their safety by sensing whether the environment is too cold or too warm. They're constantly searching for food and, hence, developed taste. Even the simplest movements require quite an amount of "computing power" to calculate, plan, and put into action. That is why worms have actual brain cells, called neurons, all over their body, just under the body wall.

If you look at our interior, from our mouth and through the esophagus, the stomach, and intestines to the anus, we are basically a large worm about thirty feet long! Our worm is neatly folded in our stomach and performs basic, but essential functions there. Our worm performs all the functions its ancient ancestor invented over half a billion years ago. It senses cold or heat, tastes and smells potential food, and digests the food. To process all these observations, compare them with previous experiences, and convert them into action, a lot of computing capacity is required. And who does all of that? The powerful network of neurons in our gut wall. We have about five hundred million brain cells in our belly. This is our oldest brain and, therefore, our primal intelligence.

Evolution continued. Worms expanded their mobility and grew additional functionality to swiftly travel the seas. Thus, fish were formed some five hundred million years ago—fairly complex multicellular creatures. In the meantime, the primordial soup had calmed down and land formed on Earth. To explore new opportunities, the fish went ashore and evolved into reptiles some three hundred million years ago—just over two hours ago on our twenty-four-hour timeline.

When reptiles further developed on land, more computing power was needed. The worm, folded into the fish's body, was enriched with legs, a more developed spine, and a head. More coordination was needed to enable life on land, such as respiration, heart rate, safety, and more advanced reproduction. Perhaps you have heard about the reptilian brain, which is our brain stem. Well, that's the reptile that's alive and kicking within you. It is a masterpiece of ingenuity by itself. Our reptilian brain caters for all our basic physiological functions. It does so autonomously, without our direct interference. It operates instinctively, based on patterns that have proven to be safe.

Our reptilian brain and the neural network in our gut wall are always in direct contact. Combined, they form our gut brain. They are all about the "I." "Am I safe? How do I survive? What are my limits?" Relaxation, well-being, and intuition are also capacities of our gut brain. We don't have to think long about the important decisions in life. As we learn to feel what's right, we just know what to do. And yes, if we are too much in our head, we have lost contact with our gut brain. We can no longer really feel what our intuition tells us. The highest expression of our gut brain is courage. It is our ability to overcome our fears and pursue our dreams.

Brain 2—Follow Your Heart!

Over time, reptiles diversified into turtles, crocodiles, and even birds. And, of course, we're inspired by the legendary dinosaurs. In the movie *Jurassic Park,* you may have seen how immense and bulky these animals were. Until about sixty-five million years ago—less than half an hour ago on our twenty-four-hour timeline—a huge meteorite hit what is now Mexico. Life became unbearable for many animals as the atmospheric debris darkened the sun. But a small, agile animal found ways to survive and was given the space to develop—a mammal.

Mammals are in many ways a wonderful example of how adverse external circumstances trigger life to innovate. Mammals can regulate their body temperature. They typically have hair and are warm blooded, which means they produce their own heat. They can live in cold environments where cold-blooded reptiles cannot survive. When they are too hot, their sweat glands help them to cool down. Mammals developed specialized teeth for tearing and grinding food. Unlike reptiles, mammals don't hatch eggs but give birth to live young.

Mammals are all about movement. They're motorically much more advanced than reptiles. And there's a very special capability that truly sets them apart from their reptilian ancestors—they have a wide myriad of emotions. E-motions are "energy in motion." They're the physical sensations that entice a living being to display certain behaviors. They make a lioness feed her cubs (while reptiles have no issue eating their young), an elephant mourn a deceased relative, and a cat purr with pleasure when stroked.

As humans, we are mammals ourselves. Our body hosts the evidence of this momentous steppingstone in evolution in two places—our mammalian brain in our head and a brain that's placed in our heart. Yes, there is also a neural network in our heart! Neuroscientists estimate there are about 40,000 to 120,000 neurons positioned in our heart. This network processes our emotions of love, joy, and connection. The magnetic field it emits is a hundred times stronger than the field generated by our head brain.[12] It can be detected a couple of feet outside the body. Have you ever walked into a room and immediately felt the atmosphere there without exchanging a word? You've picked up on the magnetic field of the participants to the meeting.

In our heart, we find our passion. What is it that we would really love to do and develop in our life? Our heart is the center of trust that life offers us new opportunities. It is where we feel gratitude for what we have received, which is one of the most powerful emotional expressions we may experience. You have no idea how much impact you will have if you know your true desires, are fully confident they will be fulfilled, and feel grateful for what is already manifesting.

Our heart brain is closely connected with our mammalian brain, which comprises both the cerebellum and limbic system. The cerebellum (Latin for "little brain") can be found just above our neck, while the limbic system is placed on top of the brain stem in the center of our head (see exhibit 4). The cerebellum is anatomically a complete brain in and of itself. Although it's merely the size of two peaches, it hosts more than 70 percent of all brain cells in the body. It accounts for our balance, the coordination of movements, and muscle tension. While the brain stem only distinguishes between light and dark, the cerebellum can discern basic colors.

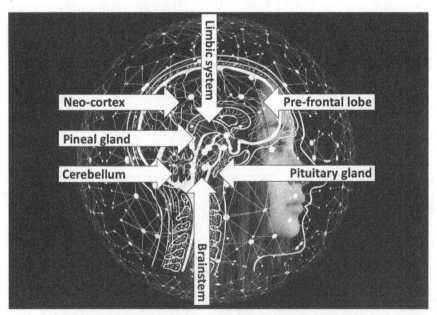

**Exhibit 4—The cerebellum and limbic system
are positioned below the neocortex.**[13]

In recent decades neuroscience has unveiled that the cerebellum plays a key role in emotional and cognitive functions. Harvard Medical School has conducted groundbreaking work in this field.

Its research confirms ancient Taoist wisdom that visual-spatial awareness, working memory, mental flexibility, and attentional and emotional control all find their root in the cerebellum.[14] The quality of our thinking is directly linked with the functioning of our cerebellum. That is why Taoist practice aims to strengthen the cerebellum-heart connection. By actively training both our basic color and spatial awareness, we enhance our emotional stability and clarity of thought.

Why do we experience emotions? This is where the limbic system comes in. It is a network of glands and other nuclei that manage our physiology (the functioning of our organs and tissues). All our sensory inputs are assessed by the neocortex (our head brain) by comparing them with stored memories. Depending on the outcome, the cortex sends a signal to the limbic system, which will activate the body accordingly. This is managed by chemical processes in the body. Specific glands release certain chemicals that enter the bloodstream. If these chemicals connect with receptors of cells in our organs, they may alter their functioning. Through the nervous system, our head brain becomes aware of these changes in the body. Only then do we really feel these emotions.

While the limbic system is a complex network, we can simplify it as being a factory with an incoming and an outgoing gate. Two glands only 0.4 inches in size, the pineal and pituitary glands, can be thought of as these gates. All the other nuclei (such as the hippocampus, amygdala, and thalamus) represent the factory process. The pineal gland—the incoming gate—has a pine-cone shape and produces melatonin, which regulates our sleep pattern. The full functioning of the pineal gland is still a mystery to today's scientists, yet it is increasingly appreciated for creating the optimal condition for our entire hormonal system to function. In ancient wisdom, the pineal gland is known as the "third eye" or "heaven's eye." It is stimulated during meditation to calm the mind and establish an increased state of awareness. The pituitary gland, representing the limbic system's outgoing gate, is in direct control of all other glands in the body as it stimulates or inhibits their hormone production.

The combination of the neural network in our heart and our mammalian brain makes up our heart brain. In its highest expression, our heart brain harbors compassion—a deep desire to help people become the best version of themselves. While the gut brain is about "I," the heart brain is all about "we."

How do I connect in a meaningful way? What do we have in common? Can I merge into a group?

Since our challenge as humanity is to learn how to collaborate and create benefits for all, it is evident that our ability to tap into the intelligence of our heart brain is of paramount importance.

Brain 3—Head Over Heels!

Mammals were granted space to evolve further. A new balance between predators—such as saber-toothed tigers and wolves—and their prey emerged. The prey had sought refuge underground (moles and rabbits) and back into the sea (dolphins and whales), or they formed a shield by staying in herds (buffalo and zebras). One animal fled into the trees—the monkey. And again, this had huge implications for the evolution of our bodies.

What happened? Wolves were smart and waited patiently for the monkeys to descend from the trees. Tigers might have gone a step further and climbed the trees to chase the monkeys, and the monkeys could only escape one way—from treetop to treetop. Just imagine the magnificent computing capacity that's required to do this. In a split second the monkey had to gauge the strength of each branch (by means of color, thickness, and flexibility). A fabulous spatial insight is crucial, combined with the ability to coordinate speed and movement.

All of this gave a huge impulse to the development of the cerebrum—the neocortex—a magnificent calculator with enormous processing speed. Our neocortex and cerebellum together have about a hundred billion neurons. These neurons constantly produce combinations that are stored as memories. What fires together, wires together! In this way, our brain converts our sensory perceptions into information that feeds our consciousness. There are more potential combinations between these neurons in our head than the number of molecules in the entire universe!

The main role of our head brain is to provide for cognitive functions. It helps us give meaning to everything we perceive with our senses. There is nothing our head brain would rather do than solve problems. It's great at analyzing issues, slicing and dicing them completely, so we understand exactly how they work. It is super curious and always looking for new inputs to ponder. In its highest expression, our head brain manifests our creativity, meaning the fresh, new "high quality" thoughts that arise in a state of focused relaxation. These fresh ideas pave our way in realizing our desires.

Our giant neocortex is immensely powerful, and that is exactly our problem. What do I mean by that? When the head brain has too little to do, it looks for problems to solve. We start to worry about minor issues, make a mountain out of a molehill, and lose our sense of reality. I coach many leaders who try to use their head brain to perform tasks for which it was not designed. They expect to motivate people by showing them smart and detailed plans. They think about important decisions by making extensive pro and con lists. Because they are out of touch with their heart brain, they do not make a real connection with others. And since they don't tune in to their gut brain, their intuition cannot guide them. The head brain is a powerful device to help you make your dreams come true. But it needs a boss, and that's you. It's a liberating experience once you realize that you are not your thinking.

—TRANSFORMATION EXERCISE 1—
Discover Your Yee Power

The Taoists discovered that the phase between being awake and asleep is the most energizing. Moreover, they developed a simple process we can apply throughout the day to bring our body in this state while being fully active. The Chinese character used to express this gentle force is pronounced "Yee." We therefore call this process attuning to your "Yee Power." In doing so, we do not get absorbed in habitual thinking and keep a focused attention in the present moment. We recharge our batteries while engaging with our environment.

It is easiest to learn how to tap into your Yee Power by closing your eyes. In due course, as you recognize the feeling, you can easily do this with your eyes opened while doing other activities. Here are the steps:

1. Close your eyes—become fully aware of your breath.
2. Relax your forehead, your eyes, tongue, jaw, and shoulders.
3. Focus three times for ten seconds on a sound in your environment (or your own breathing).
4. Imagine two invisible lines connecting the corners of your mouth with your ears and visualize this line creating pointed corners at the top of your ears.
5. If you get the sensation, it will seem as if your ears hear much sharper. You may notice a basic, pleasant "roar." This is called *shen*. You have connected with your creativity.
6. Now take this energy with you as you move your attention to your heart. Think of someone you love dearly. How does this person make you feel?
7. If you get this sensation, you heart will resemble a rose that opens. A warm feeling of love fills your chest. This is called *chi*. You have connected with your compassion.

8. Now take both the shen and chi energy with you as you move your attention to your belly. Feel how life is breathing in you as you concentrate on the area below the navel.
9. This sensation connects you with your *jing*. You have connected with your courage.
10. Now feel all three simultaneously. As your shen, chi, and jing energies mingle, you will feel alert, engaged and sharp. You're tapping into your Yee Power.

Before long, you will be able to feel your Yee Power and hold it for ten seconds or more. As you're busy doing other things, you easily drop out of Yee Power. What do you do? Just go through the process and restore it—with a little practice it will only take a moment.

Even experienced Tao practitioners drop out of Yee Power every ten to fifteen seconds. The difference is, they notice it within seconds and get back in right away. This self-awareness will grow over time. So just get going and notice what this does to you!

The Caveman Is Still Alive!

The first humanoid was born about five million years ago. That is, their DNA was so different from that of the great apes that we can speak of a human as a new species. On our twenty-four-hour timeline, that was about two minutes ago. These people were far from resembling what you and I look like. For millions of years these primal men and women lived as hunter-gatherers. They were nomads who moved in groups of twenty to fifty people and mainly lived in tents or huts. In the food chain they held a rather benign position. They gathered wild plants, nuts, and other food that was available in nature. They were also scavengers who ate some leftover meat and marrow from bones when predators had left their prey. And who did they find there? The canines! Is it any wonder that the bond between humans and dogs has grown so strong over millions of years?

Slowly but steadily, they improved their capabilities to hunt small- to medium-sized animals about two million years later. They did so, of course, by developing tools—such as pointed sticks and knives—but also by relentlessly chasing these animals. While the animals got overheated at some point, the human species had the ability to sweat in order to cool down. That was a major advantage as they walked on average six to nine miles a day, which could extend up to twenty miles in pursuit of a prey.

The control of fire some three hundred thousand years ago massively impacted the development of our ancestors.[15] It gave them dominion over other species, even when those other species were faster, stronger, or more ferocious. The use of fire also had major implications for the way food was prepared. All kinds of turnips and starches were more easily digestible, and ancestral barbecue feasts must have seen the light in those days. The intake of calorie and protein-rich food boosted the growth of brain capacity and the shortening of the digestive system. Controlling fire gave rise to early forms of cognitive development—the division of tasks and collaboration, and the ability to plan ahead to avoid negative situations. As discussed in Chapter 1, viruses are likely to have played a catalyst role in expanding the prefrontal cortex and, thus, thinking power.

Modern man—Homo sapiens—has existed for about two hundred thousand years. That's just the last five seconds on our twenty-four-hour timeline! If we were to put these human beings on an operating table to analyze what their bodies looked like inside, we would find that their physiology is exactly the same as ours. That primeval man is still alive because that's you! While a number of other human species—such as Neanderthals and Denisovans—also existed in those days, Homo sapiens ultimately precipitated the extinction of those species.

Our forebears spread from East Africa to Eurasia about seventy thousand years ago.[16] Despite a less muscular and vigorous physique,

Homo sapiens had a unique trait in comparison to other human species—their ability to think in abstract terms. They developed fictive language to communicate, applied symbols and other forms of art, created music and dance, and taught their children about the mystery of life through games and rituals. In other words, they invented culture to enhance their chances of survival.

Abstract thinking gave Homo sapiens a high degree of flexibility. The capacity to believe in certain imaginative concepts allowed these people to live in larger groups, expand their collaboration, and allow group members to specialize on specific tasks. And so, they discovered that certain plants and animals could be domesticated. Along the big rivers of the Middle East, a revolution took place some twelve thousand years ago. For the first time in history, human beings exchanged their nomadic lifestyle for an early form of farming settlements. They established agricultural societies, allowing people to live in permanent villages and towns. Deforestation, irrigation, pottery, and further domestication of animals took a surge. Ownership, trade, and political structures started to develop, advancing into the first forms of kingdoms, polytheistic religions, and money in the millennia that followed.

Why is it so important to be aware of this succinct overview of our human evolution? Our lives and challenges today couldn't be further apart from the way our ancestors spent their days. But as mentioned, we're biologically optimized to function in our direct environment. Just think about how recently we were still living as hunter-gatherers. The first humans transitioned from their nomadic lifestyle only twelve thousand years ago. On our twenty-four-hour timeline, that's only 0.3 seconds! Or expressed differently, this was merely 350–500 generations ago. Only minimal biological mutations will have taken place in this timeframe, as it takes a much longer timespan for our DNA to adjust to our environment. For millions of years, our forebears were subject to the laws of the bush. Our brains, nerves, muscles, our sophisticated hormone household, all our internal biochemical processes—in fact, every cell of our body—is perfectly attuned to our survival as a hunter-gatherer in the wild.

Indeed, we have completely changed our environment, and continue to do so at an ever accelerating rate. But the caveman still rules our physiology. The food we eat, our daily exercise, our sleeping patterns, and above all, the broad range of stimuli (social media!) we are exposed to at work and in our private lives—we are simply not designed to deal with them. They slowly but steadily wear us out. Stress, lack of energy, a full head, and the feeling of not being happy are largely because we have to function in an environment that isn't natural to us.

Does this mean we have to go back to the bush? Certainly not. We can enjoy the luxury of the environment we have created. But it's important that we understand how we are designed to function optimally. By understanding how our physiology functions, we can learn to master the triggers that lead to our disarray. Cut the caveman in you some slack! A few simple adjustments will do miracles. The upcoming chapters of Part I will hand you the tools for your physical transformation—a solid foundation that will serve as a platform to reach for the stars and manifest what you really want.

TOP THREE TAKEAWAYS

1) We do not just have a brain in our head. Neuroscience is unveiling that our heart and gut also have neural networks with an intelligence of their own. Their highest expressions are creativity, compassion, and courage, which carry us into a state of flow.

2) We can tune into our Yee Power by activating our three brains in a simple process. Thus, we keep a focused attention in the present moment and recharge our batteries while engaging with our environment.

3) All living creatures have a physiology that is optimized to function in their direct environment. Our body is designed to operate as a hunter-gatherer in nature. By studying our physiology, we can make a few simple adjustments to our daily routine that will make us more energetic, focused, and relaxed.

SHAPE YOUR PARADISE *ONLINE*

How do you apply your Yee Power at any time of the day? What does it take to trust your gut brain? And when are your instincts *not* effective? Enrich your understanding with the first lesson of the online module "You Too Are A Caveman!"

4

JUST BREATHE

"Listen. Are you breathing just a little and calling it a life?"
—Mary Oliver

The Breath of Life

Breathing properly. It's the simplest, yet most fundamental, activity we can imagine. As long as you're breathing, you are alive. We all get this basic concept.

As a matter of fact, you're not breathing at all. Life breathes in you. Breathing is an incredibly sophisticated technology that enables our lungs to absorb about 5 percent oxygen from the air in our vicinity and exchange it for carbon dioxide. In perfect alignment, our cardiovascular system distributes the oxygen to every outskirt of our body. Oxygen feeds every organ, muscle, and tissue—virtually all 50–75 trillion of our body's cells.

Yet we manage to screw up even this basic function. Let's do a little experiment. Just breathe as you normally do. Please count your number of breaths—inhalation and exhalation combined counts as one—in the next thirty seconds. Take your time, I'll wait ...

... Have you done it? Now double this amount to determine the number of breaths you take per minute. Were you at sixteen or more? Twelve or more? Eight or more? Less than eight? If you're below eight breaths per minute, you are an abnormal breather. That is, most people breathe faster than you do. But the truth is, that's the way you're supposed to breathe. It's perfectly normal.

Due to our daily pressures and for cultural reasons, we have unlearned our natural belly breathing. We put our chest forward and hold in our stomach as this posture is considered more attractive and powerful. We use our willpower and tighten our diaphragm to get through life. Some 80 percent of people in the Western Hemisphere use chest breathing. This implies an oxygen absorption that is up to three times less efficient.

Even worse, when chest breathing, we are, in fact, using our emergency breathing system. Our nervous system sends signals to our brain that we are in a stressful environment. We create a significant part of the stress we experience because we unlearned how to breathe naturally. I always loved to watch our children sleep when they were babies—the soft cadence of air flowing through their nose, and the peacefulness by which their belly went up and down. A complete surrender to life breathing in them.

—TRANSFORMATION EXERCISE 2—
The Breath of Life

How do you relearn belly breathing? It's simple. When you go to bed at night, lie down, put your right hand on your chest and your left hand on your belly. Now breathe deeply through your belly. You should see only your left hand moving up and down with the flow of air, while your right hand doesn't move at all. Do this for ten minutes. If you didn't fall asleep already, by now you will probably sleep very nicely. In the morning, wake up ten minutes earlier to do the same exercise again before you get up. During the day, check a few times whether you are breathing through your belly or chest. After four to six weeks, your diaphragm should have strengthened and you will have converted to belly breathing. It's as simple as that!

Bonus tip—if you want to train your diaphragm even faster, just place one or two heavy books next to your bed—those good old Yellow Pages used to do a marvelous job. As you do the ten-minute deep breathing in the morning or evening, put these books on your belly and your left hand on top. This makes it even easier to see your left hand moving up and down as you're breathing deeply!

Frequency Matters!

Have you ever watched a dog breathing in a completely relaxed state? It has its mouth open, tongue out, and a fast pumping of air from the belly area. What is the frequency of its breathing?

And how about a horse? An elephant? Or a turtle for that matter?

Why on earth would this be relevant for you? Well, the answer may be quite shocking and entice you even more to return to your belly breathing factory settings. The average dog breathes about twenty-four times a minute. And how old do dogs get? Usually between ten to sixteen years. Take a look at this simple table (exhibit 5), where I have put together a number of animals to compare their respiratory rate, life span, and total number of breaths in their lifetime.

	Respiratory rate	Life span	Lifetime breaths
	Breaths per minute	In years	Average in million
Mouse	80-230	1-2.5	143
Chicken	28-35	8-10	151
Dog	20-35	10-16	191
Cat	20-30	13-18	197
Horse	10-24	25-30	241
Elephant	4-12	50-70	252
Blue Whale	6	80-90	268
Sea Tortoise	4-6	80-150	302

Exhibit 5—Breathing frequency and life span of animals.

In general, the table shows that the lower the breathing frequency, the longer the life span. An interesting insight is gained when we calculate the total number of breaths each animal will take in its lifetime. There appears to be a range of 150–300 million breaths. The total number of breaths increases when the respiratory rate per minute is lower.

If we bring heart rate into the picture, we notice a direct relationship with the respiratory rate. Whereas mice have a heart rate of 450–750 beats per minute, a sea tortoise is characterized by a cardiac pulse of only five to six. In other words, the more efficiently the body absorbs oxygen by breathing, the easier it spreads this energy source to every cell by pumping blood, and the better the system is equipped to live a long life.

By lowering our respiratory rate, a wonderful opportunity to "double dip" presents itself. The "normal" respiratory rate for an adult at rest today is twelve to twenty breaths per minute, reflecting a chest breathing pattern typical of most people today. Just imagine the impact of proper belly breathing as you reduce your number of breaths to a range of six to eight breaths at rest. Not only will you feel more at ease throughout the day, but you'll get a second benefit—a strong impetus to a significant extension of your life in much better health!

—TRANSFORMATION EXERCISE 3—
Remove Your Physical Blocks

There are three physical signs by which you can immediately tell you are tense and not "in the moment." The first is bracing yourself by tightening your diaphragm. You pull your stomach in and, as a consequence, cannot breathe freely through your belly. Secondly, you raise your shoulders one or two inches to subconsciously give yourself a bit more space for chest breathing. This tension burdens the muscles in your neck and shoulders and prevents your arms from moving freely. Thirdly, you flex your jaw muscles as if you need to "bite through" the situation. In due course, this may lead to grinding teeth or even an irritation of some facial nerves. How to address this and relieve tension? Inhale deeply—using the belly—and relax the diaphragm, shoulders, and jaw by exhaling completely exclaiming "huh," as if you've successfully completed a difficult task. Rotate your shoulders and move your jaw back and forth a few times. Now drop your jaw and shoulders in a relaxed way, focus on belly breathing, and resume your activities.

Watch Your Parasympathetic Breathing

"Paul, remind me again of how I can bring my heart rate down?" my colleague Bob (not his real name) asked me. We were in a sales conference auditorium in Malta and I checked out his face. He was about to get on stage to deliver a speech in front of a thousand people for the first time in his life. He would have paid any price to be able to leave this place right now, yet he knew there was no escaping. "Breathe in for three seconds, breathe out for six," I told him. It's an old trick that always works. As Bob walked the stairs and took center stage, he turned his face to the audience and smiled. He stood rock solid. I noticed him regulating his breath for nine seconds. Then he showed the participants both his palms as he seemed to be saying, "Let me enjoy this moment for a few seconds, you have no idea how it feels!" Carried by the cheering crowd, Bob relaxed even more and conducted a marvelous performance. I was impressed!

The key to balancing your system is exhalation. How is that so? Your breath directly influences your autonomous nervous system. As you inhale, your sympathetic nervous system gets activated. It's like hitting the accelerator of your car. Your heart rate increases, more blood is pumped through your body, and your body temperature rises slightly. As you exhale, you stimulate your parasympathetic nervous system. It's like taking your foot off the accelerator and hitting the brake. Consequently, your heart rate decreases, your blood pump function slows down, and the temperature in your body drops a bit.

Most people today have an erratic breathing pattern. They feel busy, experiencing constant pressure, with one event following the next. Not only has their breathing moved upward from belly to chest—at a much higher frequency—but also their breathing pattern is irregular. Most concerning is that their exhalation is much shorter and far shallower than their inhalation. The pattern seems jerky and capricious. Imagine what it would be like if visibility were limited to only two yards and you had to drive by hitting the gas and the brakes all the time. Well, that's what you may be doing throughout most of your day when it comes to your breathing pattern.

By reapplying your belly breathing, you return to your factory settings. Naturally, you will also adopt a more balanced rhythm. If we measured your breathing pattern, we would see a nice sine graph with a short, automatic pause just before the next inhalation (see exhibit 6). Don't force anything. Just watch your breath whenever you have an opportunity.

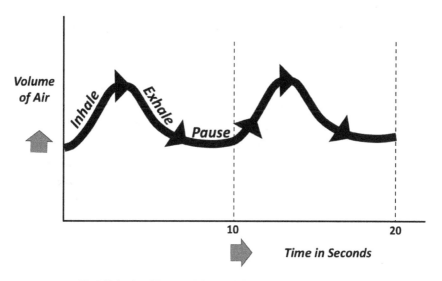

Exhibit 6—Normal breathing pattern in time.

Now that you've reconnected to your natural breathing, there is no need ever to be bored again. Do you find yourself stuck in meetings with too many participants beating around the bush? Play a funny game. Concentrate on belly breathing and watch the chests of the other participants. Rest assured the vast majority of them breathe twice or three times as often as you do, and you see their chests moving up and down. Watch the frequency of their breaths increase and that they hardly seem to be exhaling. That shows they're nervous.

Take the wonderful step to relearn how to breathe naturally. You literally get more air, and it saves a lot of energy. And super important—you shift your attention to your gut brain. Do you remember what we discussed in Chapter 3 about your gut brain? It provides you with the courage to realize your desires. This capacity is greatly enhanced when you start breathing naturally again. And how about your intuition? Do you want to be completely clear about what to do? That inner voice also gets a lot more oxygen to make itself heard and not be overwhelmed by the busy thoughts in your head.

—TRANSFORMATION EXERCISE 4—
The Joy of Waiting

Next time you are in line at the supermarket or waiting for a green light in traffic, don't get worked up thinking you're wasting precious time. Just relax and check if your breath pattern is regular at belly level. Enjoy the soothing experience of exhaling fully. Your parasympathetic nervous system will get an opportunity to balance the tension in your body. Soon, you will love these mini breaks that life is constantly offering us. It will put you in a completely different state of mind throughout the day.

As discussed, our nervous system has two opposing forces. Our sympathetic nervous system activates us in times of danger or stress. Once the situation has normalized, our parasympathetic nervous system restores balance. An equilibrium in our breathing ensures we continue to perform in a balanced way without burning out. Both nervous systems are activated equally and reinforce each other. Interestingly, these two opposing nervous systems both operate in each of our three brains. Let's take a look.

Sympathetic Nervous System

What happens if we detect a problem? The sympathetic nervous system springs into action. This system particularly stimulates the head brain. We start to think faster and faster. We try to analyze the situation from all angles and come up with solutions. However, our thinking deviates more and more from reality. We jump to all kinds of conclusions about how bad the problem is and what to do. We get into survival mode.

As our head brain projects an image that our safety is at stake, our gut brain instantly responds. The sympathetic nervous system ignites the "fight or flight" mode. This is about survival, our body thinks, so we need to be physically ready for combat or to run away. Now there is no acute need for regular activities such as digesting food or relaxing. We feel our stomach contract. Our adrenal glands use the energy in our kidneys to produce cortisol (the stress hormone) and adrenaline. We become impulsive. Our intuition is ignored. Action is required!

Our heart brain swiftly joins the action. Our heart rate increases, and our blood pressure rises. We need to maximize the oxygen that is transported to our muscles to get ready for the battle. We begin to feel angry, jealous, or anxious. The fear of missing out is another great example of an emotion that emerges with the sympathetic stimulation of the heart brain. We feel separated from the world. We disconnect from others and become aggressive or defensive.

From an evolutionary perspective, our sympathetic nervous system does an outstanding job guiding us through dangerous situations. Fighting or fleeing was a functional mode when we stood face to face with a wolf. Today, our overactive head brain identifies all kinds of dangers that are not perilous. It is crucial to realize that stress, jealousy, fear, and anger are all emotions that indicate we are stuck in our own conditioning. Without being aware, we activate certain patterns that were mainly formed in early childhood. The large number of burnout cases indicates what can happen if the sympathetic system is activated for a long time without balancing from the parasympathetic system.

Parasympathetic Nervous System

What happens if the parasympathetic nervous system is activated for a long time when there is hardly any activation of the sympathetic nervous system? It can eventually lead to a depression. If we suffer from depression, we appear to have lost our connection with life. We withdraw and feel dejected. Reasoning over and over in the same mental circles has numbed our mind. Everything turns dark. It's our system's final attempt to heal itself. No new impulses are accepted and we blindly stare at one point.

The gut brain stops all activity. We become lethargic. Whatever we still do is based solely on established habits. We vegetate. The heart brain in this state provides an emotionally flattened feeling. We become indifferent. The feeling of being separated translates into apathy. We don't connect with others anymore. There is a kind of chronic sadness that dominates our feeling. Life pushes us against the wall to wake us up to see beyond the illusion of our separation. Part II will examine the underlying mechanisms and the opportunities to set us free.

An overstimulation of the parasympathetic system can also occur as a reaction to a stressful situation. This is the "freeze" mode. Out of fear, we no longer know what to do, so we stop all activity, like a rabbit caught in the headlights of an oncoming car. We may even go into a state of shock when experiencing a complete loss of control over the situation.

Freezing was actually an effective stance in prehistoric times when we came face to face with a saber-toothed tiger—felines hunt for movement. But it's a protection mechanism that no longer serves us, similar to the "fight or flight" mode. We already won! We have wiped out our natural enemies, such as the saber-toothed tiger. Or we domesticated them, like our cats and dogs. Except if we're out in the wild, these animals are in wildlife parks or zoos, where we admire them as a weekend or holiday getaway.

Rebalancing by Breathing

It is evident that a proper balance between the two systems makes for a healthy mind and body. Deep belly breathing, where the exhalation receives as much attention as the inhalation, is the engine for a healthy life. It automatically aligns our sympathetic and parasympathetic nervous systems. This, in turn, fosters a physical and emotional balance in each of our three brains.

—TRANSFORMATION EXERCISE 5—
Alternate Nostril Breathing

The left side of your body is strongly connected with your parasympathetic nervous system. It represents your passive side—slow and receiving energy. Your right side is strongly linked with your sympathetic nervous system. It is characterized as active, fast, and transmitting energy. Did you know you can check at any moment whether both nervous systems are balanced in your body?

Gently close your right nostril with your right thumb. Now check if you can breathe freely through your left nostril. Maybe the airflow is blocked? Now do the opposite. Use your right pinky to close your left nostril. Can you breathe freely? A closed left nostril means your parasympathetic nervous system is not being activated. The same applies to your sympathetic nervous system if your right nostril is closed. When we are at peak performance, both nostrils are completely open. Our sympathetic and parasympathetic nervous systems are perfectly balanced. We're active, yet relaxed, focused, yet fully connected to everything around us.

You can easily rebalance your nervous systems by a simple exercise:

1. Breathe in. Now gently use your right thumb to close your right nostril.
2. Exhale slowly through your left nostril. Wait a second or so without breathing.
3. Inhale slowly, again through your left nostril. Now gently close your left nostril with your right pinky and remove your right thumb.
4. Exhale slowly through your right nostril. Again, wait a second or so without breathing.
5. Breathe in slowly through the right nostril. Gently close your right nostril with your right thumb and remove your right pinky.

6. Exhale slowly through the left nostril.
7. Continue the exercise for about five minutes. Make sure to end with step 6.

Note: Our head brain (the neocortex) is wired in the opposite way from the rest of our body. The left side (thinking, ratio) is linked to our sympathetic nervous system. The right side (feeling, connection) relates to our parasympathetic nervous system.

Heart-Head Coherence

We need to break our habit of activating our hereditary stress reactions—both the sympathetic and parasympathetic versions. They are illusory, false projections of the mind that put us on an unhealthy, completely unnecessary trail. In the previous chapter we learned how to use our Yee Power. We are now able to enhance this experience. Go through the steps again, but this time breathe deeply from the belly in a balanced way. This is a perfect moment. Go ahead, I'll wait …

… As you do this for a few minutes, you create coherence between your three brains. Can you sense it?

Both the heart brain and the head brain produce electromagnetic fields. These fields can be measured by an echocardiogram (ECG; heart brain) and an electroencephalogram (EEG; head brain). Here's the magic. Taking six breaths a minute in a balanced way means your breathing frequency is 0.1 hertz (Hz).[17] Your gut brain's vitality will beat the drum for your entire bodily system at the perfect pace. The electromagnetic fields of your heart and head brain tune in to the same frequency. You create heart-head coherence. The measurements show a remarkably congruent pattern between your ECG and EEG.[18]

It gets even more exciting. The Earth has a magnetic field of its own. The primary frequency of the Earth's magnetic field is … 0.1 Hz! By creating heart-head coherence, we allow ourselves to connect with the complete ecosystem. All of humanity, in fact, all living systems, are connected via the Earth's magnetic field.[19] It is all quite logical. Over billions of years we have evolved from the Earth's most basic elements to the complex beings we are today. We're not a separate, but an integral part of the Earth's ecosystem.

If we learn to operate in heart-head coherence, our intentions will yield positive benefits. Not just for ourselves, but for all systems of which we are part. By establishing this inner coherence, our experience improves drastically. It's a complete alignment of our energy system. Our intentions become like laser beams. In Part II we will enter the world of quantum physics to learn how to actively work with the energy of our intentions.

TOP THREE TAKEAWAYS

1) Our factory settings include breathing through the belly instead of the chest. Since our oxygen absorption will be three times higher, our breathing frequency will come down. A comparison between a range of animals suggests that the slower we breathe, the longer we live.

2) Most people have an irregular breathing pattern. It is important to exhale for the same length of time as we inhale. This stimulates our parasympathetic nervous system, which rebalances our body if, in response to external stimuli, we build up stress.

3) "Fight, flight, or freeze" is a functional response when we come face to face with a natural enemy in nature. Our head brain mistakes our daily private and business challenges for danger of survival. It helps to interrupt the situation for a moment and rebalance.

SHAPE YOUR PARADISE *ONLINE*

What are practical ways to convert your chest breathing to belly breathing? How can you balance your sympathetic and parasympathetic nervous systems throughout the day? How do you maintain your heart-head coherence at a deeper level? Week 2 of the online module "You Too Are A Caveman" provides a set of powerful exercises.

5

BE A GOOD SPORT

"You can discover more about a person in an hour
of play than in a year of conversation."
—Plato

Get Up from Your Chair

The cavemen never practiced any sports. They didn't need to. They were out all day in nature. They walked, ran, and hunted. They had to in order to survive. After millions of years, our entire physiology evolved to function optimally when we walk or run six to nine miles a day. It doesn't even matter that much whether we walk or run. As long as we cover this distance—or have a comparable calorie-burning effort—on a daily basis, our health flourishes. Our body and mind remain balanced. Our bones, muscles, and joints stay strong. As we get out of our head and into our body, we feel at ease with our environment and happy to be alive.

Sports have become an indelible part of our lives. It's wonderful how playing a game revives our inner child. Our energies start flowing, we get creative, bond with our teammates, and lose our sense of time. That is, if we are not too preoccupied with winning and scoring points. Unfortunately, most of us merely watch sports. We root for our favorite team, dream about our heroes, feel great when "we" win and miserable when "we" lose. Many of today's sports using a ball originate in monasteries, universities, and nobility, where people had excess time and explored ways to gain personal strength and raise team spirit.

The ultimate in idling time away must be cricket. It is easy to imagine how British colonists, bored to death in Australia, India, or Kenya, enjoyed this game on some gorgeous meadow, dressed in impeccable white outfits. On a trip to India, my business partner tried to explain how "Test" cricket games are the unsurpassed challenge—a match could take up to five consecutive days. India was playing the prestigious Anthony De Mello Trophy against England and had just finished the first day. When I asked which country was leading, my partner gave me a compassionate smile and said, "I couldn't tell you. England has yet to finish batting in their first innings!"

Our forebears indeed walked and ran long distances daily. They collected food and chased their prey. Over millions of years, their bodies became incredibly efficient. What a huge contrast with the way many of us spend our lives today. We enjoy the comfort of our cars to run errands, visit friends, and go to work. We park our cars as close to the office as possible. We sit on our chairs many hours a day, our minds so occupied with issues to solve that we even forget we have a body. When we get home, we drop dead on the couch, grab a fast snack, and surrender our intelligence to some brainless distraction on YouTube or TV.

I am exaggerating, but for a reason. If the caveman still rules our physiology, why is it so tough for us to get active and exercise for fun?

The answer is simple. Since primal humans had to walk and run so much to survive, they learned not to waste energy. In other words, we are programmed to avoid exercising. For our ancestors this was a logical measure of nature to keep their balance. Now our environment has changed completely. Food is available within a few steps, so this program no longer serves us. Our DNA has not been able to keep up with the rapid pace at which we changed our external conditions. We need to motivate ourselves and adopt an active lifestyle.

Check for yourself what you can do. For instance, run small errands on foot or by bike, and if possible, adjust your commute as well. If you work from home, take frequent breaks to do some stretching exercises. At the office, fetch your coffee or tea at the farthest machine in the building. Ask for a desk that is easily adjustable to a standing position so you can alternate between standing and sitting. For lunch, take a half-hour walk. Even better, have your one-on-one meetings while strolling outside. Replace all sitting meetings by stand-up workshops and kill those tedious PowerPoint reviews. It's an effective way to cut to the chase and save yourself a ton of time! Lastly, learn from my old man. As a young doctor, my father vowed to never take an elevator. At the day he retired at age sixty-eight, he still walked the stairs between all floors at the hospital.

Born to Run?

I have always had a love-hate relationship with running. The image of a pack of hunters, swiftly progressing in a balanced cadence through nature, seemed to be the ultimate exercise to me. It is amazing how evolution rewarded people for running long distances. Our pituitary gland secretes endorphins—a kind of endogenous morphine—to soothe our pain and bring us to a euphoric state (the "runner's high"). How I longed to experience it.

But my body proved hopelessly inefficient in comparison to others. After a mile or so, my face would turn red, my breath would get shallow, and the rest of the run was nothing short of a trip to hell. My knees would start aching and I couldn't imagine why anyone would do this for fun. So I switched to rowing and cycling and sports using a ball like tennis. Yet it always puzzled me why I had lost the caveman gene when it came to moving myself on two legs.

A few years ago, my wife and I met up with our friend Sandra. She showed us pictures of an incredible trail run she had just finished in Switzerland, conquering Mount Jungfrau with a height difference of twelve thousand feet. On one of the photos I zoomed in on her feet. Her colorful "shoes" looked like gloves as each toe had a separate "finger" into which to fit. "How do you like my barefoot shoes?" Sandra asked. "I bought these eight months ago and they're fabulous.

It took some time to change my technique to a more natural running style. I've been free of injuries ever since!"

I asked Sandra to show me the shoes and was quite amazed when I studied them. They had absolutely no resemblance to the Vaporfly shoes that Eliud Kipchoge recently wore when he became the world's first man ever to run a marathon under two hours. There was no special heel collar to shield the Achilles' tendon. No arch support for stability and motion control. And definitely no air cushions to absorb impact forces on the knees. These shoes truly were back to basics. A thin sole protected the runner against puncture wounds, but other than that, they seemed little more sophisticated than molded plastic socks. "It's quite logical if you think about it," Sandra explained. "We were born to run, so you can trust your feet to perfectly deal with the road. We simply need to unlearn to land on our heels. A forefoot landing naturally absorbs the impact as we gradually let the heel come down. Virtually all nerves in our body have endings in our feet. Do your organs a big favor and let the road massage them!"

* * *

"Running is the greatest metaphor of life, because you get out of it what you put into it."
—Oprah Winfrey

* * *

The very next day, I visited a barefoot running shop. I bought two pairs—one for normal walking and a pair of "funny finger shoes" to practice running. I needed to strengthen all kinds of muscles that had been pampered by wearing conventional shoes for more than four decades. The shop owner checked my running style and gave me some instructions. Elated, I started to practice three times a week. Soon, the initial muscle pain disappeared and my knees felt absolutely fine. But it annoyed me that I still got exhausted within ten minutes. I carried on for a few more weeks and then decided to drop my efforts altogether. It was no use. I clearly wasn't supposed to run.

On a dinner with Sandra last year the topic came up. She asked me a simple question: "Are you able to keep up a conversation while running?"

"Hell no, I would be gasping for air after just a few minutes," I replied.

"Keep up your fast pace but take smaller steps," she said.

Although I was skeptical, I decided to make a final attempt. I slowed down to a ridiculous speed of perhaps five mph. I focused on the right technique, keeping my head right above the balls of my feet as they touched the ground. I ran for five minutes and felt perfectly fine. Another five minutes and I had nicely gotten into the cadence. I continued for yet another ten minutes and really enjoyed my workout. Soon enough, forty-five minutes had passed, and I felt I could continue forever. My legs were light, my breathing smooth, and my mind completely balanced. Here I was, at forty-seven years of age, and it had finally dawned on me how nature intended me to run. I was on top the world!

The secret of running was to get out of my head and into my body. I had to forget about speed and distance, or fear of wearing myself out. My barefoot shoes put me in contact with my environment. As I let ease and fun determine the speed at which I ran, it was as if my body itself took over. I was in flow, witnessing the scene, sensing what happened both around me and within me. As running is 50 percent muscle action and 50 percent elasticity of tendons and ligaments, the investment in my daily yoga practice paid off. I could feel my life energies freely moving up my spine, balancing my body and mind and making me a very happy man. I smiled as I, all of a sudden, heard a deeper and probably unintended layer in Bruce Springsteen's song: 'Cause tramps like us, baby we were born to run!

Let's Get Physical

In recent years, working out at the gym has become a popular, yet often temporary, pastime. In the aftermath of a hearty Christmas dinner, we make our New Year's resolution to visit the gym three times a week. It's a wonderful intention, as we lose about 5 percent of our muscle mass every decade following our thirtieth birthday. This decline of muscle mass, called sarcopenia, accelerates above the age of 50. Exercise is known to be effective in counteracting the negative effects.

A popular way is to go to the gym. I have tried it many times and so have many colleagues with whom I have worked. We would pump up muscle with a few series of short and frequent pushing or pulling of weights. We would get excited by the more aesthetic shape of our bodies. We'd feel invincible as we broke personal records and felt stronger every week. And then ... something would happen that would prevent us from going to the gym. An urgent deliverable at work or a private obligation demanded that we revisit our priorities. Or an injury forced us to rest for a few weeks. And at the height of the pandemic, the gym was closed for months!

If we don't maintain the routine, after just three weeks our wonderful six-pack and Terminator chest begin to disappear. Then we feel bad about ourselves and find a million excuses. We resume our old lifestyle, claiming "it's not quite my thing anyway."

How do we sustainably rejuvenate this decaying body of ours? How do we ensure keeping our energy levels up even in busy times? I found that a set of simple yet very effective exercises work miracles for me. This daily practice takes me some forty-five minutes in the morning. And the good news is—I can do it anywhere. All I need is six by eight feet of space and a towel or yoga mat.

These exercises date back thousands of years. Yogic *asanas* and Taoist *chi kungs* were designed from a deep understanding of how our body functions. They were refined by sages in and around the Himalayas. These sages found the natural postures that work not only on a physical level, but also on an energy level. They realized that lasting strength is not in pumped-up muscles. Such muscles make our bodies stiff and inflexible and consume a lot of protein. The sages developed endurance through flexible muscles, tendons, and ligaments. They knew we thrive when our spine is loose and resilient as it connects all our organs and energy centers.

As the energy flows freely through our spine, it regenerates every part of our body. By clearing our physical blockages, we prepare our body as a platform for mental, emotional, and spiritual growth. In this way we have the opportunity to maintain our full vitality into old age.

—TRANSFORMATION EXERCISE 6—
The Five Tibetan Rites

The Himalayas are considered the cradle of human wisdom. For thousands of years sages lived in these mountains and attained ways to raise their consciousness. Yoga—which means union with the creative potential—is the practice to realize inner balance. As Indian sages crossed the Himalayas and visited Tibet since the eighth century CE, they shared their 112 asanas—yogic exercises. Tibetan lamas derived the five fundamental exercises from them that connect the energy systems of mind and body in an extraordinary way.[20] These Five Tibetan Rites are called the Fountain of Youth as they enhance metabolism, cardiovascular function, strength, energy, and flexibility. I always do them at the end of my yoga practice.

These exercises only take about 10–15 minutes and should be done on an empty stomach. Breathe in through your nose as you start the exercise and out as you return to the starting posture. Start by doing each exercise once during the first week. Then repeat each exercise two additional times every week (three times during week 2, five times during week 3, and so on). You may want to build up to the optimum of twenty-one times per exercise. There is no better way to start your day!

Note: After each rite, stand with both feet next to each other and place your palms flat on your hips. Inhale deeply through your nose and exhale through your mouth as your lips form an O. Do this twice.

1st Rite—Spinning.
Benefit: Enhance Your Balance Mechanism

Stand up straight, spread your arms horizontally with your palms facing downward and fingers together pointing outward. Now start turning clockwise around your own axis (unless you are on the Southern Hemisphere, where you turn counterclockwise). Do it at a pace that is comfortable for you. These are "push-ups" for your inner ears to keep balance.

2nd Rite—The "J."
Benefit: Strengthen Abdomen and Enhance Digestion

Lie on your back on a towel or yoga mat. Stretch your legs, ankles touching each other, and toes pointed. Put your arms next to your body with your palms facing downward and fingers touching each other. As you inhale through the nose, bring your legs up to make a ninety-degree angle with the floor. Lift your head up and tuck your chin tightly into your chest. Your body is assuming a J shape. As you exhale, slowly drop your legs to the floor. For even more impact, lower your legs to just above the floor.

3rd Rite—Arching.
Benefit: Enhance Respiration and Digestion

From a standing position, kneel down, with the back of your toes still touching the floor (balancing on the balls of your feet). Keep your knees four inches apart and your back straight up. Place the palms of your hands at the back of your thighs, just under your buttocks. Straighten your spine by tucking your chin into your chest. Inhale through the nose and arch backward from the waist. Carefully drop your head backward. As you exhale, straighten your neck and back and tuck your chin in again.

4th Rite—The Table Top.
Benefit: Strengthen the Lower Back

Sit upright with your legs stretched, toes facing up. Place your palms flat on the floor next to your hips. Tuck your chin into your chest. As you inhale through the nose, carefully drop your head backward and lift your hips up while bending your knees and placing the soles of your feet flat on the floor. Your upper body and upper legs represent a tabletop, while your arms and lower legs are vertical. As you exhale, return to the sitting position while keeping your hands next to your hips. Straighten your neck and tuck your chin in again.

5th Rite—The Two Dogs.
Benefit: Improve Blood Flow and Strengthen Spine

Lie down with your face, stomach and legs flat on the floor. Place your palms next to your chest, with your elbows bent back. Now lift your body by extending your arms, leaning only on the balls of your feet and your palms. Keep your legs and hands shoulder-width apart. Your legs should be horizontal above the floor, while your arms should be vertical, just above your hips. Keep your head bent backward while looking at the ceiling. This is the starting position. As you inhale through the nose, move your buttocks up while keeping your legs and arms stretched. Tuck your chin into your chest and form a perfect triangle with your body (your buttocks are the top of the triangle). Now exhale and return to the starting position while remaining on the balls of your feet and your palms.

Relaxation—The Child's Pose (Balasana).
Benefit: Stretch Hips, Thighs, and Ankles

After you have finished all Five Tibetan Rites, relax for a few minutes. Kneel on the floor with your feet together facing upward. Keep your knees hip-width apart. Now stretch your arms straight up and lower your upper body and arms to the floor, bending from your lower back. Relax for a few minutes. Breathe quietly through your belly and observe the sensations in your body.

From Disease Care to Prevention

As a physical manifestation of our underlying energy system, our body is a perfect reflection of what we think and how we feel on the inside. Every organ, gland, or joint relates to particular emotional states. If our energy is jammed due to certain convictions we're not even aware of, we'll sense it in our body. If we ignore the signs and allow the pressure to build, it may develop into an infection.

My pneumonia, for example, had a direct impact on my breathing. Problems with our lungs are a clear indication that we are alienated from the essence of our being. I was working day and night, outpacing everyone in my environment. But for what reason? Fear of survival had sparked an internal conviction that I wasn't enough. I constantly had to prove myself to consider myself valuable. A deep sense of insecurity was hidden behind a shield of apparent *joie de vivre.* My pneumonia forced me to do what I had never done—let go, appreciate myself for my uniqueness, and take the space to live my life in accordance with my heartfelt desire.

Where is the coronavirus attacking us? Exactly, on our respiratory system! It puts our immune system to the test, making our seniors and younger people with latent lung problems particularly vulnerable. It magnifies the problems for people walking around with a life not lived by one's inner GPS. A strong signal to humanity as a whole—we are alienated from the essence of our being. The thoughts we think, the emotions we feel, and the behaviors we display are all of a quality that is miles below our potential.

Our Western healthcare system has reached a professional standard unprecedented in history. The scientific knowledge of the physiological processes in the body is unparalleled. The range of treatment methods to cure acute disease or turn it into manageable chronic illness is impressive. But the word "healthcare" is poorly chosen. What we have built is a "disease care" system. It's fully equipped to deal with known illnesses as soon as they manifest. Yet this disease care system is unsustainable. As a population, we continue to grow older, fatter, and sicker. Costs continue to rise at twice the rate of the economy, even without taking into account the coronavirus. And in America, a considerable percentage of the population is excluded from the system.

In a genuine healthcare system, prevention would be central to all efforts. Schools would teach children the true nature of who they are. Pupils would learn how to move out of their head and listen to their body. To sense what their body really needs in terms of breathing, eating, drinking, exercising, and sleeping. This would lay the foundation for preventing lifestyle diseases at an early age. Companies and other employers would seriously invest in their employees' well-being with flexible work schedules, facilities for exercise and meditation, healthy food, and regular health checks. Without patronizing, governments would protect people from commercial marketing that responds to people's fears and incites them to consume what's not in their interest.

The impact of people's pent-up emotions on their well-being is far greater than most of us realize. We are all charged with subconscious patterns and learning to overcome them is an essential part of our human experience. Part II delves much deeper into our mental and emotional transformation. On a physical level, we can do a lot to free the body from the blockages caused by our fears. Using the power of our awareness to magnify a physical experience has a surprisingly liberating effect.

TOP THREE TAKEAWAYS

1) Our body expects to walk and run six to nine miles a day to collect and hunt food. Therefore, we are programmed not to waste energy. It takes some effort to incorporate an active lifestyle into our daily rhythm. All of us are natural runners. We have simply forgotten how nature intended us to run.

2) We lose about 5 percent of our muscle mass every decade following our thirtieth birthday. A set of basic exercises— yogic asanas and Taoist chi kungs—helps us maintain strong and flexible muscles, tendons, and ligaments.

3) Our body is a perfect reflection of what we think and how we feel on the inside. Every organ, gland, or joint relates to particular emotional states. If our energy is jammed due to subconscious patterns, we'll sense it in our body. In the long run this can even lead to illness. Asanas and chi kungs are powerful tools to overcome these blockages.

SHAPE YOUR PARADISE *ONLINE*

How do you become a barefoot runner? How do you "clear your issues from your tissues?" I have compiled a perfect mix of asanas and chi kungs to keep you energized and strong. Check out Week 3 of the online module "You Too Are A Caveman" for guidance on your natural daily workout.

6

LET IT DIGEST

*"The heart of the home beats in the kitchen and
a healthy one beats three times a day."*
—Bangambiki Habyarimana

We're Tougher than We Think

A mobile phone started buzzing. "I'm sorry, can we take a short break?" asked one of my colleagues while we were in the middle of a heated team discussion. "It is time for my healthy snack." Surprised, I checked the time and paused the meeting for five minutes to stretch our legs. As I was curious about her dietary rhythm, I walked over to my colleague and inquired about her approach.

"Yes, I went to see a dietitian as I want to lose some weight and gain more energy," she said. She explained about the yo-yo effect that uneven eating patterns had on her digestive system. "So now I have a calorie diary which I maintain in my health app. I am scheduled for eight healthy snacks a day at regular time intervals."

You probably guessed my thinking at this point: "How would the cavemen have dealt with this?" They probably did eat healthy food as everything they found was purely organic. Yet did they gather food at regular time intervals? For sure they did not record their intake in their health app, which may have been a missed opportunity on their part!

I was pleased to see that my colleague took her food consumption seriously. But is it the most natural and effective way to go about it? What about this yo-yo effect? Are irregular eating patterns really that harmful to our digestive processes? Does the choice of food we eat matter all that much? How about vegetarian or even vegan lifestyles or, for instance, the raw food movement? Is there any guidance we can retrieve from our stout-hearted forebears?

Just imagine for a while what eating food must have meant for the early humanoid species. The first two to three million years, they weren't actually hunting that much. It was mostly the gathering of food that preoccupied a good part of their days. They were at the lower end of the food chain. Physically not that impressive to most predators, these primeval humans were mainly collecting fruits, plants, vegetables, leaves, nuts, seeds, and flowers. They would occasionally eat animal protein by hunting smaller vertebrates. And they consumed the leftovers of half-eaten preys as unabashed scavengers.

In the Stone Age (starting some three million years ago), they steadily developed weapons, allowing them to hunt larger animals. And the occasional use of fire (as from one million years ago) and full control of it (around three hundred thousand years ago) allowed our forebears to become the dominant species in nature. In generations thereafter, they learned how to cook their food. Consequently, certain starches and occasional meat would be more easily digested, unlocking the nutritional value in terms of calories and protein. Consequently, their digestive system shortened, while their neocortex brain developed—a monumental gizmo in their quest for control. In Chapter 1 we discussed how viruses likely stimulated this development. The first modern man—Homo sapiens—was born, probably two hundred thousand years ago in the southern part of Africa.

Until the day the first people settled to become farmers—some twelve thousand years ago—their hours were filled with collecting a meal. They certainly didn't eat eight small healthy snacks during the day, let alone devour the fast food and soda drinks so many of us take in daily. For millions of years, these primal men lived as nomads. They moved to new places when it became too hard to feed their tribe. Food wasn't readily available. It took many hours, if not days, to gather and hunt. Preparing the food was another tedious endeavor. There were no refrigerators to store any meals. Once ready, the food had to be enjoyed within a matter of hours. Throughout the day, most activities were dedicated to this single event of having a meal together.

Here's the crux of the matter. Wild animals are never overweight. They take in as much as they need to function optimally. The same can be said of primal humans. They ate once a day or whenever food was available and could easily cope with long hours without food. In our present society of abundance, we need to take certain measures to maintain our body well. Our bodies are designed to deal with shortages, not with abundance. Our physiology has developed this incredible tenacity to cope with a complete lack of food for the larger part of the day without any issue.

Dr. Herring's Experiments

Based on this innate capability, Dr. Bert Herring, a family medicine specialist in Jacksonville, Florida, experimented for himself with a diet he labeled Fast-5.[21] For nineteen hours a day, he abstained from eating any food or drinking any calorie-rich beverage. By first skipping breakfast, and then lunch as well, he awakened an internal mechanism that made him feel strong and healthy throughout the day. In the remaining five-hour window, he allowed himself to eat anything for which he was craving. Should he eat some unhealthy food, he could rest assured the body would burn it off during the nineteen-hour fast. And the magic is that the digestive system converts the food into "brown fat," a healthy fat that evenly releases energy to the bloodstream throughout the day. Being a physician, Bert Herring measured his vital signs—pulse, blood pressure, blood glucose level (HbA1c), and amount of inflammation (HS-CRP). They all remained perfectly stable throughout the day without any observable yo-yo effect. Many people have followed Herring's example and as a benefit lost their excess weight at a rate of about one pound per week.

I can hear you thinking, "Aren't they hungry at all? I really feel hungry if I haven't eaten for just a few hours!"

Again, the beauty of the evolutionary design of our body in response to our environment becomes evident. Have you ever told yourself you wouldn't eat potato chips, a cookie, or a candy bar only to find yourself really craving it after some time? You decide to take just one bite to get the flavor of it. That heavenly fulfillment of the fuzzy taste in your mouth and stomach! You just gotta have one more bite. Before you know it, the whole bag, box, or roll is empty and thoughts of guilt start torturing you. How could this happen? You were so determined not to do this!

You just experienced a limbic hunger attack. As we explored in Chapter 3, our limbic system is the part of our brains we share with other mammals. Our social emotions and memory are processed in this brain center, with organs such as the pineal and pituitary gland. As we are designed to deal with shortages in nature, our limbic system is activated the moment we find food that contains either sugar, fat, or salt. These base ingredients were hard to find in the environment of hunter-gatherers. Hence we are programmed to eat as much of them as we possibly can the moment we taste them. It could easily take days before our forebears would have the chance to indulge in them again. It also explains why we tend to compensate for our hurt feelings by robbing the fridge—the same emotional brain center is involved.

My Personal Experience

I have frequently experimented with fasting for nineteen hours a day and found it fairly easy to do. Indeed, the hunger sensation subsides after a few weeks. It makes things easy if you let the clock decide whether you can eat something or not. You won't fall prey to limbic hunger if you simply don't take that very first bite during fasting hours. If you are overweight, I recommend you try it yourself. My only caveat is I became really skinny. Unlike most people, my metabolism is very fast. I therefore searched for some sensible adjustments to this valuable habit of daily fasting.

In the yogic science, extensive focus is dedicated to the frequency of food intake as well. Our digestive system is astonishingly complex and perfectly attuned to the specific food to be processed. The acid cocktail that your stomach releases is exactly geared to raid the meal you just consumed. This process takes about four hours to complete and should not be disturbed by new food entering the system in this time slot. In fact, our system will need at least another hour to do some internal cleansing before it's ready to process a next batch. Any sensation of hunger before this five-hour time slot purely is a mental compulsion, which disappears if you ignore it. A little training will easily extend this period of fasting to eight hours, which is optimal for the system to maintain itself well. It is no problem to feel a bit hungry; in fact you are much sharper and more intuitive on an empty stomach!

Lately, the "16/8 intermittent fasting" diet has become hot. Lots of celebrities and social media influencers have endorsed this daily rhythm of sixteen hours of fasting and an eight-hour eating window. I apply a pragmatic variant of this regime. As I want to optimize my energy level, I eat two to three times a day. I try to sense how much food my body really needs. If I am outdoors playing sports, I am likely to enjoy all three meals of the day. When I do office work indoors, I usually combine breakfast and lunch for brunch at 11 a.m. In any case, I will not eat anything for five hours straight after I have had something to eat. Even a little snack, however organic it may be, means another disruption to my digestive system. It is much better served with a little restriction on my part.

Carb-Less Cavemen

So many diets are proposed these days. Given the fact that 50 percent of Americans are overweight, while more than a third are obese, it is obvious some changes are needed. The relationship between excessive carbohydrate consumption and weight has become evident. People look for solace in the Atkins, Zone, Weight Watchers, South Beach, or Raw Food diets, which are all low on carb consumption. The latest hype is the ketogenic (or keto for short) diet. The diet suggests that we should replace almost all carb intake with fat. It's meant to teach the body to become efficient in burning fat rather than sugar. This metabolic state of burning fat instead of sugar is called ketosis. As a result, people are reported to lose weight and, in case of diabetes (type 2) patients, are able to reduce their insulin intake. Others warn that it's a very strict diet that includes lots of meat and processed food, which often contains a lot of salt.

As with all issues pertaining to our physical health, I'd like to look at the environment in which our body is optimized to function. Primeval humans certainly ate organically, as the use of pesticides, genetic mutations, and preservatives did not yet exist. A first important step is therefore not to eat processed food. Any package with a label is suspect, as it most likely contains too much salt, sugar or fat, and all kinds of preservatives. You want to know what you eat!

The majority of our ancestors' diet consisted of fruits, vegetables, nuts, and seeds. What about carb consumption? Some tubers may have been part of people's primal diet, especially after they managed to control fire. When people exchanged hunting for farming, their diet became more one-sided. Carbohydrates (grains, rice, potatoes, and nowadays, processed sugar) and dairy became more dominant elements of their daily consumption.

Our body extracts glucose from carbs, which serves as fuel for running and other activities. Excess glucose is converted to fat and stored for times of shortage. The body first burns the glucose when it requires energy, and only then turns to fat. A large carb intake significantly raises the sugar level in our blood every time we eat, to which the body overreacts by producing too much insulin. Hence, we get our highs and lows throughout the day, especially if we don't exercise much. A stable blood sugar level is facilitated by eating fewer carbohydrates, forcing our body to burn fat instead of glucose.

I concur with concerns about high carbohydrate consumption. The good news is if we train ourselves to fast for at least five hours in between meals, we will already achieve most of our diet objectives. If we learn to drink mostly water throughout the day, and quit eating snacks after dinner, we'll burn most of the excessive carb intake right after our meals. Fasting builds up the brown fat that allows for a most healthy and natural state of ketosis throughout the day.

—TRANSFORMATION EXERCISE 7—
Budweiser or Guinness?

I cannot help but smile when I see people bringing their water bottles along wherever they go, taking a zip every other minute or so. It is, of course, harmless to drink water that way, but it is pointless. As mentioned, our body is fully geared to deal with shortages, not with abundance. Drinking a couple of glasses of water every few hours is in fact more effective, as it leaves your digestive system completely at peace for distinct blocs during the day. You have an excellent measuring device—check the color of your urine when peeing. If it looks like Budweiser or lighter, you're at a perfect drinking pace. If you're producing Guinness, it's time to take your cup to the water tap as you have some catching up to do.

Bonus tip—after filling your cup, leave it there for ten to fifteen minutes before drinking. Tap water has a way of settling, which makes it much more agreeable for the body to take in. They're still the same H2O molecules, but there is more to it than meets the eye!

Food Favorites

The ideal generic diet for human beings does not exist. Different bodies react differently to certain types of food, especially when it comes to the rate at which different types of starch—and products containing refined sugar—influence blood sugar level. Check this out for yourself. After a meal, do you feel very active and a few hours later rather listless? This is a clear indication your body is producing lots of insulin to absorb the glucose in your bloodstream. Try a different type of food, for instance containing more fiber—you may want to replace bread with oatmeal, regular potatoes with red potatoes, and cookies and candy with fruit.

One nutrient to check for yourself is your magnesium intake. Our carbohydrate digestion is significantly facilitated by magnesium, and this mineral stabilizes our nervous system. Do you experience muscle cramps, a vibrating eyelid, or palpitations? These are clear symptoms your magnesium intake may be too low, as is the case for more than half of the American population. Our contemporary Western diet does not include a lot of magnesium-rich food, but with a little effort you can easily find them. Primal humans ate lots of nuts and seeds, which are a rich source of magnesium. Other sources are certain vegetables (broccoli, spinach, and cabbage), fruits (figs, bananas, and avocados) and legumes (kidney beans, chickpeas, and black beans).

What more can be said about healthy food? Do you really have to adopt a vegetarian, vegan, or raw diet? Or can you still enjoy a piece of meat? How do you optimize your energy level?

For primal humans, eating meat or fish was quite an event, as it took considerable effort to hunt or catch them. Our forebears probably did not eat animal protein more often than a few times a week. More than that is not needed in a balanced diet. Now let's shift our time machine to only a hundred years ago and consider the diet of our great-grandparents. They probably didn't eat meat or fish much, either. Most of their food would have been organic, although perhaps quite biased toward some starch or bread, dairy, and basic vegetables. The thought of having to eat meat daily has little to do with our nutritional requirements. We connect meat with health and like the taste of it. As we can afford to eat it more often, we do.

The truth is our digestive system has great difficulty consuming red meat. In fact, the closer animals are to our own DNA—as is the case with all mammals—the tougher it is for our body to process their meat. The next time you eat a steak, just notice the amount of energy it takes for your stomach and intestines to process the food. You initially may not even be able to fall asleep. And once you do, you most likely are so tired from digesting the meat that waking up in the morning becomes an ordeal. Red meat makes you long to sleep all day, just like lions do in the savannah.

You must be watching the news and notice what we're doing to the world. In order to produce four ounces of beef on your plate, five hundred gallons of water are consumed. Large stretches of rainforest are chopped each year. The land is converted into soy plantations to feed cows for meat production, while we are in dire need of trees to convert carbon dioxide into oxygen. What we're doing to cows, pigs, and goats in the bio industry is cruel and unworthy. The least we can do is make a small contribution by removing red meat from our diet. I hardly ever eat red meat. I occasionally have a bit of organic chicken or fish and I consume limited carbs (mostly cereals). But I have lots of nuts, fruits, beans, and vegetables as I wish to keep my energy level up all day.

The Iceman

"Give me the binoculars, it's my turn to look!" my son Joshua said impatiently as his sister stared at a group of elephants approaching the pond. We had parked our rental jeep on the other side of the water. What a vacation it had been! We had traveled the east side of South Africa for two weeks and were about to experience our final act at the Kruger National Park.

Four giant elephants then stepped into the water. It was time to bathe! What could be more convenient than having a trunk that serves as your built-in shower? We didn't actually need binoculars; we could easily observe the scene with our naked eye. After about ten minutes, they slowly exited the pond and I was about to start our engine. "Wait!" Joshua yelled as he pointed to the front animal, which was using its trunk for the next task. We all watched in amazement as she threw dust all over her body to protect her from the sun's ultraviolet radiation. Josh's reaction could have come straight from a movie: "Now you're all dirty again, Dumbo!"

All animals use water to clean themselves. Even in winter, they don't mind the cold as their bodies are set to withstand it. Animals have a layer of "brown fat" that serves as insulation. It prevents ducks, bears, and deer from freezing to death in winter. Here's the thing—so do we! The cavemen didn't pamper themselves. They couldn't take a hot shower. They would jump into a river for their bath. Their body would burn their brown fat to protect them from the cold. It's the same brown fat we generate by fasting for multiple hours during the day—a natural mechanism that helps us stabilize both our sugar level and body temperature.

Wim Hof is a Dutch adventurer who has put this insight to the test. For years, he trained himself in ice baths and arctic environments to build his tenacity to withstand the cold. At fifty, he ran a half marathon above the Arctic Circle barefoot and shirtless. He regularly conducted scientific experiments, measuring his vital signs with electrodes on his chest and head while standing in a container filled with ice cubes. These achievements have earned him the nickname "The Iceman." In recent years, Hof has been training groups to control their nervous systems and unleash their inner power, for instance by climbing Mount Kilimanjaro wearing shorts only.

What are the proven benefits of exposing our body to cold water? Cold therapy trains all the muscles in our cardiovascular system.[22] When exposed to the cold, these muscles close the veins and capillaries to protect the organs and other vital parts as their temperature cannot drop below 95 degrees Fahrenheit (35 degrees Celsius). When the body returns to a warmer environment, these minuscule muscles open the veins up again. It is cardiovascular fitness training! This offers several powerful long term advantages:

> Exercising the muscles in the veins lowers the blood pressure. According to the American Heart Association, nearly half of all Americans are hypertensive (blood pressure above 130/80 mm Hg). Coronary artery disease—narrowing of the blood vessels—is the world's number one deadliest disease as reported by the World Health Organization. Number 2 is stroke, when an artery in the brain leaks because the blood flow is blocked.

> Cold therapy appears to reduce inflammation in the body. Inflammation is a rather rudimentary mechanism that the immune system applies to fight bacterial, viral, or toxic attacks. By raising the temperature, the body tries to shake off intruders. Many diseases are related to chronic inflammation, which happens when the immune system mistakes the body's own cells for invaders. Examples of these diseases are diabetes (type 2), asthma, arthritis, psoriasis, hepatitis, Crohn's disease, and Alzheimer's.

> Cold water stops our habitual thinking and takes us right back to the now. It is a perfect opportunity to strengthen our concentration. It boosts our metabolism and provides an additional source of energy as brown fat is built up, which is slowly released throughout the day. It's a refreshing start of the day!

—TRANSFORMATION EXERCISE 8—
A Cold Shower a Day ...

Next time you take a shower, be brave and finish with cold therapy. If you do it for thirty days, it will become part of your system and you won't want to miss it!

Here are the steps:

1. Shower warm first, as this opens your veins, arteries, and capillaries.
2. When you're about to finish, activate your Yee Power. Focus on deep belly breathing and connect your head, heart, and gut.
3. Now lower the water temperature to about 60 degrees Fahrenheit (16 degrees Celsius). Concentrate on your breathing. Make sure your exhale is twice as long as your inhale. Try to control your breathing: two seconds in, four seconds out.
4. When you try the first time, a thirty-second cold shower is a fantastic effort. You will find that you can gradually extend the time for the following days.
5. Once you're able to hold it for two minutes in a fully balanced, normal breathing pattern, it's time to go even colder. The next time you take a shower, lower the temperature to 57 degrees Fahrenheit (14 degrees Celsius).
6. Once you smoothly manage this temperature for two minutes, move to 54 degrees Fahrenheit (12 degrees Celsius). Now you can train yourself to extend the cold shower to five or even ten minutes. Do this at least three times a week and notice the difference!

TOP THREE TAKEAWAYS

1) Our body is designed to deal with shortages, not abundance. Our digestive system functions optimally if we don't eat anything for at least five hours in between meals.

2) Sugar, salt, and fat are scarce in nature, but not in our diet today. We crave them the moment we taste them. The only way to eat less of them is to not take the first bite. Our body doesn't function well on large amounts of carbohydrates. They are stored as fat and clog our system.

3) Our body doesn't thrive if we pamper it too much. It has a built-in mechanism to close our veins when exposed to cold water. Frequent cold showers have proven benefits, such as lower blood pressure and a reduction in inflammation in the body.

SHAPE YOUR PARADISE *ONLINE*

In Week 4 of the online module "You Too Are A Caveman," you'll make your first attempt to enjoy a cold shower. You will also explore the yogic science of "pranic" food. Prana means life energy, which is chi in the Tao wisdom. Learn about the deeper backgrounds of a natural diet!

DANCE TO THE RHYTHM
OF THE DAY

*"Follow the natural rhythm of your life and you will
discover a force far greater than your own."*
—Oprah Winfrey

Born to Sleep?

My business appointment this afternoon was a few minutes late, providing a wonderful opportunity to be quiet and watch my breath. I was revisiting my intentions for the meeting to come. I would be open, warm hearted, and genuinely interested in my visitor's story. The door swung open. In a somewhat boorish way, my colleague—let's call him Fernando—rushed in.

"Those idiots at maintenance put both elevators out of use," he moaned. "Both of them! I had to climb five flights of stairs. As if I wasn't tired already!"

"Sorry to hear that, Fernando," I replied. "Glad you made it anyway. Tell me, what made you so tired today?"

"Oh, it's not just today," he said. "I haven't slept well in years. It wears me out. But that's not why I'm here. Let's get started."

For a second I considered getting down to business. I decided that I shouldn't. "Fernando, before we begin, what kind of help are you getting?" I asked.

He gave me a hesitant look. "I'm serious," I said. "It must be debilitating to not have a good night's rest. I'm sure there are experts who can help you."

Fernando paused for a few moments while he let my comments sink in. "You know, my wife said the same thing this morning," he remarked. "I guess it's time to seek professional support."

A Serious Issue

Fernando certainly wasn't the only one suffering from a sleep disorder. One in three American adults report at least mild insomnia, and about 10 percent suffer from it on a chronic basis. Many take medication on a regular basis. The total cost to society in terms of treatment, medication, work loss, and accidents for the United States are estimated to be at least $63 billion.[23]

These striking numbers are not limited to America. Stanford University reviewed more than fifty epidemiological studies of insomnia worldwide. They paint a worrying picture.[24] Generally, 16 to 21 percent report either difficulty initiating sleep (DIS) or difficulty maintaining sleep (DMS) as occurring at least three nights a week. The insomnia lasted for more than a year in 85 percent of cases. Between 8.5 percent and 13 percent of the respondents associated their insomnia with daytime symptoms such as sleepiness, cognitive impairment, irritability, mood swings, or anxiety. The 24/7 economy and rapid growth in the use of smartphones and tablets are contributing to insomnia growing to epidemic proportions.

I was quite surprised when I met Fernando about a month after our conversation. A specialist had prescribed sleeping pills. Also, this doctor advised Fernando to stay up until midnight in order to "build up sleep pressure," which should facilitate falling asleep. I asked Fernando how he felt. "The pills do their work," he responded. "But I feel quite dizzy during the day and have difficulty concentrating."

This was no real solution in my eyes. It was merely a way to cope with the problem. You're probably guessing the question that popped up in my mind—how would primal men and women have dealt with sleeping? Since our physiology still reflects the circumstances under which our ancestors lived for millions of years, let's explore this further.

Our Circadian Rhythm

When it comes to sleep, the obvious difference between us and primeval humans is the absence of electricity and artificial light in the old days. When the sun set, everything slowly turned dark. The use of fire in the last three hundred thousand years somewhat extended the day, but generally, darkness meant it was time to be quiet and fall asleep.

All living organisms are regulated by a circadian rhythm that organizes their sleep-wake cycle. The word "circadian" is derived from the Latin words *circa* (which means "around") and *dies* (the word for "day"). It's a highly refined system that optimizes energy levels, metabolism, and physical recovery throughout the day.

Our human physiology has developed two mechanisms to support the process of sleeping in the dark and waking when the sun comes up. Our hormones lend a hand, as does our internal thermometer. As soon as it notices the absence of light, our pineal gland—remember it's the gateway to our limbic system—triggers the release of melatonin. The chemical is a magnificent internal "sleeping pill" that makes us drowsy and want to sleep. In the morning, a different hormone called cortisol is secreted in our bloodstream, which activates our system. Cortisol is sometimes referred to as the "stress hormone," which is true if our body is producing an overdose during the day. Under normal circumstances, cortisol is a wonderful hormone to get us active in the morning.

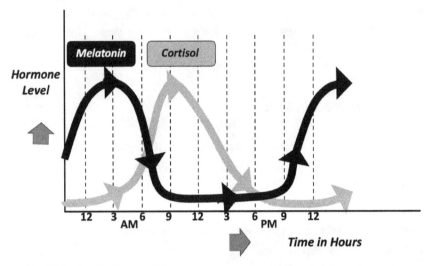

Exhibit 7—Release of hormones supports the sleep-wake cycle.

Our internal thermometer is running a basic cycle of warming our body up, roughly between 5 a.m. and 7 p.m., and cooling us down during the next ten hours. A warm body is needed to get active, while the drop in body temperature facilitates falling asleep. The spread of only two degrees Fahrenheit (just over one degree Celsius) makes all the difference in getting us in an active or passive mode.

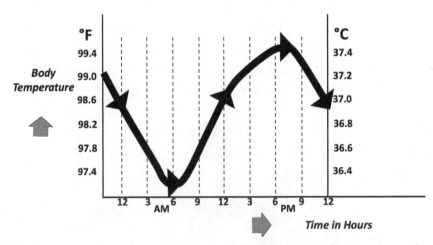

Exhibit 8—Body temperature greatly facilitates the sleep-wake cycle.

These two mechanisms—the release of hormones and our internal thermometer—naturally adapt somewhat to the seasons. Broadly speaking, they provide a perfectly natural rhythm to organize your day:

1) Physical recovery—10:30 p.m. to 2:30 a.m.
2) Mental recovery—2:30 to 6 a.m.
3) Peak action—6 a.m. to noon
4) Easy action—noon to 6 p.m.
5) Relaxation—6 to 10:30 p.m.

Physical Recovery—Hit the Sack Early

If you want to sleep well, make use of your natural rhythm to facilitate a good night's rest. Sense when your body is producing melatonin in the evening and go to bed at that time. For most, this is around 10 p.m., much earlier than people generally hit the sack. You can support this process effectively by ensuring you shut down all screens—TV, laptop and desktop computers, tablets, and mobile phones at least an hour before you go to bed. These screens emit blue light, which the pineal gland mistakes for daylight. Read an entertaining book, have a social conversation with your beloved ones, or just sit quietly and let the time pass. Try it for yourself! You will naturally fall asleep and the quality of your sleep will be much improved. The advice Fernando's doctor gave him to "build up sleep pressure" until midnight only confuses the body. It made Fernando resist his natural inclination to go to bed. It would be even worse if he were doing so by watching TV or checking social media on his smartphone.

You actually sleep in ninety-minute cycles. In each cycle you go through different sleep levels. The first levels are light stages of sleep in which you rest somewhat but often with a busy mind. It's when you hit the deeper levels of sleep that the body really recovers. The quality of your sleep is optimal when your cognitive functions shut down completely. During this deep sleep stage, your brain waves, breathing pattern, and blood pressure operate at their lowest levels. Your muscles and other parts of your body get a chance to fully recover, helped by the hormones that are released in your bloodstream.

At the end of each cycle you return from deep sleep to a lighter level. You may not even notice it and just roll to your other side to start your next cycle. The first two to three cycles (three to four and a half hours) of sleep revolve around your physical recovery. If you have spent a good deal of your time in the deeper stages, the key purpose of sleep is already fulfilled.

A lot of people who suffer from insomnia have fallen into a psychological trap.[25] Their preoccupation of having to sleep dominates their mind. They have decided for themselves they have a sleeping problem. Thus, their head is racing to resolve the issue. The truth is we were all born to sleep perfectly. Our subconscious mind has but one goal—to deliver what we are thinking about. If we tell ourselves we have a sleeping problem, and are worrying about it all day long, guess what? We're instructing our subconscious mind to ensure we have crappy nights. It is striking that the English language uses the words "falling asleep" to describe how we transition to a sleeping mode. "Falling" implies surrendering to gravity. We confide in mother nature taking care of us. There is no problem, nothing to control. We simply let go.

Mental Recovery—The Magic of the Night

After your body recovers during the deep sleep stage, you are likely to remain in lighter stages of sleep. The most intriguing level is called the REM (rapid eye movement) stage. This is a powerful mode, fully geared toward mental recovery. The brain is very active during this stage, while the body is temporarily paralyzed. You may witness vivid dreams, which help you process experiences of the previous day. As you go through two more sleep cycles (of ninety minutes each) in the second part of the night, up to twenty minutes apiece of these cycles may be spent in REM mode. This is fabulous as REM stimulates your creativity and mental sharpness.

* * *

"Our truest life is when we are in dreams awake."
—Henry David Thoreau

* * *

As the cognitive functioning of the brain during REM resembles a waking state, quite a few people do actually wake up at this stage. At times when I worked until late in the evening at the computer, I would wake up after a few hours of sleep with a racing mind—usually around 2:30 a.m. I would be pondering all sorts of things to solve at work and there was no way I would fall back to sleep any time soon. I used a simple rule of thumb—if I were still awake after fifteen minutes, I would get out of bed and go downstairs. In my crazy years, I would open my laptop and work for an hour or two and return to bed for two more hours of low-quality sleep. I hardly realized the tremendous value of being awake for a while to listen to my inner voice.

When I studied the habits of primal humans, I got a fascinating insight. They actually got up in the middle of the night (a natural time is between 2 and 3 a.m.) to enjoy the nocturnal magic! It is only since the use of artificial light that we go to bed later and think we ought to sleep seven to eight hours in one shot. The night is a wonderful time to be up for an hour or so. With everything quiet around you, it is easy to be in contact with your inner self.

So next time you are awake and worry about not being able to sleep, get out of bed! Do some light physical exercises for ten to fifteen minutes to move your energy from your head to your body. The Five Tibetan Rites (Chapter 5) are a perfect practice. Then just sit and focus on belly breathing. A centering exercise (which you will learn in Chapter 9) will help you to get out of your spinning head and find your balance. All of a sudden, you may get a powerful insight that's the solution to your concerns—a comprehension at an advanced level. It'll put you at ease. You know what to do. You're now ready to return to bed. Don't worry about sleeping. I bet you'll fall asleep at some point. Your dreams will be much more vivid and easier to recall in the morning: a sign that indicates you were in a regenerative REM state!

Peak Action—You Snooze You Lose

How well you sleep at night depends on how wisely you live your day. There is a right time for everything, so learn to ride the cycle of nature. Wake up every day around the same time, say, 6:30. Try to align it with your ninety-minute cycle so you won't wake with a start when your alarm bell rings while you are in the midst of a vivid dream. A wakeup light that reflects an actual sunrise works wonders! Although extremely tempting, you do not want to snooze. No matter how comfortable it may feel to turn around once again, you're seriously impacting your ability to fall asleep the next evening. Imagine the mixed signals you are giving your body when every ten minutes the alarm clock wakes you up and you decide to doze off again. Hormonal production of cortisol and melatonin will become a complete mess. And the value of the added sleep is very poor as you will be neither in deep sleep, nor in REM sleep, but at one of the light levels with little impact.

Set your alarm at the time you want to wake up, get out of bed, open the curtains for direct exposure to daylight, and start your morning ritual to welcome the day. It is certainly advisable to do some exercises for fifteen to thirty minutes to fully wake up the body. Take your time in the morning so you don't start the day feeling stressed and pressed for time. Having breakfast with slow carbohydrates, fruits, and nuts also gives the body a signal it is time to ramp up. It is fine, however, to postpone your breakfast by a few hours in order not to waste energy on the digestion of food. Check it out for yourself—you will be razor sharp! Even during the weekend it is wise to get up within an hour of when you do on weekdays. You can't make up for lost sleep during the week, or due to a party. Just get up and bring your system back to its natural rhythm and go to bed by 10 p.m. again.

—TRANSFORMATION EXERCISE 9—
Meeting-Free Mornings

The morning is the time to translate your nightly insights into practical action. All bodily processes are accelerating to facilitate your peak performance. The morning is creation time. Do only what you want to get done. Don't waste this time on simple tasks that don't require you to be at your sharpest. Block these hours in your agenda to write that message that requires all your eloquence, to sort your thoughts on how to grow sales, or to detail your strategic plan for the coming years.

Until noon you really do not want to be responsive to the demands of others. If there is an email culture in your organization, spend a maximum of thirty minutes addressing the most pressing issues. Avoid being drawn into meetings and discussions you can still handle when you are at only 75 percent of your energy. By finishing what you wanted to do before lunch, the rest of the day will flow naturally. Of course, you may encounter resistance from others. Simply explain how you organize your day. It won't be long before others will follow your example. Thus, you create a "meeting-free morning" culture.

Easy Action—Connect and Empower

After noon, our energies rapidly decelerate. Especially after a carb-rich lunch, many people have a hard time concentrating as all their energies are immersed in digesting food. There are a few things you can do. First, have a light and fiber-rich lunch (for instance, a salad with fruit). Lunch is a great opportunity to spend time with your team in a relaxed atmosphere, though it's slightly more challenging at a six-foot social distance. It is definitely refreshing to have a walk with your colleagues right after lunch for half an hour. What better way to connect and exercise at the same time? If you're a coffee (or cola) drinker, this is the right time for your last cup for the day. Caffeine in the system shortens your sleep and impacts the quality of your rest, so use your last cup to shake off your after-lunch dip.

Then get rid of some easy tasks you postponed, such as responding to emails, making courtesy calls or visits, or walking the floor to check on things with colleagues. One of the benefits of the coronavirus crisis is that we will likely continue to work from home at least a few days a week. This is a golden opportunity to do what's most natural about an hour after lunch—take a nap! Power naps (ten to thirty minutes) are very effective in the early afternoon. They reenergize you in the run-up to your afternoon appointments.

From 2-5 p.m. is a good time to organize the meetings or other sessions that are needed to empower your team. You will gain time (and energy!) by having these discussions while standing. At 5 p.m., call it a day. Except for some very simple tasks, you will not be productive anymore. Close the day by reviewing your accomplishments and checking your planning for the next day. Have a drink with colleagues, play sports, go home to cook food, or watch some videos or programs you enjoy. If you haven't taken your nap yet, now is the time.

Soccer star Cristiano Ronaldo is said to extend his early afternoon nap to a full ninety-minute cycle—a true siesta, which is in style with his Portuguese roots. It allows for a shorter night's sleep and keeps him more energetic all day long. At age thirty-five he seems just as fit as he was ten years ago. Ronaldo even has a sleep coach, Nick Littlehales, who has guided many top athletes to better energy management and performance. He also supported the Sky cycling team, which achieved great success in the Tour de France.

Littlehales advocates polyphasic (more than one period) sleep over the monophasic (one period) standard in our current society.[26] This also provides a wonderful alternative for night owls. If you go to bed well after midnight, just spend three cycles during your nocturnal sleep. Rise and shine with the larks to take full advantage of the morning's energy boost and have two separate early and late afternoon cycles of sleep. Indeed, between 5 and 6:30 p.m. is another natural time slot for a full sleep cycle if you wish to shorten your nights. It's a much more effective use of your time and energy than sleeping in! So the next time you doze off in the afternoon and your partner is calling you names, just tell them this is the first part of your training schedule to play soccer like Ronaldo!

Relaxation—Let Your Hair Down

The key theme for the evening is relaxation. It's a time to rest your busy mind and shift your attention to your body. Dinner is an important moment to reward yourself for your active engagement during the day. You will fully experience this when you try to eat slowly and really taste the food. You may wish to take a minute to be grateful to all the people who contributed to make sure you have this meal on your plate. Digestion is a miracle in itself as food submits itself to your system and recharges every cell in your body.

Have you ever noticed you get a boost of energy right after dinner? It is perfect timing for sports, hobbies, or reflection. Can you feel how the day has been for you? What events gave you energy and when did you lose it? What emotions do you sense? In exceptional cases, if there still is work to be done, you can have one or two more productive hours. In any case, you really want to finish around 9 p.m., shut down all screens, and unwind. Sort out the things to take with you the next morning. Read a light book. Have a social conversation or take a warm bath. Give your pineal gland every reason to secrete tons of melatonin.

Alcohol has a major impact on our bodily functions, including sleep. In fact, it is so toxic that your body misinterprets alcohol as a direct threat to survival. As the body registers it may die, you experience a temporary expansion of consciousness. Your mind stops worrying, you no longer feel your shortcomings, and you feel as if you're in a state of bliss. But there is a serious price to be paid. Your body burns a lot of energy to dispose of the alcohol, a process that takes five to six hours. As you go to bed, you drop straight into the deep stages of sleep. Your body needs to physically recover from the attack. Heavy snoring is a typical symptom of alcohol use, especially for overweight people. Did you know that this habit may develop into sleep apnea over time?

After two to three sleep cycles, you shift from your comatose state to a lighter stage of sleep. Now you're likely to wake up, unable to sleep anymore. You miss out on your REM sleep—a missed opportunity for mental recovery.

I therefore apply a simple rule. During weekdays, I avoid drinking alcohol altogether. On weekends, I enjoy a glass of wine at dinner. Of course, I make sure it is a nice one. Life is too short to drink bad wine!

TOP THREE TAKEAWAYS

1) There is a natural time and rhythm for all our activities during the day. There's a delicate balance between the release of melatonin at night and cortisol in the morning. If we organize our activities accordingly, we are bound to sleep well.

2) We can bust the myth that we need to sleep seven to eight hours in one shot. We can divide our sleep into a physical and a mental recovery phase. In between is a wonderful window to get up for an hour or so to get in contact with our inner self.

3) It's smart to have meeting-free mornings to work on activities that require all our energy. The afternoon is the perfect time to get in touch with colleagues, have meetings, and finish some lighter work.

SHAPE YOUR PARADISE *ONLINE*

What can you do to fall asleep smoothly? How do you benefit even more from the magic of the night? What are smart moves to be more effective during the day? Week 5 of the online module "You Too Are A Caveman" covers all these questions and more!

Ready to Cocoon?

Congratulations, you have transformed yourself physically. You are integrating the "caveman" in your daily life. You have returned to your factory settings while you have relearned how to breathe through the belly. You adopt a healthy lifestyle when it comes to embedding regular exercise in your daily schedule. You pay attention not only to what you eat, but especially when you eat. And you follow the natural rhythm of the day to get the most out of your energy flow. Do you feel like making an inward journey? Ready to transform yourself mentally, emotionally, and spiritually? Let's enter our cocoon and prepare for an "inside-out" retreat!

—PART II—

CONSCIOUSNESS? AWESOME!

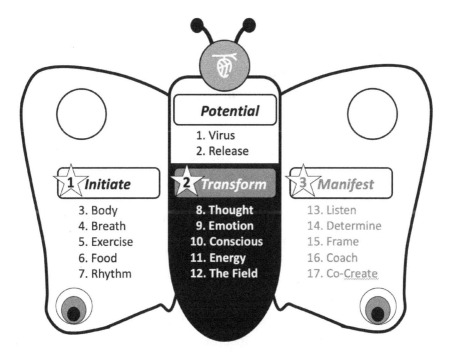

You have been operating under an illusory conception
of how the World and Life at large tick.
Go back to Start. Do not pass Go.

TRANSFORM

Cocooning for a Deep Inward Journey

... the Pupa

"Cogito, ergo sum." (I think, therefore I am.)
—René Descartes

In this Part you will move inward and focus on your personal transformation. We will dive into the world of our thoughts and how they shape our reality. Some 95 percent of our thinking takes place when we're not conscious and controlled by patterns in our system of which we're often not even aware. We will further explore why most people are so afraid of their emotions when in fact they are a perfect GPS to navigate our lives. We will learn about consciousness and how it directly relates to the quantum energy field that feeds us if we know how to tap into it. This Part contains five chapters that enable us to explore our inner world and apply some powerful techniques that hand us the key to Shape Our Paradise.

❖ Chapter 8 explores the natural journey from "outside-in" to "inside-out" thinking. We'll find that in every moment, we have an opportunity to connect to our inner wisdom. If we choose not to fall prey to our subconscious patterns, our thoughts will be of higher quality. And we'll feel a whole lot happier!

❖ In Chapter 9 we'll dive deeper into our subconscious mind. We'll learn about our childhood conclusions and how, in our innocence, we have built our thought patterns on false assumptions. We'll discover how emotions can help to navigate our life.

❖ Chapter 10 takes us through the eight stages of consciousness. We'll unveil how our personal growth from birth to adulthood follows the same steps that human society has gone through over the past two hundred thousand years. And we'll look at our imminent transition to the next level, which is taking leadership to a whole new ballgame.

❖ In Chapter 11 we will revisit the magical world of quantum physics. We will explore how, in essence, everything in our world is pure energy. We will directly apply this truth to our daily life by visualizing our New Tomorrow.

❖ Chapter 12 will address the force that has been most misconceived by people throughout history. Modern science is suggesting that the source of life, or universal Field of Intelligence, does exist and creates our physical world. As we learn to tune into its frequency, we become masters in Shaping Our Paradise.

I Think, Therefore I Am

The Renaissance, which started in the fourteenth century in Florence, Italy, heralded a new era. For almost a full millennium, the Middle Ages had tormented the European people with feudalism, religious indoctrination, technological standstill, mass disease, and little hope you could ever escape your fate. *Now the times they were achangin'*.[27] A new culture emerged displaying a rediscovery of ancient philosophy, art, and science. Civilians with a bright set of brains proved to shape their own destiny as businessmen, artists, or scientists.

A tremendous boost of energy spread across the continent. The idea took hold that human progress was boundless if man—yes, emancipation of women's rights would take quite a few centuries longer —would apply and develop his cognitive capacity. The zeitgeist was eloquently phrased by Descartes' above quote. I am relevant, I exist, because I think. This notion preluded a magnificent shift in the focus of Western societies, of which we have reaped the benefits until this very day. Granted, the emphasis on education has lifted us to an unfathomable level of prosperity and freedom. It sparked an unprecedented game of scientific leapfrog fueled by mass industrialization and, most recently, digitization.

111

Incredible progress has been made. In Western societies, we live at luxury levels our great-grandparents could never have imagined just a century ago. As people were licking their wounds from World War I, a renewed optimism emerged at the dawn of the Roaring Twenties. Roads would be freed from the nasty smell of horse poo as the well-to-do acquired an "automobile." I'm sure you have seen those funny movies of drivers igniting the engine by winding up a winch in front of the car. Cross-continental travel was by ship, as commercial air travel did not take off until the 1950s.

Power plants were rapidly expanding to provide companies and households with electricity. Consequently, houses could be lit by electric lighting, replacing gas lamps. Long-distance communication, which had only been possible by writing letters or sending telegrams through Morse code, was boosted as telephone landlines were making their inroads into homes. Again, you must have seen the images of early days' communication centers where operators connected international callers by manually switching plugs. Commercial radio broadcast was first introduced in 1920, bringing the world in real time to people's homes for the first time in history.

In the one hundred years that followed, humanity has taken impressive advantage of its ability to think. We put our thinking to the test in research and development. We expanded technological frontiers at an ever accelerating pace. Our homes were filled with convenience devices such as vacuum cleaners, laundry machines, dishwashers, microwaves, razors, desktops, laptops, and smartphones. We revolutionized healthcare, transport, media, banking, music, construction, and communication. And the pace is increasing exponentially. Artificial intelligence and robotics will once again disrupt our daily work and private routines beyond our wildest dreams in the coming decades.

Are We Any Happier?

While we have created a world that's smarter, faster, safer, healthier, and more educated than ever before in the history of mankind, the big question is whether we have become any happier than the generations before us. Has all this thinking, and all the benefits it has brought us, opened a gateway to intense passion and motivation to come to work every day and help create a better world?

Extensive research by Gallup (2017) is painting quite a different scenery. Two-thirds of global employees are not engaged. As "their engagement needs are not being fully met, they're putting time— but not energy of passion—into their work," according to Gallup.[28] What's worse, a staggering 18 percent of employees worldwide are actively disengaged. These "employees aren't just unhappy at work. Every day, they potentially undermine what their engaged coworkers accomplish."

Only 15 percent of employees worldwide are truly engaged in their work. They are "highly involved in and enthusiastic about their work and workplace. They drive performance and innovation and move the organization forward," Gallup reported.

These results only vary some ten percentage points between continents and countries. On average, only one in six employees is truly happy at work and actively creates new possibilities for the organization to prosper. By firing on only one of six cylinders, we have shaped the material world we live in today. An immense potential is left untouched. It's a human tragedy that four in six employees just put in time, while the sixth employee may even undermine what engaged colleagues accomplish.

Why aren't we any happier? Be brutally honest with yourself. How often are you really completely happy? How many times a day, a week, a month, or even a year do you truly feel free, fulfilled, loved, connected, and capable of creating anything? What portion of your life is filled with routine, a feeling that "I have to do this?" What dreams have you given up on? When have you yielded and become an executor of a system that, deep in your heart, you do not believe in?

Let's zoom out for a minute. How come, with all our thinking capacity, our world today still has so many flaws? Why does one in seven people in the world live in hunger while a third of all food is wasted? What prompts us to emit unsustainable levels of carbon dioxide in the air, which has raised the temperature by almost two degrees Fahrenheit (one degree Celsius) in the last century? For what reason are American jails filled with two million prisoners today? I could raise a zillion other questions. And I'm not trying to ignite a political debate whatsoever. I just want to direct your attention to the one underlying reason that, in the end, explains it all.

All the woes we're suffering from, all wrongs committed by one person against another, all miscommunication, lack of understanding, and missed opportunities originate from a single phenomenon—the quality of our thinking.

SHAPE YOUR PARADISE *ONLINE*

Enrich your learning experience with the second module of the Shape Your Paradise online self-coaching program. It builds on this second Part of the book, "Consciousness? Awesome!" The structure is identical to Module 1—in five weeks you actively work on your inner transformation.

Your thinking is completely conditioned by your subconscious memories. Can you break the vicious circle and take real steps? How do you function optimally in your daily activities? In this module you will experience:

> ➤ how your early childhood programmed you mentally
> ➤ how this may impede you from functioning optimally
> ➤ how quantum physics teaches us a new perspective
> ➤ how to tap into your potential and create real value
> ➤ how Paradise Shaper Leadership is built on consciousness

You will learn to effectively increase your influence, connections, and impact. Find your path to mastery of your emotions and thoughts. Learn to create what you truly desire. Go to www.paradiseshaper.com and deepen your inner discovery!

8

IT'S IN YOUR THINKING, STUPID!

"A moment's insight is sometimes worth a life's experience."
—Oliver Wendell Holmes

A Life Changing Insight

There is a crucial insight that completely changed my life and functioning as a leader. It did not come overnight and, in fact, developed in an unusual way. It is a truth not known to most people—an extremely simple axiom, yet fundamentally opposite to the mainstream way of looking at life and the world in which we live.

The insight is this—the outer world I operate in is only a reflection of my inner world. Everything I encounter is the result of my own creation. The way I create is not through my actions, but my own thinking. The success, wealth, friendship, love, and health that I experience are merely a consequence of my own thought process. Even my emotions are a direct mirror of my thoughts. It is, therefore, my inner world that really matters. The outside world is just a playground to exercise my mastery of my inner world.

Excuse me? That can't be! Everyone naturally wants to be happy and successful. We all want a world that is a paradise to everyone. If our thoughts created our experience, why do we suffer so much? No one would intentionally create the hassle we face on a daily basis, right?

You're absolutely right. There's a reason we create all our

problems. In both this and the next chapter we will go deeper into this insight. We will explore why we make our own lives and those of others difficult. And you'll have the opportunity to take the first steps in mastering your inner world. Let's start by guiding you through the phases that have helped me attain this understanding.

Phase 1—At the Mercy of the Outside World

Until pneumonia struck at age 32, my perspective on life was rather down-to-earth. I thought that with my five senses—sight, hearing, taste, smell, and touch—I perceived the world as it is. I had the opportunity to interact with many people and have many experiences and sensations. If I worked hard and supported others, I would generally encounter people responding positively to me, which in turn made me feel good. If, at times, I were less considerate of others and acted selfishly or in an agitated manner, people would typically be less friendly to me in return. This would make me feel bad about myself, so logically I decided to interact as positively as I could with those around me.

At times I encountered situations where people were unreasonably rude or arrogant. Or they did things I considered stupid, which irritated me. I tried to remain loyal to my personal adage to stay positive to others, especially if people I considered my senior were involved. But my internal bucket of frustration was slowly filling up. And on those rare occasions when the bucket overflowed, you didn't want to be in my neighborhood. I would be livid, make the most ridiculous accusations, and shout in profane language. Actually, this typically would only happen at home, since I would not lose my temper at work. After a few minutes I would come to terms and be overwhelmed with guilt. I remember telling my wife it really wasn't me who got angry. It felt as if I had been taken over by some devilish gnome who made me say things that were not even remotely how I felt about the situation.

I lived under the assumption that our human experience is

"outside-in." Things simply "happened" to me, which had a subsequent impact on how I felt inside. In a way, my internal well-being was at the mercy of the behavior of others and situations that occurred. I labeled them as either positive or negative. I had a few coping strategies, but whenever they proved ineffective, an ugly and destructive side of me emerged.

Phase 2—Developing Positive Coping Strategies

I had yet to learn that things never happen without reason. And neither did my pneumonia. During those weeks I was forced to stay in bed, I made a vow. I would learn how my mind really works. How could I take ownership of the way I dealt with stress? In the years that followed, I studied all kinds of self-help books.[29] I also signed up for many training courses, which taught me how to put a filter on the way I perceived my interactions with others. Positive thinking and neurolinguistic programming (NLP) contributed to a happier and more rewarding life.

I learned to replace negative thoughts by finding more productive perspectives on my experiences. I noticed that I continuously judged others' opinions. I compared the events on my path with my internal yardstick of how things ought to be. Wasn't it absurd to assume my views would be superior to those of others? I practiced looking at things in different ways, to be open to the opinions of my colleagues and business partners.

I gained interest in how others felt. At the start of a meeting, I would take time to inquire how things were going. I showed interest in their health, concerns, and advice. This approach lifted me to a higher level in my relationship management. People felt my change was sincere. They were more comfortable sharing their thoughts. They volunteered smarter ways to do things. I embraced their suggestions when I thought they were worth a try. I sowed confidence in their plans. Then I reaped the reward of their ownership of putting these ideas into practice. As a result, I got a lot more done, and I spent significantly less time doing the work myself.

While my new insights and skills boosted my effectiveness, they still didn't ease my mind. It was tiring to "work on myself" continuously. In every conversation, I tried to observe the thoughts emerging in my mind. I commissioned myself to always look at the bright side of life, to adopt a more fruitful way of looking at events. I worked from the basic conviction that I was not good enough and that life was an opportunity to work on my shortcomings. The task at hand was to become a master of my own mind. I would label my perspective as "outside-in with color filter."

Phase 3—Welcome to My Inner World

Just before my fortieth birthday, life took another amazing turn. I became head of Emerging Markets in my company. In my role, I got to watch Madhavan, my financial controller, and did so with increasing admiration. The way he interacted with our colleagues in country organizations was remarkable. Madhavan didn't bully or patronize anyone. I never heard him raise his voice. He had the twinkling eyes and contagious smile of a leader who thoroughly enjoyed his work. But Madhavan was by no means easy on people. In a subdued, persistent way, he asked questions that all hit the bull's-eye. "What is the one thing you don't do today that would totally change the game if you found the means to do it?" I remember him asking. What an empowering way to build awareness!

One morning I decided I wanted to know his secret. "Madhavan, do you meditate?" I asked, a little surprised by my own question. His response was a simple "Why are you asking?"

So I explained, "Well, I can see it in your eyes. In the focused but caring way in which you interact with our colleagues. In your balanced attitude that inspires people to be the best version of themselves. You seem to have a certain mastery over your emotions."

Madhavan smiled and replied, "I don't usually share this within a business environment, but you guessed right. For the past twelve years I've been practicing yoga. The traditional yoga that goes back thousands of years. I have learned a set of practices and meditations. Over the years, they have had a profound impact on the way I think, feel and act. I am moved that you've noticed."

Our conversation soon turned into a brainstorming session. How could we strengthen the performance of our organization? Could we give everyone an opportunity to get introduced to yoga? Upon Madhavan's request, a teacher was hired to conduct an "Inner Engineering" course at our premises.[30] The deal was straightforward—a minimum of thirty colleagues would enroll in a one-week program, attending every workday from 6 to 9 a.m. During the weekend, the program was scheduled from 9 a.m. to 6 p.m. No one was to drop out of the program. You sign up, you show up. No excuses. We were surprised when no fewer than fifty-five people registered. We decided to have both a morning and an evening group to give all candidates the opportunity to participate.

The course opened my eyes to a whole new reality. Next to our external, physical world, there also is an internal, metaphysical dimension to our lives—a dimension as vast and boundless as the external universe that humanity so fanatically explores. We learned several exercises to get acquainted with our inner world. We experienced what it means to quiet the mind.

This is where the magic hit. I suddenly realized that "I am not my thinking." If I just sat still and focused on my breath, I could shift my attention to the space in my head where all thoughts arise—a quiet place that was soon disturbed by shreds of thoughts that took me in all directions. I realized I did not generate most thoughts intentionally. Yes, sometimes they were triggered by my environment. But the thoughts themselves did not necessarily reflect what was really happening. Instead, some kind of preprogrammed script was unfolding. Certain fears hidden deep in my system projected imaginary scenarios onto the current situation. The more attention I paid to these images, the more worrisome the picture became.

There were two important observations I made, two major clues that transformed how I experienced life. First, there is no need to be afraid of my emotions. All my stress, tension, anger, shame, or sadness are not caused by adverse events taking place in the outside world. They are merely reflections of my thought patterns. Often there isn't even an external situation I can point to that causes my mind to wander. What a gift to have emotions show me exactly what's going on in my head. They are a powerful barometer of the quality of my thinking, even if I'm not aware of it.

The second takeaway was that thoughts come and go as long as I don't pay attention to them. They are like passing clouds in the sky. The sun is right behind them! There is no need to replace a negative thought with a more positive one. All I need to do is to ignore the thought, not feed it with the energy of my attention. Within moments the thought will drift and disappear from my internal sky. My mood then will improve. My inner balance will be restored.

I realized I wasn't at the mercy of the outside world. Nor did I need to develop positive coping strategies to deal with the woes of life. My experience turned into "it's all inside." I had learned to play with the mechanics of the mind.

Phase 4—Shaping My Own World

These insights had a remarkable consequence I could not foresee at the time. I loosened the grip that my thought patterns used to have on my mood, and, apparently, a space opened for a more profound and wiser "inner voice" to emerge. I found a serene, yet all-pervasive urge to step out of my daily work routine. I longed to dedicate my life to a higher calling—to raise the consciousness of leaders. I would try to create a more inclusive, sustainable, and "impact-full" society. It was evident I would move in that direction, but where to start?

I'm sure you've had those moments where you were completely relaxed and, suddenly, a brilliant idea came to mind. A spark of inspiration. The perfect answer to a problem you had been pondering. You were taking a shower, mowing the lawn, or enjoying the holidays.

Unexpectedly, the solution presented itself on a golden plate. Well, I had many of those experiences. And the frequency seemed to increase! They all gave me clues as to the task at hand. People I bumped into at the supermarket. Ads on social media I would otherwise have ignored. A certain line in the lyrics of a song. They all pointed me in a certain direction.

One morning, I woke up and asked my wife, "Years ago, you took a 'sensational selling' course. Can you get me in contact with the trainer?" She did, and within a week I had my first online session with my new business mentor Lianne. I had expected a result-oriented sales conversation. Much to my surprise, my mentor pointed out the "Three Principles"—Mind, Consciousness, and Thought. "What will set you apart as an executive coach? It won't be your ability to teach leaders some powerful skills," she explained. "By conveying your inner wisdom, you will provide them with a possibility to gain a deep and life-changing insight for themselves."

Studying the Three Principles was a feast of recognition.[31] It helped me identify the phases I had gone through. My eyes were opened to the next stage. I had found my inner balance by not putting energy into negative thinking. It created space for something else—I had connected to my inner clarity. An intelligence that only surfaces if I do not disturb it with my loud, habitual thinking. The confidence that life has marvelous things in store if I am prepared to play my part in the grand scheme of things. It's my intuition that gives me higher quality insights—and it's a much better deal than listening to the compulsive thoughts generated by my fear-driven patterns.

I realized with all my being that our human experience is truly "inside-out." My fresh new ideas offered a wonderful opportunity to put them into action. I could fulfill our highest calling as human beings—to create! I could convert my brand-new concepts into concrete actions, products, and services that enrich others. All I had to do was take ownership and connect with my inner wisdom.

The Three Principles

It was Scottish mystic (and welder!) Sydney Banks who coined the term Three Principles. They describe what he realized in an instant flash of enlightenment some fifty years ago. In that very moment, the simple truth of our human experience was clear to him. It was an astute representation of the mystery that ancient wisdom traditions have protected for thousands of years. These three interconnected forces orchestrate our experience of life.

The Principle of Thought is the force with which we create. It is the "missing link" between spirit and form. High-quality, original thoughts have the potential to Shape Our Paradise. Yet most of us are plagued by low-quality thoughts that often stem from childhood. Chapter 9 will explore the reason why we as kids were programmed to live in the outside-in illusion.

In Chapter 10, we will dive into the Principle of Consciousness, the second force. This principle reflects the degree to which we realize our full potential. To what extent are we aware of the truth of our existence? The more advanced our consciousness, the easier we will find it to navigate our life. We will then be considerably more effective in leading the people for whom we are responsible.

The third force is the Principle of Mind. This is the Field of Intelligence I referred to in Chapter 1. It is the source of all energy, the blueprint of life, the oneness of creation. By expanding our consciousness, we will sense this energy in every aspect of our lives. We will further explore the massive impact of this animating force in Chapters 11 and 12.

Paradise Shaper Leadership

Living from the inside-out has major implications for our leadership. Exhibit 9 depicts the basic choice we have as human beings. The left side displays the treadmill in which we find ourselves so easily stuck. My memories, or the stories of others for that matter, have instilled certain fears in my system. The mind wants to prevent these scary projections from happening at any cost. Therefore, it has developed a multitude of patterns. These patterns generate compulsive, low-quality thoughts. If I act upon them, my actions will be selfish and to the detriment of other people and society at large. I may experience some short-term pleasure. But sooner or later I will have to face the consequences of my irresponsible behavior.

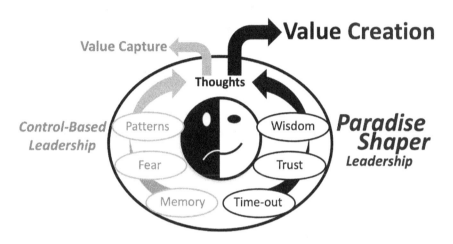

**Exhibit 9—Paradise Shaper leadership
based on the human experience.**

As a leader, I may easily fall into the trap of activating the left side of the picture. I will find myself in the business of "value capture"—pushing my organization to deliver on the financial commitments I have made. While I may believe that I'm serving others, my main concern is myself and my own interests. My subconscious programs dictate my leadership. I attach all kinds of emotional values to status and money—as security, a demonstration of my success or power over others. It's my sense of separation that makes me grab what I can and feel like I really deserve it.

I may put in place a control system to ensure people don't succumb to their laziness. In reality, I am acting out of fear. I have translated my patterns into a refined model of Control-Based Leadership. How will my employees experience my leadership? Before long, their own fear-based patterns will be triggered. This will lead to disengagement and underperformance, which, in turn, feeds my fears as a leader, and entices me to push even harder. It is easy to see how a vicious circle is established.

It is precisely this phenomenon that we are witnessing all around us. Why did nature bring the global economy to a halt by means of the coronavirus? Control-based leadership and a value-capture mentality led to an accumulation of irresponsible decisions. Companies, governments, and other organizations across the globe jointly put us in a tangle of crises. They are leading our global society to the brink of collapse. It is the key reason why 85 percent of employees worldwide are not engaged at work.

"We are collectively creating results that nobody wants," as Scharmer and Kaufer aptly put it.[32] They provide an agonizing analysis of the Age of Disruption we are devising. Three "divides" may be distinguished to portray the current situation:

- ➤ The ecological divide—Our footprint today equals more than 1.5 times the regeneration capacity of the planet and is increasing. Before long, we will have a serious aggravation of food and water shortages. The poor suffer the most from environmental disasters.
- ➤ The social divide—There is a growing disconnect between the Haves and the Have Nots. Half of the world's population own only 1 percent of wealth, while the richest 1 percent own 40 percent—and in the United States as much as 70 percent. The polarization of wealth erodes basic human rights and equal opportunities.
- ➤ The spiritual-cultural divide—The gap between what we do each day and who we really are is widening, translating into rapidly growing numbers on burnout and depression. Today many more people die from suicide than in wars.

These are big topics, and I am not suggesting we can solve them easily. But if we look at each of these symptoms, one thing is evident. People are stuck in outside-in thinking. Whether they are leaders, employees, or other individuals, their psychology totally confuses them. They act according to habitual thinking as fear-based patterns are activated. As leaders build their control-based systems, they not only keep their employees hostage on the left side of the picture (exhibit 9), but their customers, suppliers, citizens, and other stakeholders are all constantly prompted to act out of fear. Even these leaders themselves are ruled by the system they maintain. And so, we are collectively creating results that nobody wants.

The good news is that I can definitely do something—both as a leader and as an employee! As I awake to the inside-out reality of my experience, I can move to the right side of the picture at any given moment. If I take a timeout, I can easily find my inner peace. In doing so, I no longer act out of fear and short-term egoistic needs. Instead, I build on my innate trust that a solution will always present itself once I connect with my internal wisdom. Out of this inner space, the most original and encompassing thoughts will emerge, directly inspired by the Field of Intelligence. As you'll discover, the magnificent energy of this creative force is beyond compare.

And you know what? All of my colleagues have this fantastic capability, too. And since each of them has different talents, capabilities, and networks, I can avail of an amazingly creative engine if I know how to get them to shift to the right side of the picture as well. As they do their job on a daily basis, they will know what needs to be done. They will come up with fresh ideas that are so simple, yet so pervasive, I will be surprised I had not come up with them before. As we shift our perspective, our fear-free, high-quality thinking is bound to take full ownership of our impact on society. We will be in the business of "value creation," providing our customers with pure and inclusive solutions. In this way, we will be enriching humanity—and the planet we live on—with innovations that are in sync with nature and the purpose of our existence. That's what characterizes Paradise Shaper leadership.

—TRANSFORMATION EXERCISE 10—
Connect with Your Wisdom

How do you prevent your actions from being driven by fear? How do you turn negative emotions into a more constructive state? How do you connect with your inner wisdom to attract fresh and creative thoughts?

In other words, how to play with the mechanics of the mind?

These are the five steps that describe the process. Take your time to go through these steps once or twice a day. It is particularly valuable to do so when you're in "the heat of the moment" for instance at work. Notice the massive impact on how you are feeling and your subsequent course of actions!

1. Feel your emotion—"measure" the quality of your thoughts
2. Take a time-out—focus on your breath
3. Stay in the "now"—let your thoughts pass
4. Wait until your mood improves—feel if you can trust your thoughts
5. Get back in the game—build on a creative thought

Gradually it will become second nature to "check your temperature" and take a brief time-out to ensure you are in the right state of mind to pursue action. Let your inner wisdom shape your world!

TOP THREE TAKEAWAYS

1) The outer world we operate in is only a reflection of our own inner world. Everything we encounter is the result of our own creation. The way we create is not through our actions, but by virtue of our own thoughts.

2) The Three Principles of Thought, Consciousness and Mind represent an ancient wisdom about the nature of our human experience. At any given moment, we are able return to our factory settings, a natural state in which we're blissful, joyful, and relaxed.

3) Control-based leadership and a value-capture mentality have led to an accumulation of fear-based, irresponsible decisions by organizations across the globe. When leaders learn to connect with their wisdom, they will be in the business of value creation, providing people with pure and inclusive solutions.

SHAPE YOUR PARADISE *ONLINE*

Online module 2 "Consciousness? Awesome!" will help you become more familiar with your inner world. How do you perceive your environment today? What does it take to connect with your wisdom? Reading about it is one thing. Experiencing it for yourself ignites your metamorphosis!

9

UNDER THE HOOD

"It isn't what you have, or who you are, or where you are, or what you are doing that makes you happy or unhappy. It is what you think about."
—Dale Carnegie

The Principle of Thought

Everything ever created in the world originates in a thought. Thought is the "crayon" through which all manifestation in the world takes shape. That's the Principle of Thought. Through thought we create our personal reality. In other words, how we experience the world around us reflects our thinking about ourselves and our environment.

The issue is that we tend to blame situations and other people for the way we feel. This is the outside-in illusion, lived by the vast majority of people on a daily basis. The other day I heard one of my sons yell at his brother, "Stop it, you are making me angry!" I was considering how corny it would have sounded if he'd said, "I am allowing my mind to produce thoughts of being mistreated by you. As a result I'm feeling frustrated." It would, however, have been a much more accurate statement!

Our experience of the world isn't outside-in, but inside-out. Nothing that happens to us can ever make us angry, stressed, unhappy, sad, or lonesome. Every emotion we feel is a mirror of our own thinking. It is only we ourselves who are generating thoughts of danger and unfairness, of being a victim, left out, or simply not good enough to deserve love and appreciation.

Why would we choose to do that? In truth, we don't really opt to think negatively. It is a compulsion we have developed, especially in early childhood. Let's look under the hood to enter the realm of our subconscious mind.

Our Early Years

Let us return for a moment to the day you were born. Until then, you were in paradise. In the comfort of your mother's womb, life was perfect. In an unconscious way, you just lived in the moment, enjoying the darkness. The familiar beating of your mother's heart. The muffled sounds from outside. The temperature around you always nice and warm. The umbilical cord providing you with the exact level of nutrients you needed at any moment. For you, this was eternity.

Then everything changed. By massive pressure, you were pushed out of paradise. Exposed to tremendous light, you were equally overwhelmed by penetrating sounds. The temperature around you was freezing cold, and then the umbilical cord was cut. You were robbed of the lifeline that connected you to your source. You cried your lungs out in your struggle to live. Your first breath marked the start of your stay on Earth. It was a traumatic experience with a clear message: "I am helpless and at the mercy of others for my survival."

As a baby, every time you were hungry or in need of clean diapers, you felt unhappy and started screaming for help. Your parents, or others taking care of you, served you milk or changed you. Then all was fine again. The simple projection you derived from this experience was "I depend on others to feel happy." Consequently, you developed all sorts of strategies to draw the attention of others. As a toddler you had your first engagements with other kids. You explored even more ways to assure yourself of the support of others. You may have been dominant, used flattery, or perhaps been submissive. Depending on your success rate, you further explored certain paths in pursuit of survival and happiness.

It is important to realize that, roughly until age six, children do not have a self-conscious mind. The brain activity of children develops over the years.[33] In the first six years, their brain waves display delta (0.5–4 Hz), and theta (4–8 Hz) frequencies. This is the lowest EEG frequency range. It implies they spend their lives in a "hypnotic trance." They mix their imaginary world with the events that are really happening. Their perceptions are directly downloaded into their subconscious mind, without any self-conscious filter. A child in this age is in a "programmable state." This condition facilitates fast learning and the development of complex motoric skills. But there's a downside. These perceptions and beliefs become the basic subconscious programs by which the child navigates the rest of its life.

Self-consciousness and the ability to think only develop after age six. The child's brain activity shifts to the alpha (8–12 Hz) frequency range. At middle school age, it transitions to beta (12–35 Hz) frequencies. In beta, the brain is completely externally focused. The door to the subconscious mind closes and for most people only opens during sleep, especially in the REM state.

Being a rational adult, you have overcome your physical dependence on others. You are fully capable of making a basic living, getting your food and drink, and visiting the restroom when needed. So there shouldn't be any factual reason to be concerned or unhappy.

Yet the voice in your head tells you something different.

Voice in my head? What voice do you mean?

Exactly, that's the voice! During your earliest childhood years, you unconsciously developed a strong belief that your survival depended on the support of others—a conclusion that was directly programmed into your subconscious mind. You developed many strategies to attain the support of others and avoid what you perceived as "danger." These strategies have become patterns that can be activated at any moment. As soon as your five senses (sight, hearing, taste, smell, and touch) record a certain activity in your environment, your mind will check if there is any danger. If it perceives your survival may be at stake, it will trigger a recorded pattern to "protect" you.

Once these patterns become active, you are no longer "in the moment." Instead, you are reliving the programs you "downloaded" in your early childhood. Lots of negative thoughts come to mind (the voice in your head!). They make you feel afraid, nervous, or angry. Since you perceive these thoughts to be true, you become even more insecure. Consequently, even gloomier scenarios unfold in your mind's eye.

—TRANSFORMATION EXERCISE 11—
Centering

How do you connect with your core and find peace and balance? How can you stay "in the now" while conducting your daily activities?

There is a simple exercise called "Centering" that helps you to disengage with your habitual thinking. You allow your breath to guide you to your "inner world". If it is your first time doing some basic form of meditation, just go with the flow. It may be surprising to experience that a source of peace and calmness is just around the corner. In fact, you are always carrying it with you and have access to it at any given moment.

Read these steps a few times so you will remember them as it is easiest to do them with eyes closed. If you forget the next step, it's fine. Just open your eyes to read and resume the exercise. In due course, you will find it no problem to do this even with eyes open.

1. Close your eyes and sit straight up without leaning on the back of the chair. Feel that you're sitting on your "sit bones." Focus your attention on belly breathing.
2. Now move your chin slightly to your chest and sense that your spine is erect. Create an imaginary Eiffel Tower between your sit bones and the back of your head.

3. Relax your forehead. Imagine it becoming as smooth as a piece of silk. Relax your eyes, cheeks, and tongue as well.

4. On your next exhalation, feel how warm air is leaving your nostrils.

5. On the following inhalation, feel fresh and colder air coming into your nostrils.

6. Stay with the sensation in your nostrils of warm air being exchanged for fresh air for two to three minutes.

7. On the next inhalation, follow the flow of fresh air and, in doing so, shift your attention to the imaginary center of your head.

8. Feel the calm and vastness of the center of your head. Welcome to your inner world! This is the space where all thoughts arise. If a thought appears, don't pay any attention to it. Just let it pass, as if you're watching a cloud fade away against the sky. Keep your attention at the center for some five minutes.

9. If you find you got carried away by your thoughts, no problem. Just focus on your nostrils again. Feel how warm air leaving your nostrils is replaced by fresh air coming in. After a few breaths, follow the flow of fresh air to the imaginary center of your head and keep your attention there.

10. Cover your eyes with your hands. Now open your eyes and slowly remove your hands so you can readjust to the outside world.

Bonus tip—This exercise deliberately connects the sensation of air leaving and entering the nostrils with the actual centering of your attention in your head. Throughout the day, whenever you remember, just feel the air movement in your nostrils. Every time you do so, you will immediately be "in the now" and connect with your inner world while being active in the outer world.

Our Childhood Conclusions

The subconscious programs we "downloaded" in our early childhood are strikingly common. Nearly a century ago, Austrian psychoanalyst Wilhelm Reich discovered that most people harbor the same kind of negative thoughts. In fact, there are only a handful. Five "childhood conclusions" can be distinguished that produce destructive self-talk throughout our adult lives.[34] Of course, the degree to which these apply varies from person to person. I haven't met a single person yet to whom not one of them was relevant.

1. I'm not welcome, I must go elsewhere.

We may have experienced birth itself as a traumatic event. As a newborn, we want to return to our dreamy state in our mother's womb when we were in heaven. We don't belong here! We cannot focus on worldly affairs that don't interest us. Our high sensitivity drains our energy when we're exposed to multiple stimuli. And so we flee to our internal *La La Land.*

2. There isn't enough, I'm not enough.

As we crave for food and cuddling, we create a fear of deficiency when our parents do not show up. All our life, we'll be longing for attention, confirmation, and appreciation. But we don't want to ask for it, as it wouldn't feel real. It's the sheer fear of survival that makes us very uncomfortable in queues and traffic jams. No matter how successful our careers are, we will always be plagued by "FOMO"—the fear of missing out.

3. What do I know—have it your way.

As toddlers, we are afraid to lose the love of our parents. Our boundless creativity leads us to do things that arouses their anger. We feel misunderstood, but swallow our objections to keep them happy. When our boundaries are crossed, we are unable to resist the force. We feel like a powerless victim. And so we don't take ownership, nor dare to show our true colors. We hide our feelings by pleasing others.

4. I must be in control.

Our hearts were broken for the first time when our childhood fantasy of being mom or dad's life partner proved to be an illusion. The wound still hurts. We don't trust life or other people without inhibitions. We see life and relationships as a power struggle and swear to always be on top. We're quick to see others as enemies and prepare for combat. We seem fearless, but are terrified to open our heart.

5. I must conform to fit in.

As a child, our uninhibited behavior caused a painful moment of embarrassment. We have decided we are the odd one out. We feel like an impostor, who will soon be exposed. Sensitive to the opinion of others, we endlessly scrutinize our behavior and appearance. We constantly scan our environment for local conventions. And then we blend in like a chameleon, afraid to show our authentic self.

None of these childhood conclusions could have been further from the truth. Each of us was born joyful, talented, playful, passionate, and creative. They are false beliefs we created when we lived in a dream state, unable to properly assess the actual situation. And so these conclusions have drawn neural pathways into our subconscious mind. They are easily triggered by adverse daily events. Our childhood conclusions aren't rational at all. But most people are not aware how strongly these convictions dominate their emotions and, therefore, behavior.

As soon as you enter this state of mind, your subconscious mind and body (especially the gut brain) begin a pattern that simply takes over. Stress hormones such as cortisol and adrenaline are produced and injected into your bloodstream. All energy in your body is directed to getting out of this "dangerous" situation by defending or running away—which is the sympathetic nervous system's response. Alternatively, you just freeze and stop all activity—the parasympathetic "solution." At best, you cope with the situation by using your rational mind. You tell yourself that the situation isn't so bad. You have done it before and are able to deal with it, aren't you? Thus, you try to replace the negative thoughts with more positive ones. The stress is still there, but you endure it.

All forms of stress are part of a very natural defense mechanism our system developed. Over millions of years of evolution, our mind and body figured out a highly effective way to deal with the rare occasions when we are in real danger. In today's society, our minds misjudge the situation multiple times a day. Our childhood conclusions get triggered all the time. Work deadlines, targets, or the social media circus are but a few examples. Our stress reaction is ignited, yet there is no danger whatsoever. We just unconsciously *think* there is.

And that, in fact, is the core implication of the Principle of Thought. You are not really stressed, angry, sad, lonesome, scared, or any other negative emotion. You just *think* you are. If you learn to stay present, you can mentally press the pause button. Just notice your patterns are causing negative emotions. You're no longer a victim of your own past. You have the freedom to connect with your core and find your balance.

The three childhood conclusions I had strongly wired in my subconscious mind were numbers two, three, and five. I was looking for confirmation and attention for decades. I tried to please others and make sure I fit in with the group. My subconscious patterns literally made me work until I dropped. Do you remember the introduction story when my feelings were hurt by a rude comment from my parents' friend? It resonated deeply with my limiting belief that I'm not good enough.

Over the years, I began to realize how much I was operating based on fear. I learned how to defuse these internal bombs easily by staying consciously in the now. I started making choices for myself instead of meeting (my projections of) the wishes of others. I dared to show my authentic self. My relationships became more meaningful. My work became so much more enjoyable. And as a result, my energy levels replenished much faster.

Emotions—Our Energy in Motion

Many people are afraid of their emotions. Since emotions often make us feel uncomfortable, we try to avoid them. Our emotions seem to be erratic in nature. They suddenly appear, sometimes for no apparent reason. Feeling bored, dejected, jealous, anxious, guilty, or angry exhausts our energy. Once we are in a certain emotion, it can be difficult to get out of it. Emotions make us feel like we're not ourselves.

So what do we do? We look for distraction. We try to fill our feeling of emptiness by eating. We numb our brain by indulging in YouTube or Netflix. We leave nasty comments on social media. We lose ourselves in a Fortnite epic game. We party at festivals. We blow our minds on pills or booze. We go skydiving, bungee jumping, or helicopter skiing. Anything to escape our emotions. It's our main driver—move away from pain and seek pleasure.

Isn't it absurd that we are so scared of such a powerful tool that is always at our disposal? As we saw in Chapter 8, emotions are a wonderful barometer of the quality of our thinking. Our thinking and feeling are in fact two sides of the same coin. Certain emotions that we perceive as negative tell us that we are thinking the corresponding destructive thoughts. And where do these thoughts come from? Exactly! The childhood conclusions that we have hardwired into our subconscious mind. We have fallen victim to our past.

With a bit of practice, we will learn to observe our own behavior, emotions, and thoughts. To be both an actor on stage and a spectator in the balcony. To be both a football player on the field and a coach who watches every move from the sideline. When we realize that we are not our behavior, emotions, or thoughts, it becomes a liberating experience to see through our patterns. As human beings, we have about sixty thousand thoughts a day. Around 95 percent of them are the very same thoughts we entertained the day before. They are habitual thoughts, produced subconsciously while our five senses activate our patterns.

But here's the thing—our emotions provide an impeccable service. They make us aware of the vicious circle we're in. Now that we're awake, we no longer need to feed our low-quality thoughts with the energy of our attention. When we connect with our wisdom, the thoughts fade, and so do the unpleasant emotions.

Distinguish Emotions that Matter

If our emotions were only an alarm clock to wake us from our habitual state of mind, a uniform, nasty feeling would suffice. Instead, we have a multitude of emotions. Most experts distinguish six emotions—anger, disgust, fear, happiness, sadness, and surprise. Recent research by the University of California at Berkeley elicited twenty-seven distinct emotions.[35] They were categorized in gradients based on a few thousand short videos. This research builds on research by Duke University.[36] This study was able to detect different neural activation patterns in the brain corresponding to different emotional states. Participants were presented with either a film or music clip, while their brain was scanned during functional magnetic resonance imaging (fMRI). Why do we have all these different emotions?

To learn from our emotions, it is essential to distinguish between primary and secondary emotions. Primary emotions are pure, honest ones that arise in the moment. They usually stem from early-life trauma and reflect our childhood conclusions. Typical examples are fear, pain, grief, resentment, and, on the positive side, joy.

Secondary emotions often surface as sudden "eruptions" that

seem out of proportion to the specific situation. These secondary emotions actually hide a primary emotion. Because we don't dare feel our primary emotions, we cover them with a secondary emotion that is easier to handle. Examples are frustration and anger (our red buttons!), anxiety (good old stress!), and guilt.

Often the culture in which we live has a significant impact on our flight to secondary emotions. In many societies, men still do not easily show their vulnerable side. When they are scared or feel lonely, they hide their primary emotion under a burst of aggression. If others react impulsively, they may end up fighting when, in fact, both are just as scared.

I don't find it useful to dwell on secondary emotions. Many spend hours discussing their anger or anxiety as they think it will help ease their troubles. All they really are doing is beating around the bush, feeding their ego with attention. So the next time someone yells at you or complains extensively in response to a minor mistake on your part, just realize it is a secondary emotion. If this happens in traffic or at the supermarket, simply apologize and move on.

If you really care for the other person, which should be the case at work, see if they're willing to open up. Ask questions like, "I notice you're annoyed, where does your anger really come from?" Or, "You seem concerned, what are you really afraid of?" If your relationship is more established, you can inquire, "What has happened in your past that is being activated in this moment?" In this way, you guide the other person from a secondary emotion to the underlying primary emotion.

A Gateway to Growth

Only our primary emotions are a gateway to growth. Each of our primary emotions holds a key to learning about ourselves. They want to move us in a certain direction. The Latin word *emovere* means "to stir up" or "to set in motion." Behind every highly charged emotion is a profound and calm feeling that is the voice of our soul. It's our deeper wisdom, our intuition that is always in the present moment. It is always spot on and aids us in navigating our lives.

What it takes is not to push your primary emotions away, flee into distractions, or try to explain what caused your fear, grief, or resentment. Those are all compulsive reactions. All you need to do is just welcome the emotion. Embrace it. Feel it in your body. Don't rationalize it by putting words to it. Stop coming up with all kinds of scenarios that only live in your imagination, triggered by your subconscious patterns.

If you're resentful, don't waste your time yelling all kinds of accusations you will later regret. It only distracts you from the present moment. There is a deeper reason for your rage. Someone has crossed your boundaries and your gut brain tells you this is not acceptable. So, take a timeout and feel your anger physically. Stamp your feet on the floor, clench your fists, scream your lungs out. I promise, it won't take more than a minute for the sky to clear. It will help you feel your innate power. And then there will be a calm determination. You simply know how to resolve the issue in a steadfast, yet respectful way. You base your actions on the values that fully resonate with your innermost core. It's an effective way to be guided by your emotions!

Have you ever felt immensely sad about missing an opportunity or losing someone dear? There's no point in being strong and biting your lip. You suffered a loss and now need to face that reality. Your energy wants to flow. I know from experience that men are not inclined to cry for their loss. Anyone who has ever given way to grief by crying deeply from the gut knows what a hugely liberating experience it is.

Most of us literally swallow our tears and create an energy block around our diaphragm. Step by step, we lose contact with our feelings and, thus, with our intuition. Our hearts bleed under a veil of indifference. Just as we're tough on ourselves, we become tough on our environment. We become insensitive to the needs of others and offer instant rational "solutions" when all they want is a listening ear. We have frozen our heart and shielded our gut and consider every emotion to be an omen of weakness.

Once we learn not to run from our emotions, but rather to embrace them, the opposite of what we think actually will happen. We will not lose our balance and become emotionally unstable. We will become like surfers who have learned to ride the waves as they emerge. Underneath our deepest fears we will discover our excitement for life's adventures. And in the boredom of our existence we'll find the purpose of our being—our creativity.

TOP THREE TAKEAWAYS

1) In our early childhood, we felt helpless and dependent on others for our survival. We have scripted fear-based patterns that still get triggered every day. Our childhood conclusions prevent us from living our true potential.

2) The Principle of Thought sends a powerful message. We are not really stressed, angry, sad, lonesome, scared, or any other negative emotion. We just think we are. If we learn to stay present, we can mentally press the pause button.

3) Our emotions are a yardstick for the quality of our thinking. If we notice our fear-based thinking is triggered, we can choose to take a timeout and let our thoughts pass. Behind every primary emotion we find a deep and calm feeling that helps us navigate our lives.

SHAPE YOUR PARADISE *ONLINE*

In week 2 of the online module "Consciousness? Awesome!" you will experience the Centering exercise in a guided meditation. You will further explore the transformation potential of emotions. What are the childhood conclusions that are hampering you? What wisdom is hidden behind them? Seize the opportunity to actively work with this powerful material!

10

EVER MORE CONSCIOUS

*"Reality is that which, when you stop
believing in it, doesn't go away."*
—Philip K. Dick

The Principle of Consciousness

The previous two chapters were dedicated to the transformation in our thinking. We saw how everything in our perception is created by thought. Even our emotions reflect the quality of our thoughts. In our early childhood we all experienced traumas that created patterns in our subconscious mind. If we're not conscious about our habitual thinking, we are likely to suffer and act out of fear of survival.

What exactly is Consciousness? What would such a New Age topic have to do with leadership? Can't we simply look at some hands-on, practical concepts that explain how we can be more effective as (personal) leaders?

To me, these are fair questions that require clear-cut answers. That's the reason we spend this entire chapter on the Principle of Consciousness. In Chapter 8 I described that this principle "reflects the degree to which we realize our full potential." And I asked, "To what extent are we aware about the truth of our existence?" This may sound as if we're presently not seeing reality as it is. As if we're stuck in the dark without having clear vision. It took me quite a few years to recognize that this is indeed the case. All my life I have been critical about any theories that people tried to impose. I didn't want to get lost in unproven fantasies. Just take things at face value. What you see is what you get. To me it seemed like the most honest way to go about life.

In this light, traditional science and the medical profession also look at the word "consciousness." The Oxford Dictionary provides a straightforward definition: "The state of being aware of and responsive to one's surroundings." It couldn't be any clearer. If I'm able to interact with things happening around me, I am conscious. However, I am (temporarily) unconscious if I'm sleeping, sedated during surgery, or in a coma.

This definition does not attach a dynamic quality to the word consciousness. It seems more like a digital switch on our smartphone. We swipe either "on" or "off." When we're awake, we're "on." During sleep, narcosis, or in a coma, we're "off." The word "awakeness" does a perfect job to represent this distinction.

On my journey from an outside-in to an inside-out perspective on my experience of life, I have come to see consciousness in a more subtle way. It's an awareness that provides me with concrete guidance throughout the day. At thirty thousand feet, my best effort to provide a definition of consciousness is "The degree to which I realize the Truth—I am part of something greater than myself." I'll be able to uncover this Truth if I become familiar with my inner world.

Here's the key. The moment I realize I am a unique cog in a magnificent timepiece, I open the gateway to realizing my full potential. I will thoroughly enjoy developing my personal strengths and the unique talents with which I have been endowed. Yet I'll do so to the benefit of everyone in my vicinity—a priceless contribution to the rise of humanity as a whole. The ultimate destiny for each of us is to become the sugar that dissolves in the tea. Its unique quality can be clearly distinguished. In fact, it turns the bitter tea into a sweet and enjoyable drink! But it surrenders its individuality to help shape the perfect drink.

This requires a confident, yet humble way of engaging with others. It implies we clearly see that everyone, and I literally mean everyone, holds a piece in solving the puzzle of our existence. Our weaknesses can be easily compensated for by the strengths of others, and vice versa. Our position in the hierarchy of organizations, our financial wealth, our imagined status, the reputation of our family, the club, rank, caste, religion, nationality, race, gender, or any other distinction we may apply to feel better or worse than another human being simply conveys that we are operating at the lowest levels of consciousness. Striving to win at the detriment of others has the effect of the world losing as a whole. In the cocktail of humanity, there is unity in diversity. The task at hand is to celebrate our differences and learn from each other.

The more we perceive the Truth in the present moment, the better it will guide us in choosing our behavior. We will find it increasingly easier to coach and lead the people for whom we are responsible. And we will reap the benefits of stronger results, better relationships, and a hell of a lot more fun.

Societal Transformation in Eight Stages

Let's establish some picket posts in our journey of consciousness transformation. A great number of scholars have conducted groundbreaking work in this field. Ken Wilber has incorporated the common denominator of their work in his Integral Theory.[37] I will therefore use his description as a basis to distinguish eight different levels of development.[38] We will first focus on the collective perspective of societal development. The individual, psychological perspective follows in the next section.

It all begins where we left off in Chapter 3—the first modern human, *Homo sapiens*. They walked the savannah in Africa about two hundred thousand years ago. Take a look at exhibit 10. The colors of the rainbow that match the eight stages reflect the myriad of development that has taken place since. Let's first review stages one through six, which are called Tier 1. We will then cover our imminent transition to Teal (stage seven), which is a momentous leap to Tier 2. And finally, we'll take a brief look at our future transition beyond Teal.

The 8 Stages of *Collective* Development
The Sociology of Consciousness Transformation

	Color	Culture	Emergence (yrs ago)	Metaphor (organization)	Mode	
					Thrive	
8	Indigo	Unified	Now			Tier 3
7	Teal	Integral	50	Organism		Tier 2
6	Green	Postmodern	150	Family		
5	Orange	Modern	300	Machine		Tier 1
4	Amber	Traditional	5,000	Army		
3	Red	Tribal	12,000	Wolf pack		
2	Magenta	Indigenous	50,000			
1	Infrared	Archaic	200,000		Survive	

Exhibit 10—The eight stages of collective development.

Infrared (stage one) represents the first 150,000 to 190,000 years when people lived in family kinships of just 20 to 35 people. Relationships became too complex beyond this size of society. There was no hierarchy, no organizational model. Few people lived beyond their twenties; an age of forty was seldom reached. Life was about survival—the typical hunter-gatherer era.

In **Magenta** (stage two), people started to form tribes of up to a few hundred people. Rituals were developed, led by shamans, to appease the magical world of spirits. Task differentiation was still limited and there was no serious form of organization yet. People lived significantly longer, sometimes up to fifty or older. The use of tools and knowledge of plants must have contributed to this development.

Red (stage 3) marks the time when people settled down and started early forms of horticulture about twelve thousand years ago. The first chiefdoms appeared. The form of organization was like a wolfpack. The chief demonstrated great power and bent others to his will. When his power faded, he was history. He therefore assembled loyal family members to protect him by keeping the others in line. Public punishment was part of the indoctrination. Still today, street gangs and mafia operate by this paradigm.

In **Amber** (stage 4), humankind leaped to the Agrarian Age. States, institutions, and bureaucracy were formed, as well as organized religion. Classes of rulers, priests, warriors, and administrators emerged. The metaphor of an army represents the structure of organizations. We still find this setup today in public schools, the military and, for instance, the Catholic Church. Self-discipline and control are part of this static world view. There are laws and morality and the threat of suffering in the hereafter. People who aren't part of the group or society are excluded. Rigid gender differences and clear etiquettes prescribe how to think, behave, dress, and marry. Society is well organized and fairly safe, built on inequality and unchanging standards.

Orange (stage 5) induced modern culture—the Industrial Age. The Renaissance poked holes in the traditional world of religious certainties. Science became the new foundation of truth. People ought to be free to pursue their dreams. Performance should be the basis for social recognition. The industrial revolution further spurred the materialistic world view—only what is tangible really exists. Modern global corporations embody this paradigm in which organizations are viewed as machines. Engineering jargon dominates our world today—inputs, outputs, efficiency, effectiveness, information flows, scaling, blueprints, and implementation. Innovation and accountability fuel the notion that growth matters most. All activities are geared to maximizing shareholder value. Individual and collective greed are the shadow of this stage.

The Information Age saw the light of day in **Green** (stage 6). A pluralistic perspective is taken. In the postmodern world view, fairness, equality, and harmony is sought. A society in which everyone's perspectives deserve respect. It is the awakening of this paradigm that led to the abolition of slavery in the nineteenth century and the rise of feminism. The aversion to rules causes the

Green stage to aspire to an egalitarian society. This notion gained popularity during the anti-establishment movement of the 1960s and 1970s. Postmodern thinking is widely found at universities and nongovernmental organizations today. The organizational metaphor is of a family that cares for all its employees. It's all about the company culture. Empowerment, 360-degree feedback of leaders, a values-driven culture, an inspirational purpose, and a multiple stakeholder perspective are typical innovations of Green organizations. Examples of such companies are Ben & Jerry's and Southwest Airlines.

Psychological Transformation in Eight Stages

In Chapter 3 we explored that our body encompasses 3.5 billion years of evolution. With every new pregnancy, the entire evolution repeats itself at record speed. A fertilized egg is in fact a single-celled organism. It quickly divides to form a multicellular organism. Within weeks, the lungs and vital organs develop, followed by the heart, bones and muscles. Then the nervous system, skin and eyes are formed. The brain, especially the prefrontal lobe, is only fully developed at age twenty-five. It's magnificent how the same progression takes place in our consciousness development. It took modern man, *Homo sapiens*, two hundred thousand years to progress through the collective stages. We get to experience them in roughly the first quarter of our life (see exhibit 11). Our upbringing and childhood conclusions significantly impact which stage becomes our dominant level of consciousness. Our further development depends on our own eagerness to grow and the new insights we gain from our experiences.

The 8 Stages of *Individual* Development
The Psychology of Consciousness Transformation

	Color	Mindset	Potential Age (yrs)	% Adults (average)	Experience
					Inside-Out
8	Indigo	Sage	45+		Tier 3
7	Teal	Integrator	35+	<1%	Tier 2
6	Green	Relativist	21+	10%	
5	Orange	Achiever	12-21	30%	
4	Amber	Conformist	7-12	40%	Tier 1
3	Red	Opportunist	3-7	20%	
2	Magenta	Impulsive	1-3		
1	Infrared	Survivor	0-1		Outside-In

Exhibit 11—The eight stages of individual development.

Infrared (stage 1) is the level experienced by newborn babies in their first year. They are merely surviving. These infants have not developed any sense of self-consciousness yet. They depend on their mother. They live completely from the outside-in, feeling helpless and lonesome when they're hungry or in need of a clean diaper.

In **Magenta** (stage 2), these young children, roughly between one and three years old, begin to sense they are separate from their mother. As we've discussed in Chapter 9, in this phase, reality and imagination are mixed in the child's experience. There is a wonderful quality to children at this age—the art of playing. A playing child is pure, creative, and in the moment. It is not disturbed by any concern. The child reacts impulsively to its environment, which in its perception is constantly changing.[39] It will not take ownership for any situation and respond emotionally to whatever perceived wrongdoing. The infant expects others to resolve its problems.

Red (stage 3) is the time when children begin to sense they are separate from others (typically between the age of three and seven).[40] The focus of these children is an opportunistic "what's in it for me?" in every social engagement. Their desires drive their behavior. They are relentlessly persistent in getting what they want. They no longer act purely impulsively to a situation. They understand there is a price to be paid to materialize their desires. In this stage, a child is forming its opinions. It develops a notion of the rules that apply. It adopts a laser-beam focus on its self-centered needs. This filter is combined with a steadfast conviction that certain rules must be obeyed. Or to the contrary, that the prevailing order must be overthrown. The result is a critical attitude toward everyone in their environment. *You are either with me or against me.*

In **Amber** (stage 4), children from the age of seven make an important transition from being focused on their own egoistic desires to identifying with a group to which they feel connected. As such, these children are constantly looking for an outside reference to adopt the appropriate way to think and act. They are prepared to subordinate their own wishes to conform to the groups' standards.[41] In other words, they shift from Red egocentrism to Amber ethnocentrism. The "own" group is sacred, but members of other groups are despised. Different "schools of thought" exercise their influence on these children. These may be family, education system, religion, friends, or YouTube vloggers. They sometimes feel torn between all different opinions. As a result, they may feel insecure and act indecisively. It wears them down to serve multiple lords. They have not been able to integrate the various perspectives into a balanced perspective of their own.

Orange (stage 5) typically is the age of adolescence, when young people question the previously considered immutable laws. They no longer look at external authorities—parents or teachers—to determine how to think and act. People expand their ethnocentric focus to a more world-centric view. They certainly take the opinions of others in consideration, but they themselves form a perspective of how things really work.[42] Achievement is the name of the Orange game. The goal in life is to be successful. The pursuit of a career and a respected social status is an Orange trait. A passion for competition and winning over others is another feature. An Orange level of consciousness comes with excessive consumerism and a materialistic world view. People only accept what is empirically proven. They are wary of any form of spirituality. They tend to live in the future as their minds are preoccupied by reaching their goals.

Social inequality and the loss of community are the shadow of Orange. They cause a person to reflect on society and adopt a more pluralistic world view. In **Green** (stage 6), an adult realizes there is more to life than achievement. People seek harmony, consensus, and equality. They understand that all opinions count and only reveal a relative "truth." They do not feel inferior or superior to anyone. Nor do they serve others in ways that do not really help them. They operate on the basis of "I'm okay, you're okay." A true connection with others is sought, in which social classes, castes, institutional religion, and other hierarchies are no longer accepted. Green is allergic to power. It is forceful at breaking down obsolete structures, yet not strong in defining workable alternatives.

Far from Being Mature

It is crucial to note the stage at which we operate is by no means static. We actually travel between levels overnight. When at ease, for instance after a good night's sleep, we often see things from a different perspective at a higher level of consciousness. In the heat of an argument, we may lose our bearings. Our survival anxiety surfaces and we drop one or more levels. Our thoughts and emotions are transient. Having said that, we typically have a dominant level that paints the scene of how we experience life.

The eight stages of development are loosely connected with the age at which people typically have the potential to reach a next level. Several studies offer a perspective on the percentage of adults who perceive life at different stages.[43] On average, about 20 percent of adults operate as an Opportunist in Red (stage 3)—the child stage. Another 40 percent align with Amber (stage 4) as a Conformist— the elementary school stage. And the next 30 percent of adults typically function as adolescent Achievers in Orange (stage 5). Isn't it striking that about 90 percent of adults have not reached the level of consciousness appropriate for their adulthood?

It's also amazing how similar these numbers are to the earlier discussed Gallup study (2017). Their poll revealed that 85 percent of employees are not engaged, or even actively disengaged, in their work today. The majority of adults still make meaning of life on a level of consciousness that by default places them in constant conflict situations. No wonder they are not engaged in their daily work. They are stuck in never-ending, immature games that drain their energy level.

Every person's psychology is a palette of different stages of consciousness. And so are the cultures of which they are a part. Most people think they are right and the others are wrong. People tend to attach their identity to their world view. It is often difficult, if not impossible, to reconcile these perspectives. This to a large degree explains the tremendous tension that is felt in our societies today. What is needed is nothing short of a global awakening—a major boost in consciousness, and not just in the way we think when we're calm and reasonable. We need to learn how we lift our primary emotions to a trust-based level, even when the heat is on.

Our Imminent Transition to Teal

The dawn of the Transformation Age builds on our global awakening. Something special happens here. In **Teal** (stage 7), people learn to observe their own ego structure. As they see through their own compulsive thinking, they free themselves of their fear of survival. In so doing, they see the limitations of their own individuality. They start to see that beyond the differences in beliefs, identifications, and cultural values, all people are truly interconnected. And so are the systems of which they are a part.

We are not just separate individuals, interacting with each other in a transactional way to the benefit of both. It is in the relationship with other people that the completeness of human beings materializes.[44] People no longer see a need to draw a line in the sand as a sharp border between "mine" and "thine." In other words, they shift from "I'm okay, you're okay" (at Green, or stage 6 level) to the full realization that "I am you." The polarities of life fade away as they start to see the underlying similarities and our common journey. As such, they take an integral perspective. With increasingly less effort, they see an ever-expanding range of possibilities.

* * *

"An organization cannot evolve beyond its leadership's stage of development."
—Frederic Laloux

* * *

In Teal, the Transformation Age, people understand it is not about them. For the first time, they see the evolutionary nature of life toward ever higher levels of consciousness. Therefore, this progression marks the transition from Tier 1 to Tier 2. Do you remember my hunch in the introduction that organizations themselves are living organisms? Fredric Laloux uses the same metaphor to paint a mental picture of what a Teal organization looks like. He describes twelve companies that already operate in Teal.[45] Their organizations vary from one hundred to forty thousand employees. They have found an answer to the Green struggles with authority and structure. They all go by the premise that nature itself is built on hierarchies. These aren't the "dominator" hierarchies we find in Amber or Orange companies. They are built on self-organization. The complete hierarchy is nested in teams of up to fifteen people. The team makes all decisions and divides the work among themselves. This includes "overhead tasks" such as administration.

Teal organizations do not pursue growth as the Holy Grail or push for results. The organization is viewed as having a genuine purpose of its own. It's the work itself that is central to creating value for customers. Employees are inspired to develop their intuitive and emotional self and not rely only on their rational thinking. They are extensively trained to effectively work together as a whole. Peer feedback is a major contributor to establish joint values and boost improvement. There are no targets, job descriptions, or organization charts. It's the team that jointly decides about the ambition, role division, and remuneration.

It is obvious that the role of leaders is completely changing in Teal organizations. They become coaches and experts in team processes. They support their people in strengthening their self-management skills. Employee motivation rises significantly in these organizations. Companies become a magnet for staff wanting to join them. It is a wonderful paradox how these Teal organizations achieve stellar results without necessarily pursuing them.

Part III of this book is dedicated to the leadership competencies that set Teal leaders apart from there Tier 1-based colleagues. Even in companies that aren't ready to make the transition to Teal yet, these leaders will have a magnificent impact. They will demonstrate how a more natural leadership style yields more sustainable results for all parties involved. It is leadership based on a sound comprehension of what truly motivates people.

Future Transition beyond Teal

Wilber distinguishes several stages beyond Teal. I have simplified these levels of consciousness into one combined Indigo stage. This stage marks yet another significant transition from Tier 2 to Tier 3. This is the stage attained by sages all over the world throughout history. They completely transcended the illusion of separateness and experienced unity with all of nature. I can only imagine what a society operating from this level of consciousness will look like. It will embody one global unified community in which people have full mastery of their inner world. From there they directly create the outer world they wish to experience. In the next chapter we will explore a basic technique to experiment with this.

TOP THREE TAKEAWAYS

1) Consciousness is "The degree to which I realize the Truth—I am part of something greater than myself." The moment I realize I am a unique cog in a magnificent timepiece, I open the gateway to realizing my full potential.

2) We often find ourselves caught in immature games in which we play a role that depletes our energy in the long term. Once we see through our selfish needs, and understand they are caused by our illusory fear of survival, we have the opportunity to free ourselves.

3) The journey of our consciousness transformation, which took modern man two hundred thousand years to develop, is one that we get to experience in roughly the first quarter of our life. Our further development depends on our eagerness to grow and the new insights we gain from our experiences.

SHAPE YOUR PARADISE *ONLINE*

At what stage of consciousness do you typically operate? What are the kind of games in which you get entangled? How does your cognitive development differ from your emotional development? Week 3 of the online module "Consciousness? Awesome!" addresses these challenging questions. Are you ready to face your own music? It will be an insightful self-discovery.

EVERYTHING IS ENERGY

*"If you want to find the secrets of the universe, think
in terms of energy, frequency, and vibration."*
—Nikola Tesla

Up For a Surprise

Energy wants to flow. The more we sense it in our body, the
better we feel. When fully charged, we are excited to take action and
pursue our interests. But what is energy? Where does it come from?
And if it's so useful, how can I get more of it? How can I inject more
energy into the people with whom I work? We are touching the core
of what it means to transform your organization into a paradise.

Let us build it up in steps. Energy is the fuel that boosts your
manifestation in the world—just like your car runs on gasoline, the
lights in your house burn on electricity, and your lawn turns healthy
and green if it gets sufficient sunlight, water, and fertilizer. Part
of your energy comes from the quality of the food you eat and the
restfulness of your sleep.

There's much more to it at a deeper level. To grasp this, let's
examine the construction of our physical world more closely. We take
a foray into quantum physics, which will give us some magnificent
insights. At the smallest level, all matter in our physical world is
99.9999999 percent empty space. These atoms comprise electrons
swirling around a small nucleus of protons and neutrons. This nucleus

contains quarks and gluons. And here's where things get interesting—these quarks and gluons are so small, physicists have not been able to ever measure their size.

What they did find were some weird phenomena that could not be understood by "Newtonian physics." The classical laws of mechanics as defined by Sir Isaac Newton at the end of the seventeenth century accurately explain the movement of objects in relation to the forces acting on them. There always is a linear relationship of cause and effect. Therefore an object can only be in one place at the same time. When scientists studied the tiniest building blocks of physical matter, however, they were taken by surprise.

The Major Implications of Quantum Physics

The prelude to quantum physics started with the so called double-slit experiment. In 1801 Thomas Young used a light source to illuminate a plate with two parallel slits. On the opposite wall, Young noted an interesting pattern. The two waves of light passing the slits had interfered to create this pattern. It was similar to two stones thrown in a pond. He concluded that light behaves like a wave. This went against the then-prevailing Newtonian theory that light was made up of particles.

However, in 1905, Albert Einstein launched the idea that light consists of ultrasmall particles. Just over twenty years later, the American chemist Gilbert Newton Lewis (what's in a middle name?) coined the term "photon" to describe these units of light. So the jury was out—did light behave like waves or particles? Young's double-slit experiment was revisited using advanced measuring instruments. This time a most remarkable outcome was witnessed. A single photon was forced through the slits and its movement was monitored all the way to the opposite wall. No interference pattern appeared on the wall. Hence, the light continued to behave like a particle. However, as soon as the scientists removed the measuring equipment, the interference pattern returned on the wall. The light behaved like a wave again.

In 1924 the French physicist Louis de Broglie took the wave versus particle duality a giant step further. He asserted this duality not only applied to light, but to all matter in the universe. De Broglie combined Einstein's famous formula $E=mc^2$ (relating energy and mass) with Planck's formula $E=hf$ (relating energy and the frequency of a wave). Since energy is related to both mass and frequency, he theorized that the mass of an object must be related to frequency as well. In other words, any object has both particle (mass) and wave (frequency) properties.

The challenge was to observe an object displaying wave-like behavior. The calculated wavelength would be extremely small. Only three years later, in 1927, scientists were able to conduct the experiment that proved the validity of de Broglie's claim. They forced electrons through tiny holes, the size of their own wavelength, in a thin metal film. The electrons diffracted, displaying wave-like patterns. The evidence was there—objects do have small but unmistakable wave properties. As a result, de Broglie was awarded the Nobel Prize in 1929.

Just think about the consequences of these scientific insights. Depending on how they set up the experiments, the scientists could make both light and matter behave as waves or particles. As soon as they observed the waves closely, they collapsed them into particles.

Quantum physics has uncovered that in its essence, all matter simply is space vibrating at a certain frequency. Everything is energy. It is our presence that is converting this energy into the physical reality we perceive. Our mind shapes our world in the most literal sense. What an impactful demonstration of the inside-out experience!

The Higher the Frequency, the More Power

Since everything is space vibrating at a certain frequency, let's explore these waves somewhat further. We learned from Planck's formula that energy goes up as the frequency of the vibration increases. The length of the wave is inversely related to its frequency. The shorter the wavelength, the higher the frequency and the more energy it contains. However, the longer the wavelength, the farther its distance of reception.

Waves have a particular quality. Not only do they convey energy, they also are perfect media to store and transmit information. How? Let's take radio waves as an example (see exhibit 12). Information is coded in these waves through modulation. For instance, the sender is changing the amplitude (the height of the wave) or its frequency by a second wave signal. This could be a song or some other data. If the receiver knows what type of modulation was applied, the signal can be decoded to obtain the information. In this way, an almost limitless amount of information can be shared between parties. Wi-Fi, TV broadcasting, and our GPS navigation systems are but a few examples of information transmission using waves.

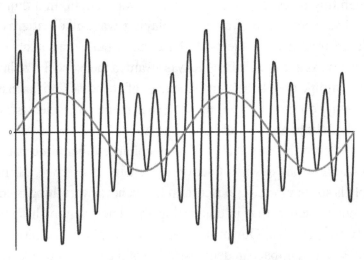

Exhibit 12—Wave modulation.[46]

Three of our five senses (hearing, sight, and touch) register certain phenomena in our environment by decoding waves to retrieve information. The sounds that we hear use air as a carrier to travel. We hear sounds at frequencies between 20 Hz and 20 kHz. The colors that we see are light waves in the visible range of approximately

430–770 THz.[47] These waves are different from sound waves as they do not require a medium to travel. That is why we can see stars whose rays of light have traveled through space for many years. Our touch can sense infrared waves as thermal energy (heat) at frequencies below the visible range.

The frequencies we are able to register by our sight and touch are limited ranges within the electromagnetic spectrum. This spectrum covers a wide range from low vibrating radio waves all the way to extremely high frequency gamma rays (see exhibit 13). All waves in the electromagnetic spectrum have in common that they travel at the speed of light. The higher the frequency of the vibration, the more energy it contains. Radio waves travel through the ether without much impact on any objects they may cross. Yet ultraviolet light is dangerous for the unprotected skin. Radiologists and operators diagnosing patients with X-ray technology stand behind shielded windows. Frequent exposure to these waves may have health implications. Atomic or nuclear radiation relates to gamma waves. They impart the highest photon energy. Their frequencies are in the top range of the electromagnetic spectrum.

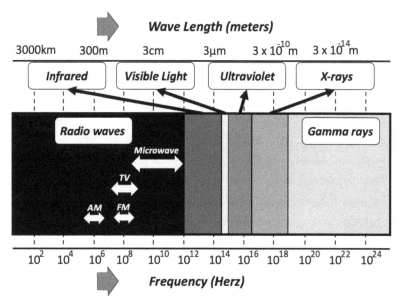

Exhibit 13—The electromagnetic spectrum.

Scientists uncovered how to modulate waves in the past century. Thus they paved the road for a multitude of applications to convey information and energy between sender and receiver. We have developed a host of devices that code and decode waves we cannot register with our own senses. Microwaves, for instance, are at the high end of the radio-wave frequencies. They are used to heat food. Infrared waves are applied in surveillance cameras. X-ray technology is used to provide an image of a patient's bone and vein structure. At an ever-increasing rate, we are learning to make use of the amazing design of the universe.

Herein lies the secret of energy management. The cosmos is home to infinite quantum vibrational waves. They serve as storage for a limitless amount of energy and information. In comparison, our ability to code and decode both sonar and electromagnetic waves is negligible. All the seemingly empty space has the potential to create anything in our perception. As we expand our ability to receive and decode these vibrations, we will gain access to levels of energy and wisdom beyond our wildest imagination. This is not done through devices and manmade technology. It is done through our extraordinary human quality—our consciousness.

You Are the Observer

Like all matter in the universe, your body is 99.9999999 percent empty space. In essence, it is pure energy, space vibrating at a certain frequency. As an observer, you have collapsed the waves into particles. Or energy into matter—your body and even your mind.

This sounds dopey. What have you been smoking?

I know, it seems kind of weird. And if it's even true, why would it be relevant for us as (personal) leaders? Well, if you fully capture this reality, it opens the gateway to colossal possibilities. Let's take it in bite-sized chunks.

As mentioned in Chapter 9, you are both the actor on stage and the spectator in the balcony. You're the football player as well as the coach who watches from the sidelines. The observer obviously is the spectator or the coach in you. In fact, it's who you really are.

Eckhart Tolle describes how, at the pinnacle of his depression in his younger years, he woke up one morning feeling dreadful:[48]

> *'I cannot live with myself any longer.' This was the thought that kept repeating itself in my mind. Then suddenly I became aware of what a peculiar thought it was. 'I am one or two? If I cannot live with myself, there must be two of me—the 'I' and the 'self' that 'I' cannot live with.' 'Maybe,' I thought, 'only one of them is real.'*

At this realization, Tolle's mind stopped, and he felt drawn into a vortex of energy. When he woke up, everything had changed:

> *"That day I walked around the city in utter amazement at the miracle of life on Earth, as if I had just been born into this world."*

Most people never reach Tolle's level of clarity as their daily lives don't push them against the wall hard enough. Tolle's depression left him with no other option. His desperate desire to get out of pain was even stronger than his fear of survival. His decision to give up on life sparked a sudden breakthrough in his consciousness. He switched from matter (his body and mind) to energy (his consciousness). And then his perception of life changed completely as he suddenly grasped a reality—it was not about him.

The "you" that you know is not the essence of your being. Your familiar "you" is the product of many years of compulsive recycling of your own beliefs. Your patterns have molded your personality. Your fear of survival has turned neural goat paths into six-lane mental highways that instantly activate your stress response to any perceived danger. They cause you to relive the very same loops over and over again. The tentacles of your subconscious memory restrain you from living your full potential. You only get what you always got. Yet the fear of losing what you have in terms of possessions, status, and convictions keep you hostage to your illusory world of scarcity.

You don't have to wait for life to force you to relinquish your mental attachments. You have a standing invitation to choose a different course. You can literally Shape Your Paradise. Right here, right now. What it takes is for you to shift from matter to energy. To stop being concerned about "you." To give up on driving for results and trying to control the outcome. That's just the world of consequences. If you learn to shift to the world of causes, you enter the quantum reality of your existence.

Creating a Quantum Mind

How do we shift from body to consciousness, so from matter to energy and from particle to wave? The shift to becoming a wave can be taken in the most literal sense. In Chapter 4 we discussed how coherence between our head and heart brains aligns our energy system. This alignment can be simultaneously measured by recording both an EEG (head brain) and an ECG (heart brain). Thus, we synchronize our thoughts (head) and emotions (heart) using deep belly breathing (gut). We tune into the Earth's magnetic field and connect at a deep level with all systems of which we are part. This is called a "quantum mind." Ancient wisdom schools such as yoga or Taoism, as well as shamanic traditions from all over the world, already taught this process thousands of years ago.

By creating a quantum mind, we enter a state of flow. This is only possible if our personality disappears. It is not about us. It is about the value we wish to create in the world. We become "no body, no one, no thing, no where at no time."[49] Now we're in the perfect state to make optimum use of the one endowment that sets us apart from all other creatures—our prefrontal lobe. Home to our conscious mind, our prefrontal lobe enables us not only to reason, but also to imagine! Visualizing the future is much more than just dreaming about it. It is the way in which we create it. If we know what we really want to create and put all our attention and passion on imagining what that future scenario looks like, it is bound to happen.

I want to be a billionaire, live like a movie star, drive a Ferrari, and play golf every day. I take ten minutes each day to paint this picture in my mind's eye. Why isn't it happening?

Well, your conscious mind may outline your desired future, but your subconscious mind works against you. Your convictions and childhood conclusions have carved neurological pathways that depict an opposite future, one with limitations that assumes you had better accept that you cannot have it all. You're thinking, "I want to be billionaire." But the voice in your head, a limiting belief, is telling you, "Don't be ridiculous, just a decent salary is good enough for me." Likewise, your childhood conclusions also discard your dreams about the life of a movie star, the Ferrari, and your daily golf game.

Since you don't really believe life has all these beautiful things in store for you, your heart and head brains are not coherent. Without realizing it, you have created your present situation. You have sent mixed signals and settled for a life with obstacles. And since you're still nurturing these limiting beliefs, you continue to create a future that's rooted in the misconceptions of your childhood. You have passed from energy to matter and turned off your quantum mind.

A powerful carrier for creating a quantum mind is meditation. This isn't "woo-woo" at all. It simply is a process to become aware of your automatic, subconscious programs. Step by step, you learn to become the perfect observer. You will only materialize those thoughts that you truly desire. And frankly, the billion-dollar bank account, the Ferrari, and all the other perks it can buy are not the things that will ultimately fulfill you. You're not here to consume. You're here to create.

Rewiring Your Subconscious Mind

Some of the programs in our subconscious mind are based on a misconception of our outer world. Now that we are adults, they do not serve us anymore. How about rewriting them? Let our subconscious mind execute what our conscious mind visualizes! To accomplish this, we need to learn how to access our subconscious mind. This is where the internal alchemy starts! When did we download most of our mental programs and wire them in our subconscious mind? Exactly, in our early childhood! Now, if we want to change the wiring, how would we do it? It's quite obvious: we need to get our mind in the same state as when we downloaded these programs.

As we saw in Chapter 9, young children's brain waves display delta (0.5–4 Hz) and theta (4–8 Hz) frequencies. Only during deep sleep do our adult brains shift to the delta state. We only experience theta when we are dreaming vividly during the REM stage of sleep. When we wake up, we are still in an alpha (8–12 Hz) state. This is the dominant state for children between six and twelve. But the moment our eyes catch the first sunlight, we move our attention outward. We enter the beta (12–35 Hz) frequency range. This has been the case since our high school days.

In order to access our subconscious mind, we need to first shift from beta to alpha brain waves. In alpha, we are on the brink of entering our inner landscape. We are still fully aware of our environment. But we have access to our "dream state" at the same time. We're in the twilight zone. It's the state between wakefulness and sleep. We usually only quickly cross this state when we fall asleep, or when we wake up. It's an incredibly powerful state to linger in as everything is done with ease. We recharge our batteries while still fully present in the world. As we want to learn how to Shape Our Paradise, it is crucial we train our ability to remain in an alpha state for longer periods of time. And you already know how to do it! In Chapter 3 you learned to activate your Yee Power. You know how to connect with your head, heart, and gut brains. This is, in fact, the alpha state.

Now we're ready to take the next step. We want to become increasingly calm. We seek to transition from alpha to theta brain waves. This entails a complete synchronization of our three brains. We will activate our parasympathetic nervous system even further. The Centering exercise (Chapter 9) offers a nice pathway. This really is a transition from egoism to altruism in itself. We drop our identifications with the outer world—our body, possessions, image, and opinions. It is not about us. In this pure state of consciousness, we transform from matter to energy, from particle to wave. Hence, we enter the cockpit of creation. In this state of mind, we are ready for the next step—to shape our New Tomorrow.

—TRANSFORMATION EXERCISE 12—
Your New Tomorrow

We cannot resolve our current problems with our present level of consciousness. It is time to shift to a more advanced perspective that offers genuine solutions. Seize the opportunity to transform and create a lighter version of yourself and of your organization. You can effectively connect to the infinite Field of Intelligence to help you find new ways. One way is by using the gateway of your subconscious mind. Your subconscious mind never sleeps and, if instructed correctly by your conscious mind, will go all the way to realize your dreams.

Step 1—Visualize Your New Tomorrow

In the morning, before opening your eyes, allow yourself fifteen minutes to make use of the creative state you are in. In this dream state, your conscious mind has easy access to your subconscious mind. It is the perfect time to visualize your New Tomorrow.

a) Activate your Yee Power by connecting your head, heart, and gut brains
b) Enter your inner world by Centering your attention
c) When you notice you are free from your body and mind, maintain the observer position:
   ➢ What reality do I want to create?
   ➢ Where will I be? What will I do? With whom do I spend time?
   ➢ Sense all the details—What do I see, hear, taste, smell, and touch?
   ➢ Who will benefit in my New Tomorrow?
   ➢ How can I create even more value for even more people?

Don't try to interfere by actively thinking about answers. Just see what images come to your mind. In the beginning, it may feel odd, and you may be distracted by other thoughts. Just bring your awareness back and see what happens. If you make this a daily routine, you will soon get vivid images of what your New Tomorrow looks like.

While you're still in your dream state in the morning, continue with step 2.

Step 2—Feel Your Passion

Your subconscious mind cannot distinguish between what's really happening and your imagination. It wants to direct you from pain to happiness. When you really feel the passion for your New Tomorrow, you instruct your subconscious mind to make it happen. That's the key to realizing your dreams.

a) Focus your attention on your heart as if you are breathing through your heart.
b) Feel how much you love your life in your New Tomorrow. How it excites you to do what you're really passionate about. How wonderful it is to spend time with the people you love. How fulfilling it is to have an impact and to grow. You are truly adding value!
c) Experience how it fills you with gratitude to live in your New Tomorrow. What an amazing gift it is to be able to Shape Your Paradise!
d) Experience how this feeling of gratitude is transported to every cell in your body on an inhalation. All negativity is cleansed in each cell on an exhalation. Repeat for a few minutes.

Be confident about your New Tomorrow as if it is already a reality. You're Shaping Your Paradise. Don't worry about planning the steps to get there. Leave it to your subconscious mind to guide you in taking the right steps. And by the way, that guidance is called intuition. Try this for four weeks in a row. You'll be amazed by the progress you're making in becoming a lighter version of yourself.

TOP THREE TAKEAWAYS

1) Quantum physics has uncovered that all matter simply is space vibrating at a certain frequency. Everything is energy. It is our presence that is converting this energy into the physical reality we observe. Our thoughts shape our world in the most literal sense.

2) Entering our quantum state means that we make optimum use of the one endowment that sets us apart from all other creatures—our prefrontal lobe. Visualizing our New Tomorrow is the way in which we Shape Our Paradise.

3) The quantum state really is the dream state in which we downloaded our mental programs into our subconscious mind as a child. If we truly feel our passion for our New Tomorrow, we rewire our subconscious mind with this powerful program update.

SHAPE YOUR PARADISE *ONLINE*

The Law of Attraction has become immensely popular. What's the real secret of making it work for you? How does your level of consciousness impact results? You will actively practice with the building blocks to enter your quantum mind. Have fun with Week 4 of the online module "Consciousness? Awesome!"

12

TAPPING INTO THE FIELD

"The meaning of life is to discover your gift.
The purpose of life is to give it away."
—Pablo Picasso

Free at Last

The Light was there. Brightly as ever.[50]
Offering its grace abundantly.
Boundlessly. Wholeheartedly.
In a realm beyond time. Beyond space.
Pure energy, bustling with life.
Effervescent. All pervasive.

Then a single thought put things in motion.
'Why bestow if no one enjoys my offering?'
Or put even more precisely:
'What would it be like to experience me?'

And so, the Light created a vessel.
A container to receive its blessings.
Now there was perfect union.
Send and Receive. Give and Take.
A Paradise.

Yet the vessel grew uncomfortable.
'What would it be to be like the Light?'
Or put even more precisely:
'How can I learn to become a creator?'

The Light heard this plea, thought it over and asked:
'How badly do you want to learn?
Mind you! It is opposite to your nature.
You'll earn it by blood, sweat and tears.'

The vessel gave it a second thought.
'Am I prepared to give up all of my comfort?
Strong enough to withstand my own compulsions?
Will it be worth my painful suffering?'

Then it looked in awe at the Light.
'Imagine if I could Shape my own Paradise?
And master the power of enchantment?'
'Bring it on, I want it all!'

'So you have chosen,' the Light responded.
'I'll create a place devoid of my presence.
You will tumble to the darkest spot,
and live at the mercy of extremes.'

'There'll be many veils that obscure my Light.
These veils will be lifted, one at a time,
as you learn to convert your selfish nature.
And a little more of my Light will shine upon you.'

Before the vessel could change its mind,
it felt itself pulled towards one single point.
An uncertain beginning in a different dimension.
With a Big Bang it shattered into countless pieces.

These first particles were swimming
in a brand-new physical universe.
Disoriented, they embarked on their journey,
an endeavor they have yet to complete.

These particles formed atoms.
Atoms became molecules.
Molecules turned into living cells,
which evolved into all plants and animals.
And eventually—human beings.

Thus, the shattered pieces come together,
as they learn to share all they receive.
Slowly becoming ever more conscious
and at an ever-increasing speed.

Now, at the summit of evolution
we're getting ready for the final act.
One last clue in our quest to create,
when we realize—It's NOT about me!

A Paradise that's built on trust,
as we overcome our fear of survival.
We'll arrive just where our roundtrip started
and know the place for the very first time.

The Light will be there. Brightly as ever.
Offering its grace abundantly.
Boundlessly. Wholeheartedly.
As a loving parent to hear all our stories
Reunited. And free at last!

Inspired by the wisdom of Kabbalah[50]

The Purpose of Life

You were born into this world as a uniquely talented, complete, and fulfilled human being. You don't need to prove or acquire anything nor become anyone in order to be happy. You are already perfect—you just don't realize it. These are your factory settings. It is of crucial importance that you fully grasp this.

Your need to beat others, to seek adventure, or to reach certain milestones, your quest for wealth or physical things, to build a particular reputation, or even to gain knowledge—these are all erroneous goals in your pursuit of happiness. By all means, have fun as these opportunities present themselves. However, there is no point in thinking that your next-level job will give you a lasting sense of satisfaction. Nor will your more advanced degree, your admission to a reputable club, or any other attainment in the outside world. It is the illusion of your own outside-in thinking that keeps you hostage in your self-created cage. If you can look at this objectively, you will see that your drive simply is a bunch of thought patterns that are rooted in your fear of survival.

There is nothing to be accomplished, no recognition needed for anything, and no earthly pleasure that will ever provide you with bliss. The moment you release your thinking and just stay in the present moment, you will be blissful just for being alive.

Wait a minute. This all sounds way too airy-fairy. I need to work to make money as there are bills to be paid. And actually, I often enjoy my work and get a kick out of achieving the targets we have set. I can't just lay on the beach, drink piña colada, and expect life to sort itself out, can I?

For sure there is a reality with which to deal. The question is whether you expect your happiness to come from your achievements in that reality. That would be a waste of effort. The truth is it works the other way around. If you allow yourself to simply be you, you are already fulfilled from the outset. There evidently is a reason you are here. You have come to this world to have an experience. To discover and grow your talents. To connect with others and their special gifts. And to jointly create something of value to share with the world.

In order to create, all that's needed is to be your true self. To not let your compulsive patterns take control of your thoughts. Many top sports athletes and performing artists have discovered how to invoke the best version of themselves at the *moment suprème*. Of course, they still needed to take action to accomplish something. But by not allowing their psychology to get involved, the work itself no longer felt like an effort.

Inviting Genius

A few years back I watched a most intriguing interview with master pianist Wibi Soerjadi. If I recall correctly, the interviewer asked, "Wibi, the curtains open and you enter the stage of Carnegie Hall. There's a twenty-eight-hundred-people audience expecting an evening of divine piano music. You are to play by heart, with all your passion, for an hour and a half. You cannot make a single mistake. As you take your seat behind the grand piano, what are you thinking?"

What do think his answer was? Things like, "I know I can do it, I have practiced long enough?" Or maybe, "Let me just get through the first five minutes and it will all become easier?" Or even better, "I'm gonna rock this place like they've never seen before in the world of classical music?" None whatsoever! His simple answer was, "I actually don't think at all. I simply sit straight and do not interfere. I just watch my hands as they play the music they know so very well." It sounded like he was pleased to have scored the best tickets in the entire concert hall!

Many top sports athletes and performing artists have discovered how to invoke the best version of themselves at the *moment suprème*. Ask Serena Williams how she did it—return to the tennis top ten and win a WTA tournament in Australia as a 38-year-old mother! Ask LeBron James about his secret formula. How did he become the only basketball player in history to win the NBA championship with three different teams? Talk to any leader in sports, music, or any other creative discipline. I guarantee you will get a similar story. Ignore your thinking. Be in the moment. Do your thing.

What sets a genius apart from other people? Wolfgang Amadeus Mozart, Marie Curie, Albert Einstein, Oprah Winfrey, Bruce Lee—what was the cause of their extraordinary contributions? An incredible talent combined with hard work? Certainly, but there's another crucial element to their success. What all exceptional people throughout history have in common is their ability to directly tap into the Field of Intelligence. The state of flow they experienced is nothing short of a dexterity in interacting with the creative force.

Is this only possible for people who seem "superhumanly" gifted? If you study their biographies you will learn they were normal folks like you and me. They also had struggles and weaknesses. Yet they dared to follow their intuition. They developed their ability to connect with a dimension beyond their thinking. Genius as such wasn't who they were—it's the frequency into which they tuned. Genius *is* the Field, and it's available to all of us. If only we know how to invite it into our lives.[51]

The Field Is Always Present

The Field of Intelligence is not only recognized as the creative force by ancient wisdom traditions. Fact-based science, observing strict protocols to underpin its hypotheses, has made amazing progress in support of the existence of the "Quantum Field."[52] These researchers empirically found that space is not empty at all. It comprises an energy field from which particles (matter) briefly pop up. They instantly disappear back into the Field as waves. The lowest possible temperature in the universe is zero degrees Kelvin (minus 459 degrees Fahrenheit or minus 273 degrees Celsius). When all cosmic activity becomes inert, the Field is just as active. Hence, the frequently used term Zero Point Field.[53]

The Field provides atoms, the building blocks of all physical presence, their stability. It ensures the entire universe is in equilibrium—a perfectly coherent state of energy exchange. But there is more. The Field is an infinite network of waves. As we saw in the previous chapter, waves are a perfect repository of information. The interference of these waves forms a hologram. This is an astonishing phenomenon—all information stored in waves is available at any point in the Field. And all this intelligence is "nonlocal," meaning it is not bound to time and space. Therefore, information is shared instantly. It is not limited to the speed of light, as is the case in the physical universe.

World-renowned physicist David Bohm placed a hyphen in the word "in-formation."[54] This connotes that the Field is the source from which all matter is formed.[55] Once a connection is made between things, they are instantly informed about each other's developments. Both time and distance between them are irrelevant. As such, these connected elements are part of an implicate order. This applies to atoms and molecules, but also people.

Every atom and molecule in the universe and every cell in our body is directly interacting with the Field. It is hard to fathom what it takes to keep a living organism as complex as our body in perfect coherence. Each of the 50–75 trillion cells in our body conducts thousands of biochemical reactions every second. If any of these are off by only a fraction of a second, our body system will immediately destabilize. Just imagine the ridiculously extensive computational and coordination power required to keep these processes aligned.

The Field seems to play a masterful guiding role in our evolution. We looked at the major steps by which organisms evolved into higher levels of complexity (in Chapter 3). Paleontologists study the history of life on Earth. They are puzzled by "missing links" in the gradual evolution of species. Advanced evolutionary leaps seem to have taken place within relatively short periods of time. It is evident they cannot be the result of random mutations. The statistical chances of successful adaptations are nil. They require the coordination of a highly advanced intelligence.[56]

What if these jumps are direct interventions by the Field? A clear push to take life to an ever-growing consciousness? Do you recall the role viruses played in the human genome (Chapter 1)? Indeed, there is every reason to view the coronavirus as yet another twist of "parental guidance" by the Field.

Modern science is taking promising steps to explore the secrets of our existence. These are the mysteries that were fully grasped by ancient wisdom traditions. The wisdom of Kabbalah refers to the Field as the "Light." What a powerful metaphor! Light, with its quality of being both wave and particle, was the gateway to quantum physics. The sun's light energizes us. It is indispensable in enabling life on our planet. Light provides clarity. It shows us what was hidden in the dark. Every second of the day we have an opportunity to defy our selfish nature. Thus, we earn the right to lift a veil from what obscures our inner Light.

The Principle of Mind

In previous chapters, we took a deep dive into the Principles of Thought and Consciousness. Thought creates our world. Consciousness is an expanded awareness. We realize that we're part of something greater than ourselves.

But *what* is greater than ourselves?

We now have a clearer picture. It's the Field of Intelligence, which Banks calls the Principle of Mind. He's referring to the universal mind. The spirit of nature that brings us to life. The creative potential. The all-embracing power that is yearned for by every religion on the planet.

The bloodiest of wars have been fought over belief systems trying to grasp this principle. Many people today have dropped their pious feathers. They are disillusioned with the excesses caused by organized religion. Their existence has been reduced to what they can perceive with their five senses. They are limited to the world of matter. Only by pushing hard do they believe results can be achieved.

Yet the physical reality in which we live is a world of consequences, a place created by thought. As we have seen, our fear-driven patterns trigger low-quality thinking. They result in actions to capture value at the expense of others. True value creation, however, is the result of high-quality thoughts.

Now, what is the source of truly creative thoughts? I asked this question in one of my creativity workshops. A participant explained, "My most creative thoughts appear out of the blue when I take my dog to the forest." When I asked her, "What is the 'blue?'" she thought for a couple of seconds. Then she replied, "It feels like I'm an antenna for ideas that want to become reality."

She couldn't have phrased it more accurately. This source is beyond your thinking. Only if you allow yourself to time out and tune into it do you become a carrier for the creative potential to express itself. You can experience it in your direct awareness at any time of the day. But you have to be in the moment, free from your habitual thinking. Every person is fully capable of doing this.

If you dare to make an inward journey, you will develop your "sixth sense." You get access to the world of causes. The creative potential, with its unlimited intelligence. True value creation always happens from within. The real work takes place in your inner landscape. In fact, it is not so much a matter of doing, as a state of being.

Tapping into the Field

How do we connect with our genius? We need to build our extrasensory perception, our sixth sense. It will enable us to consciously tap into the Field. The previous chapter presented an effective way to directly work with quantum energy. We can take this approach a step further and learn to bring the Field into our direct awareness.

In Chapter 1 I invited you to try to experience the Field. I asked you to sit still, close your eyes, and notice you're alive. You probably noticed it wasn't that easy. All kinds of thoughts crossed your mind and kept you busy. Meanwhile, we have studied the functioning of our conscious and subconscious minds. You now realize that most of your thinking is just a chatterbox. It gets triggered by your fear of survival. The transformation exercises support you in letting go of your fear-based patterns.

I'd like to provide you with some further guidance to tap into the Field. In Chapter 10 we revisited the eight development stages. They represent a lifelong journey of consciousness transformation. However, the Eastern wisdom traditions distinguish among a number of consciousness *states*. They are like the layers of an onion. We can peel them off to directly experience our authentic self. It's as if we temporarily lift the veils that obscure the Light. We get a glimpse of how it feels to be blissful and exuberant. The more we practice, the better we get at attaining our potential. And the faster we will advance our transformation.

My experience in meditation is a paradox in itself—the deeper I focus my attention inward, the more my awareness expands. The four states Wilber distinguishes, based on the Eastern wisdom traditions, aptly describe the spheres I experience.[57] These are the gross, subtle, causal and nondual states, as depicted in exhibit 14.

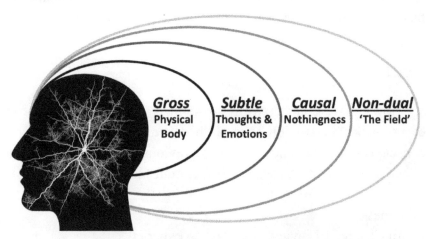

Exhibit 14—Four states of consciousness.[58]

As I sit down, I first activate my Yee Power (see Chapter 3). I become fully present in the "gross" body, which is my physical body.

I make contact with my head intelligence (shen), heart intelligence (chi), and gut intelligence (jing). Once my attention is fully focused on belly breathing, I visualize how I combine the sensations of my three intelligences into one point. This is the Yee Power, which enacts a light state of trance, meaning I move from beta to alpha brain waves.

* * *

"Every thought, every emotion is only a tourist ...
and I am not a hotel. Let them come and go."
—Mooji

* * *

I enter my inner world and continue with the Centering exercise (Chapter 9). The "subtle" body is the first layer of this inner landscape. It's the sheath at which our thoughts and emotions appear. As I become the observer, I visualize that I'm shifting my Yee Power to the center of my head. At the location of my pineal gland, the "third eye," I watch my thoughts come and go, like clouds in the sky. I sense the feelings in my body but simply "breathe through them." I keep my attention centered in my head. As soon as I find myself lost in a thought, I return to the center and continue watching. In the beginning, you may catch yourself wandering off every few seconds. Just bring your awareness back to the center, it will get easier. Guaranteed!

After some time (typically ten to fifteen minutes), my mind appears to surrender. It reduces the frequency of the thought bursts. I begin to experience a quiet and empty plain. I have arrived at the "causal" body. This is the vast space that surrounds and carries the subtle and gross bodies. It is a relaxing and liberating sensation. I am completely weightless—my breath slows down even further and I am at peace. I continue focusing my attention at the center of my head. It's as if my inner eyes slowly move backward and widen my vista, like a camera zooming out. The few thoughts that pop up every now and then are of a surprising insight. Even if I choose to explore them, I find it relatively easy to maintain the observer's position at the same time.

If I am really quiet and in full coherence, something magical may happen. It's difficult to find words for this experience. I disappear completely, totally immersed in the present moment. There is perfect harmony and connection with life itself. My awareness is crystal clear, without any limitations. I am thrilled and thrive on boundless energy. These moments are called oneness experiences. I transcend the polarities, the duality of my earthly existence, as I tap directly into the Field. Hence the name nondual state. These are intense moments of ecstasy. Isn't it cool how we can "get high on our own supply?"

The Ultimate State of Consciousness

There is actually one more state of consciousness, which I can only speak of conceptually. It's the ultimate state, where we don't just experience the Field, we dissolve in it. This state reflects the "return to the Light" of the Kabbalah, the Sufi concept that "you're the entire ocean in a drop," the "Atman merging into Brahman" in the Hindu tradition, or Christian endeavor to "enter the Kingdom of Heaven." This state is called self-realization or enlightenment. We will have come full circle. The Light's question in the introduction to this chapter, "What would it be like to experience me?" will then be fully answered. We will be both energy and matter, fully conscious while still in our body. We will master the art of enchantment as a direct extension of the Field.

TOP THREE TAKEAWAYS

1) Each of us is already perfect and won't need to prove anything or become anyone. We have come to this world to discover and grow our talents, connect with others, and jointly create something of value to share with the world.

2) Space is not empty at all but comprises an energy field with which all matter and life on the planet—including our body— is constantly connected. This Field is the Principle of Mind, also called the Light or Source in ancient wisdom traditions.

3) Meditation is a powerful practice to build our sixth sense. Beyond our thinking is a state of flow through which we can consciously tap into the Field. Thus, we invite genius to enter our life and work.

SHAPE YOUR PARADISE *ONLINE*

Meditation is a powerful way to tap into the Field. There are other ways as well. In Week 5 of the online module "Consciousness? Awesome!" you will experience a number of powerful exercises. One such practice is shadow work—"the part of me that I can't see." True dialogue, in which you learn to make a real connection, is another. Enjoy the sensation of tapping into the Field!

Ready to Spread Your Wings?

My compliments for transforming yourself mentally and emotionally. Perhaps you have even gained a spiritual insight. As a pupa you have taken a timeout in your cocoon. On the outside it seemed like you weren't moving at all. But on the inside there has been a major shift. You recognize your habitual, low-quality thinking by your mood. You understand how you can take a break and connect with your inner wisdom. You realize that everything in our universe is energy that you can connect to by raising your level of consciousness. While connecting to the creative potential, you have a GPS to navigate your leadership.

Are you ready to really connect with your team? To discover the power of vulnerability? To completely change the game? There's a small opening in your cocoon. You're strong enough to widen it and break free. Come on, spread your wings and make your mark. It's time to usher your team into the Transformation Age!

—PART III—

PARADISE SHAPER LEADERSHIP

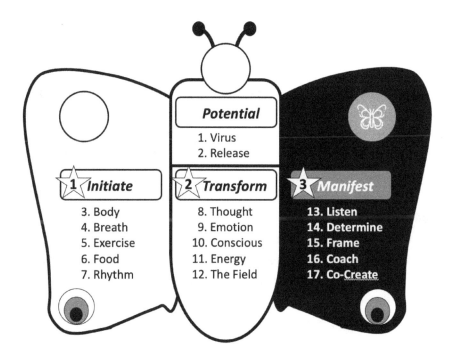

Stop pushing for results, boomer!
Crack the secret code of people motivation
and learn to pave the way for lasting impact.

MANIFEST

Spread Your Wings and Make Your Mark

... the Butterfly

*"Only a conscious leader can evoke the spirit of
unconditional responsibility in each of her followers
and in her organization as a whole."*
—Fred Kofman

In this Part you will shift your focus outward again and actively engage with your people. It is time to spread your wings and show your true colors. As you have made contact with your inner core, there is an opportunity for a completely different, and far more effective, interaction with your team. We will learn what makes people tick and how to unleash their motivation. Based on a personal case study we will experience how Self-Determination Theory is successfully put into practice. We will explore why structure and freedom form a powerful polarity. As a Teal leader—who operates at a Tier 2 stage of consciousness—we masterfully balance both sides and allow our organization to perform at its best. Leadership is understanding the true calling of the organization and orchestrating the process of team co-creation in order to answer it.

- ❖ Chapter 13 builds on the simple fact that every person wants to be noticed. Rather than sending our own message, Paradise Shaper Leadership is about deep listening. In addition to facts that are shared with us, we receive all signals—both externally and within ourselves. This builds strong relationships and helps us see the emerging future!
- ❖ Chapter 14 delves into the groundbreaking impact of Self-Determination Theory. Based on academic research at the organization I led, we'll clarify a proven path that lifts

engaging leaders to attaining improved outcomes in terms of employee motivation and business results.

❖ In Chapter 15 we will explore how we can perfectly combine the focus on both people and processes. We'll revisit the principles behind the acronym PRoFiTS, which provide a practical way to create a framework for our team. Employees will feel autonomous, connected, and competent to perform.

❖ Chapter 16 is about systemic work. We start out with the dynamic effects of organizational constellations. We will discuss how transformational coaching is a powerful leadership tool. It is all about asking "moving questions!" They bring blockages to the surface and re-energize our team. It's the art of zooming out!

❖ Chapter 17 puts all we have learned into an overall perspective by looking at nature itself. There's a repeating cycle of ever-growing consciousness—the Spiral of Creation. By actively guiding the designated work every step of this spiral, we will enable our people to enjoy their job to the fullest while achieving stellar results.

All Quadrants, All Levels

There's a fascinating story shared by Ken Wilber on the digital platform Integral Life. He elaborates on how he developed his Integral Theory. As an erudite scholar, Wilber had read every book he could lay his hands on for several decades. His arsenal covered virtually every academic field. It occurred to him that in almost every domain—biology, psychology, agriculture, economics, engineering, operations, even metaphysics—a certain hierarchy of growth could be distinguished. Yes, different words were used. But there were striking similarities between these hierarchies. Wilber decided to draw each of these "stairways" on a separate sheet of paper. He then put all these sheets on the floor in his house. They covered the entire space. For weeks he would pace around, looking at the sheets, taking mental imprints of the echelons.

One day Wilber saw a pattern. Some of the hierarchies were about the internal world. But others covered the external reality. He reshuffled the sheets. The left side of the floor was home to the internal world. And he placed the external scales on the right. He allowed his subconscious mind to ponder the picture. Then Wilber suddenly saw another criterion by which he could order the sheets— they were either about the individual or the group. Now he applied this distinction to the sheets on both sides of the room. It resulted in a Four Quadrants model (exhibit 15).

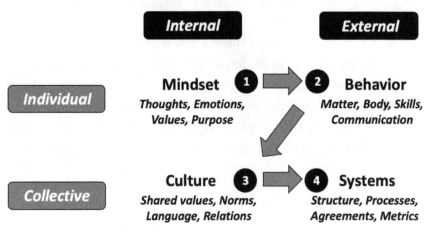

Exhibit 15—The Four Quadrants model.

Each of these four quadrants has a natural growth hierarchy. In Chapter 10 we explored what these hierarchies look like from an internal perspective, both individually and collectively. The collective applies to any group of people with a common interest. This can be humanity as a whole, a specific society, or a particular organization.

In this Part III we'll zoom into your role as a leader. For an organization to thrive, developments in all four quadrants need to keep a balanced pace. Our society today has become obsessed with the external side of the house. The relationship between employer and employee has primarily become a financial understanding. Employees rent themselves out in return for a decent package. Loyalty is subject to the monetary benefits that flash on the horizon. If a better deal is found elsewhere, professionals move on to the next band.

Our neo-liberal (Orange) society has lost sight of the existential basis for organizations. Do you remember the central theme in evolution? To grow the level of consciousness at an ever-increasing speed! What better place to do so than in companies and other organizations? They bring people together. It's a perfect breeding ground to create value to the benefit of all—customers, employees, and society at large.

The sole purpose of the previous Parts of the book was to shift your attention to the upper left quadrant—your internal world (step 1). As your consciousness grows, your mindset shifts. You'll be less driven by your fear of survival. You'll relax your focus on short-term (financial) results. Your mind and heart will open to the real purpose you wish to pursue. A powerful springboard to guide your team to great heights.

This is where we will place our attention in Part III:

> ➢ How can you improve your interaction with your colleagues, partners, and customers (step 2, upper right quadrant)?
> ➢ How will your advanced behavior lead to a healthier culture? How will you forge shared values and norms that build stronger relationships among your team members (step 3, lower left quadrant)?
> ➢ How will you establish a structure and processes that are fully endorsed by your team (step 4, lower right quadrant)?

You will find that the more you focus on the "undercurrent" in your team, the easier it will be. You will learn to co-create a framework with your people. This structure will paradoxically grant them freedom. It will be a great facilitator to put their true self into their work. And that completes the circle. Now your employees will be inspired to grow their own level of consciousness (upper left quadrant). You will have set the flywheel in motion. And that's another paradox—by not pushing for results, you will surpass your wildest expectations!

SHAPE YOUR PARADISE *ONLINE*

You can enjoy a third module in the Shape Your Paradise online self-coaching program. It deepens your experience with this Part of the book, "Paradise Shaper Leadership." Again, we have maintained a clear structure—you will actively engage your team to grow their happiness at work. And, consequently, their performance!

A crisis reshuffles the cards. How do you give direction to the new challenges of the Transformation Age? You will do so by learning about these five points:

> ➤ how you raise effective listening to new dimensions
> ➤ how people share three basic needs that match with our three brains
> ➤ the secret of motivation and how to set the right framework
> ➤ why Plan-Do-Check-Act is a vicious circle
> ➤ how co-creation is a natural process that goes through six phases

Lead your team to true innovation by freeing their passion. Discover how to convert your elevated consciousness into enhanced team results.

Go to www.paradiseshaper.com and reinvent your leadership!

13

LISTEN DEEPLY

*"Most people do not listen with the intent to
understand; they listen with the intent to reply."*
—Stephen R. Covey

When the Going Gets Tough...

"I'm sorry to say this, Paul, but you're leading a sick-making organization."

Our occupational physician looked me straight in the eye, making sure I felt the impact of his words. The doctor had requested a meeting to share his concerns. He had every reason to do so. The supply chain department that I led had serious employee health issues. Absenteeism in one of our groups had risen to 7 percent for the second time in only four months—an indisputable threshold for the doctor to sound the alarm bell.

The multinational I worked for offered our customers a wide range of cutting-edge healthcare innovations. Among them were giant diagnostic scanners, but we also provided patient monitoring and COPD care solutions, just to name a few. In previous years we had centralized order management activities in so-called Customer Fulfillment Centers. These teams processed all customer orders in the company's Enterprise Resource Planning (ERP) system, which triggered factory production. They overlooked the logistics process up to the installation at the customer site, which was usually a hospital.

The doctor's comment pertained to one of these Customer Fulfillment Centers. This organization was the home of 150 logistics officers who handled billions of dollars in customer orders across a large region. The situation over there looked bleak across the board (see exhibit 16):

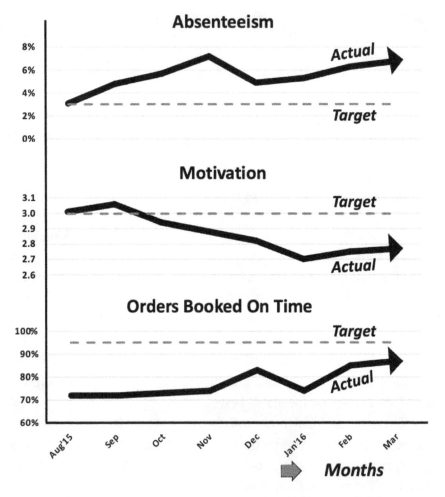

Exhibit 16—Situation at the Customer Fulfillment Center.

When I combined these statistics, I noted a few things:

- ➤ In the last eight months, absenteeism had never been below the threshold of 3 percent that defines a healthy organization.
- ➤ Motivation levels (measured on scale of 4) had plummeted after the summer and were well below the benchmark level of 3.
- ➤ Absenteeism and employee motivation appeared to be inversely related.
- ➤ The key performance indicator of orders booked on time (i.e., within forty-eight hours after customer signature) had never been even close to the target of 95 percent. The relentless focus on this metric had yielded limited results, at a high social cost.

Unsolicited Advice

When I took the job, I had been given a clear picture of the task at hand. It was taking too long to convert customer orders to realized sales. Our forecasting had to be strengthened and inventory reduced. I realized the entire value chain depended on the performance of the Customer Fulfillment Centers. How would I reverse the trend and get this organization to deliver?

The unsolicited advice that one business leader gave me was to "wage a shock-and-awe campaign." It was obvious to him that the centralized team "didn't have a clue" about the pressure in the business. As we were disconnected from our sales organizations, I needed to "beat my own drum." I should send a strong message that "playtime is over," with a list of clear instructions. We wouldn't go home until all orders were booked. And the team leaders had to check every day whether the backlog had been cleared. There would be serious consequences if they failed to complete their task. This would "get their incompetent asses moving."

Did you notice his belligerent language? Was I at war with my own organization? Did this business leader really believe these 150 logistics professionals were clueless, disconnected, and incompetent? It is obvious to me now that fear-based patterns had been triggered within him. They produced an array of combative thoughts that conditioned his behavior. Although I didn't fully realize at the time how this mechanism works, I was convinced that past experiences had seriously colored his perspective. He was taken hostage by his own thoughts. It didn't feel right to me to go by his advice. For me, leadership starts with listening deeply.

Notice Me!

When our kids were small, I vowed to never miss their soccer matches on Saturday mornings. Even if I had come home a few hours earlier on a red-eye flight, I made sure to be at the game at 9 or 10 a.m. I loved watching the kids make their first inroads into "stardom." And I would talk to the other parents. All kinds of topics were covered—the quality of the trainer, the kids' progress, school, camp, sports, cars, local politics, the latest iPhone. It really didn't matter what we discussed. We simply enjoyed this bonding opportunity.

I realized most of our Saturday morning chatter was much more about "sending" information than "receiving." I decided to conduct a little experiment. I would engage the parent next to me with open questions. These typically start with "what," "how," or "why." I would refrain from volunteering my own stories. Nor would I ask any closed questions—ones that could only be answered by "yes" or "no."

I would, for instance, open with, "How are things at work?" And indeed, the other parent would provide me with colorful details, such as "We're a supplier to the high-tech industry. We're making huge investments to fuel the growth. The negotiations are really tough." After a couple of minutes, I would ask more personal questions like, "How is the relationship with your boss?" Or, "What makes you feel stressed?" I would keep on firing open questions and listened to their answers with genuine interest. Without exception, they all would share what was really on their mind. In many cases our conversation took the entire soccer game. The other parent would often thank me for the talk. Yet I had not been asked a single question in return.

What was the lesson? All people walk around with an invisible sign on their forehead, that says "Notice me!" Our lives are only meaningful to us if someone else is truly interested. We all want to be seen, to be listened to, and have impact. A company that perfectly understands this is Harley Davidson. Years ago, I attended an enjoyable speech by one of their former executives. In each of their stores, and at every event they organize, Harley-Davidson employees have thousands of conversations with customers. They ask all kinds of questions. What is your favorite accessory? If you were to design it, what would it look like? Since Harley-Davidson's catalogue is immense, it certainly would contain an accessory that matched the customer's preferences. So they would send the customer a picture of the accessory and a "thank you" note for enhancing the experience of many other bikers. That's how you build brand loyalty. Name any other firm whose customers are proud to wear a full-size tattoo with the company logo on their back!

There's a beating heart in every customer and employee. If you want them to be engaged, the golden key is to listen deeply. To give them the opportunity to express themselves freely. To enrich your observations with what they see, hear, and feel. Withhold your opinions, your solutions, your instructions. Use your full capacity to truly understand. Yes, it is time consuming. Paradise Shaper leadership does entail a serious effort on your part. However, it is energy well invested. Trust comes by foot and leaves on horseback. Everything you put into it in this stage will pay off exponentially once your team is rocking. The commitment of your team, the quality of your plans, and the ease of execution will drastically improve. Multiplying them together gives you an idea of the return on your investment.

The Eight Levels of Listening

Mastering the art of listening provides us with a powerful tool to expand our consciousness. There is a natural scale that perfectly aligns with Wilber's Stages of Development (as discussed in Chapter 10).[59] Have a look at exhibit 17.

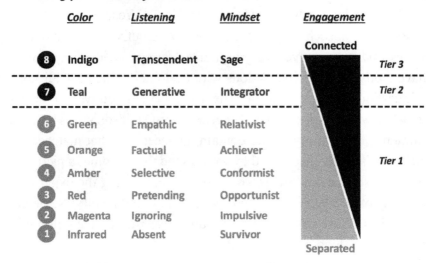

The 8 Levels of *Listening*
Raising your Level of Attention

Color	Listening	Mindset	Engagement	
			Connected	
8 Indigo	Transcendent	Sage		Tier 3
7 Teal	Generative	Integrator		Tier 2
6 Green	Empathic	Relativist		
5 Orange	Factual	Achiever		Tier 1
4 Amber	Selective	Conformist		
3 Red	Pretending	Opportunist		
2 Magenta	Ignoring	Impulsive		
1 Infrared	Absent	Survivor		
			Separated	

Exhibit 17—The eight levels of listening.

—*Absent*—

The first level, absent listening, implies we are not listening at all. We do not feel any responsibility for the other person and are not interested in hearing what they have to say. We believe there is nothing to gain by listening. We are in our own world and do not wish to concentrate on outside information. This represents the Infrared level of listening that a Survivor displays.

—Ignoring—

At the second level, ignoring, we do notice the other person but choose not to pay attention. We don't focus on what's being said, and at best wait for the opportunity to say what's on our mind. Our own thoughts are our reality, and we jump from one area of attention to the next. This listening behavior illustrates an Impulsive level of consciousness (Magenta).

—Pretending—

At the third level, pretending, we are multitasking during a conversation. This is the "uh-huh" automatic response while we are doing other things and feigning we pay attention. We're unable to recall what was shared since we're not really interested. We may suddenly change the subject and put our own perspective forward. Opportunists are often witnessed to show this Red level of listening.

—Selective—

At the fourth level, we are selective in what we hear. We listen to confirm our opinions, which we have formed in the past. We are not interested in information, only affirmation. We are downloading what we already know. And if we don't like what we hear, we'll ignore or negate it. We are looking at our own projections, not at what happens in the present moment. This is the typical listening style of a Conformist (Amber).

I recall a hilarious visit to my hairdresser when I asked him about his chats with clients. "I'm like a shrink," he said, "but for sure a whole lot cheaper!" As people recline in the chair, enjoying a moment for themselves and his personal dedication, they easily open up. "Depending on their age, I only ask one question and they tell me their story," he said, stoking my curiosity. "If they're under thirty-five, I ask, 'What festivals are you hitting?' Now, if they're somewhat older, but still under sixty-five, I inquire, 'What are your vacation plans?'"

I smiled and posed the obvious question, "So what will you ask if they're over sixty-five?"

"Ah, they all want to talk about their health," he explained, "so I poke them with, 'How is your golf game, or do you still have sex?'"

—Factual—

The fifth level is factual listening. As in scientific research, we want to know the facts. We refrain from judging and are truly curious about what we're hearing. We want to absorb everything the other person explains and listen with our full attention. It is new information that we are seeking. We therefore ask questions that give us more insights. An Achiever (Orange) often uses this mode of listening to get the complete picture.

—TRANSFORMATION EXERCISE 13—
Factual Listening

A highly effective way to practice factual listening is the following. The next time one of your colleagues wants to discuss a topic, tell them you would like to structure the meeting with a simple agenda:

1. What's the issue?
2. What's the impact?
3. What support do they need to resolve it?

Adopt an active sitting posture and maintain eye contact with your colleague. Give them three minutes to elaborate on the issue (point 1). Listen so attentively that you would almost be able to literally repeat what they said. No thinking whatsoever is required on your part.

After three minutes, intervene with the suggestion, "Now let me summarize what you are telling me." Then take less than a minute to provide the summary and ask, "Is that a correct reflection of the issue?" If they confirm, move on to the impact (point 2). If not, allow them to briefly add what you have misunderstood. Then summarize once again and move on. Do exactly the same for points 2 and 3 and take two more minutes to agree on actions.

In just fifteen minutes you will achieve much more than in most regular meetings I witness in a full hour. You leave the ownership for the issue with your colleague. They appreciate you really want to know the facts. And you have come to a clear set of actions to resolve the matter.

Bonus tip—Have the meeting while you stand. It will make it far more active!

—Empathic—

At the sixth level we listen empathically. This is a deeper level of listening as we aim to truly connect with the other person. We no longer pursue our own interests but place ourselves in the shoes of the other, and not just at a cognitive level. We want to see what the other is seeing and feel what the other is feeling. We therefore need to open our heart and establish a deep connection from within. This is how strong relationships are built. A Relativist (Green) has the capacity to listen in this way.

—TRANSFORMATION EXERCISE 14—
Empathic Listening

To become a skilled empathic listener takes quite a bit of practice. You not only listen with your head, you use your whole body to experience what your conversation partner is thinking, feeling, and needing.

There are few important things to keep in mind:

1. Arrange a relaxed and safe setting for your meeting.
2. As the person enters, observe their body language. The way they walk, talk, breathe, their facial expression. What do you notice?
3. Open the conversation with a simple question, like "What brings you here today?" Follow up with open questions. Be with your breath and keep an undisturbed focus on the other person. There is no need to think at all when your conversation partner is talking. This is not about you, it is about them.
4. While you're listening to the other person, try to sense what the other person is feeling and needing. This is difficult, as it may distract you from listening attentively. Over time, you will develop this skill intuitively.
5. Share your impression of what you sense they are feeling, such as, "This is really stressful for you, isn't it?"
6. Listen to their response. It is an opportunity for you to check whether you really stepped into their shoes. If they confirm, you are on the right track.
7. If they don't recognize the feeling you describe, it is valuable that you discovered this early in the conversation. It will give further direction in the conversation and deepen your connection with your conversation partner.
8. Ask them what they need and listen to their response.

> 9. Volunteer what you are sensing and check whether they confirm.
> 10. Close by asking what next steps they will take and thank them for their openness.
>
> You will be amazed by the engagement of your conversation partner as they experience that you really understand how they feel.

—Generative—

The seventh level is generative listening. At this level we are not only connected with the other person, but also with our inner wisdom, our intuition. Bonding at a deep level with the other person gives us access to our subconscious mind, which is directly connected with the Field (Chapter 12). A whole new perspective is generated. As we enter a state of flow, we see the future potential that wants to materialize. These are moments of magnificent insight that change us as a person and offer amazing opportunities in our collaboration with the other person. An Integrator knows how to enact this Teal level of deep listening.

—TRANSFORMATION EXERCISE 15—
Generative Listening

There is no step-by-step plan for generative listening. It is the capacity to reside in a high state of consciousness (Chapter 12) while focusing on the person speaking. You put yourself in the position of the other person and at the same time are in direct contact with your inner world. Let's revisit a couple of ingredients to develop your generative listening proficiency:

> ➢ Before the conversation, assess your intention for the discussion. How will you stay in the moment and not get distracted by your ego voice?
> ➢ Activate your Yee Power—connecting your head, heart, and gut. This is the gateway to your inner world.
> ➢ As in transformation exercise 14, observe the body language of the other person. What is it telling you?
> ➢ Ask only open questions like what, how, and, if the conversation goes well, why (questions beginning with "why" tend to activate subconscious patterns if the bond has not yet been forged).
> ➢ Observe the other person holistically. Listen to their words, tone of voice, and breathing and carefully watch for sudden changes in their body language. The physiology in the body is directly steered by the speaker's subconscious mind. It is a perfect clue to the patterns that are triggered!
> ➢ Suspend your judgment, which always is the voice of your ego. Don't put energy in entertaining low-quality thinking. Simply accept what's unfolding in this moment.
> ➢ Stay in the now by focusing on your breath and observe the sensations in your body. What do you feel in your heart and belly? Don't interpret, just feel the precise sensation—for example a cramp, a sting, or a relaxation.

- ➢ Be curious. Try to understand the potential behind the other person's issues. In their heart of hearts, what is their true desire? What is it they would like to create? What's already in their power to make it happen?
- ➢ Keep your focus on the potential that wants to emerge. Stimulate the other person to find more answers in themselves. A simple "Tell me more about..." does miracles!
- ➢ Aim to keep the other person from dwelling on their mental impediments to pursuing their desire. As soon as the conversation is well under way, feel free to intervene. For instance, "I understand this can be challenging, now let's stay focused on your dream. What does the best scenario look like?" You will be surprised at what happens if you invite the speaker to stay focused on the potential for at least ten consecutive minutes.

In such a conversation, the air typically begins to clear and both of you start tapping into the Field. You will notice the energy in your body moving to a higher, exciting, yet relaxing vibration. You will watch the speaker's body language change—their spine straightens, their arms actively support their ideas, their eyebrows and corners of the mouth rise, their voice becomes powerful, and the words flow smoothly. At the end of such a conversation, you're not tired at all. Both of you feel energized, and the other person will have gained a new perspective of what's possible. They can't wait to make it happen!

—Transcendent—

The eighth and highest level is transcendent listening. At this level, the words themselves lose all relevance. Listening is fully performed with the sixth sense, tapping directly from the Field. Every interaction becomes a plain opportunity for energy exchange. Since transcendent listeners are fully conscious, they can notice and distinguish the different flows in their body. Therefore, they can "see" the energy radiated by the other person. They sense the patterns and blocks that keep the speaker from realizing their potential. This allows a transcendent listener to work with the other person at a deeper level to learn how to free themselves. A contemporary Sage masters the art of transcendent listening (Indigo).

Reach Out to The Team

How was I to address the challenging situation in the Customer Fulfillment Center? The business leader in the beginning of this chapter had advised me to take a top-down, authoritarian stance. I chose a different course. I took time to meet with all employees in the organization, as I had done in previous jobs since I really wanted to hear directly from the people how they experienced work. What issues were they facing? Since they were the experts, they must have thought about solutions as well. What were these solutions? What was preventing them from being put in place?

These meetings proved invaluable. Without exception, people took the opportunity to talk about their jobs and what things did not go well. They explained to me who provided them with input, and to whom they sent the outcome of their work. I tried to draw simple pictures indicating how customer orders were flowing through the organization. This soon turned out to be a multidimensional spider web, and I received a lot of suggestions on improvement areas and impediments. But most importantly, I made a real connection with people on the work floor. I raised some hope that changes were indeed possible.

I collected a pile of issues during these meetings. Two central themes stood out as the core of our problem:

1. We appeared to have a leadership issue within most of our teams. A widespread notion had taken hold among employees that their team managers were "functional robots." They didn't seem really interested in their people. Communication was perceived as one directional. One colleague exclaimed in frustration, "I know exactly what information is lacking when I book an order. And I have lots of ideas on how to fix this. But no one ever asked me!"

2. Our processes had grown organically. They had become very complex. You couldn't draw them on a whiteboard. No one could provide me with a complete, real-time picture of the current status of our orders. We had generic root cause analyses of the reasons why orders got stuck. But none were directly linked to individual orders. Order-desk employees pushed back to their input providers. They needed additional information. But how and when this input would be provided was a black hole.

I focused my attention on these two themes. I adopted an innovative approach to both. The next chapter dissects our leadership issue. Chapter 15 discusses our transition to concise and effective processes. Chapter 16 explains how leaders become transformational coaches who coach for impact. In Chapter 17 this culminates in the inside-out roadmap to Paradise Shaper leadership—the art of co-creation.

TOP THREE TAKEAWAYS

1) All people walk around with an invisible sign on their forehead, that says, "Look at me!" Everyone wants to be noticed, to be listened to, and have impact. If we want our customers and employees to be engaged, the golden key is to listen deeply.

2) There are eight levels of listening that provide us with powerful tools to expand our consciousness. At level 6, empathic listening, we build strong relationships. We put ourselves in the shoes of the other person. Level 7, generative listening, uncovers the future potential that wants to materialize. We notice it by maintaining contact with our inner world.

3) Deep listening is a way to integrate our head, heart, and gut brains. We listen to the facts. We demonstrate we truly care for the other person. And we have the courage to move beyond our own fears and egoistic needs. Thus we set the foundation to resolve problems and create a new and exciting future.

SHAPE YOUR PARADISE *ONLINE*

To deepen your learning process, we have created online module 3, "Paradise Shaper Leadership." In week 1 of this module you will practice the different levels of listening—first factually, then empathically, and eventually generatively. How do you enrich your conversations? What are proven ways that always lead to a successful engagement? Enjoy a more meaningful way of connecting with your team.

14

FREE THE MOTIVATION

"The most courageous act is still to think for yourself. Aloud."
—Coco Chanel

A Moment of Synchronicity

An organization is only as strong as its team leaders. Worldwide workforce research has underscored time and again that the manager is critical to building a vibrant culture.[60] I could have as many inspiring interactions with our employees as possible, develop the most ingenious plan to solve process issues, raise remuneration, and organize cool events. But it would all be to no avail if we didn't fix one thing—growing our managers to touch the hearts of their staff.

I held a number of meetings with our team managers. How did they like their role? What was the most challenging part of their job? What would they like to change in order to have more impact? Most were millennial leaders who were on a fast-track career path. I learned that quite a few lacked an in-depth background in order management. It made them insecure. Do you remember the agitated employee who didn't feel heard (Chapter 13)? I was particularly intrigued by the words of his manager. "This job is really tough," she said. "Every evening I evaluate the day and search the internet to find solutions to our logistics problems. When I come to the office in the morning and share my new ideas, I only get lukewarm responses.

These guys are just not motivated to work. They do not respect me as their supervisor. It really stresses me out."

The team manager suffered from a false conception of what leadership is about. She thought she had to be all knowing and provide clear directions to her team. She had erected a shield to hide her insecurity and behaved in a formal, bossy way. She considered asking questions as a sign of weakness. As a result, her team did not feel she cared. They would not listen to her solutions because she didn't show interest in theirs. In addition, a lot of her proposals displayed a clear ignorance about the daily problems they faced. This team lacked the heart-to-heart connection it desperately needed to let the energy and solution flow freely. It was a vicious circle that had to be broken.

We needed nothing less than a leadership transformation. Over the years I had developed an inclusive leadership style myself. The contours of our transformation program were fairly clear to me. Yet I wanted to make sure I used the latest insights that the social sciences offered. I got in contact with Professor Willem van Rhenen at Nyenrode Business University, my *alma mater* in the Netherlands.[61] As he listened to my story, van Rhenen became more and more enthusiastic. "What you are after is to put Self-Determination Theory into practice," he suggested. "It's a very exciting field. A lot of research has been done, but especially at universities, in the public sector and in sports. Surprisingly few studies have been carried out at companies." And then he made me a marvelous proposal, "What would you say if I offered to do research in your department? It will be an eighteen-month program in which we design and implement a leadership intervention. We will measure progress in both motivational as well as business metrics. It's truly unique!"

Just a week later, van Rhenen organized a get-together with Lars van Tuin, a renowned team trainer and coach. Lars had just completed his research into engaging leadership in companies. He was looking for an organization to put theory into practice as field research for his doctorate. This was one of those defining moments of synchronicity. What I wanted perfectly matched what Lars had to offer, and vice versa. There, in the picturesque university garden, we laid the foundation of what would become the Paradise Shaper method.

Self-Determination Theory

I invited Lars to join my leadership team in a brainstorming session. How should we approach the two themes we identified? What would be the next steps to take? As a warmup, I asked Lars to outline the background to his research. "If there's one thing that stood out in my fifteen years of coaching, then it's this," he said. "Everyone has a soul deep inside, and it yearns for connection."

Lars was silent for a moment to make his words resound.

"Over the past two years," he continued, "I have begun to answer my calling. I long to provide the underlying evidence for the countless cases I have witnessed with my own eyes. A leadership style that fosters strong connections between people is not only conducive to a pleasant working environment, but it also renders unparalleled business results."

In his quest, Lars had come across a research field within organizational psychology. Van Rhenen had also referred to it during our first meeting—Self-Determination Theory. Launched in the 1980s by Richard Ryan and Edward Deci, this theory broke new ground in organizational psychology. Until then, organizational psychology had primarily focused on how motivation and behavior could be controlled externally. Ryan and Deci were more interested in how people and organizations naturally learn and behave. They concluded that "human motivation is functionally designed and experienced from within."[62]

A central theme is the notion that all human beings share three basic psychological needs. These are the needs for:

> ➤ autonomy—I want to influence the way I organize my work;
> ➤ relatedness—I want to be part of a team where members build on each other; and
> ➤ competence—I want to be good at something and develop myself.

The degree of fulfilment (or frustration) of these needs significantly impacts the intrinsic motivation of employees to do their job. The sense of purpose and happiness they experience is connected directly to boosting their performance.

Lars proposed starting our collaboration by measuring the degree of fulfillment and frustration on these three psychological needs. We would also survey "engaging leadership" and "employee work motivation."[63]

We applied a pragmatic research model as depicted in exhibit 18. On the left, we hypothesized an Engaging Leadership style to be a driver for positive outcomes on the right. We distinguished two sets of outcomes—work motivation, and some clear-cut business key performance indicators (KPIs). For example, the number of customer orders booked within a twenty-four-hour period. In the middle, we were interested to learn how basic psychological needs satisfaction could act as a catalyst to enhance outcomes.

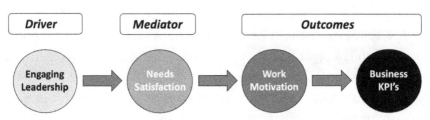

Exhibit 18—Engaging Leadership research model.

Engaging Leadership

Engaging leaders give substance to their people's call for freedom and responsibility in a modern way. They promote the fulfillment of their employees' basic psychological needs for autonomy, relatedness, and competence. Four behaviors can be distinguished that characterize engaging leaders.[64]

> ➤ They strengthen their employees by encouraging them to develop their talents and by delegating tasks and responsibilities.
> ➤ They connect their employees by fostering collaboration between colleagues and aligning them behind the same goals.
> ➤ They empower team members by inviting them to share their opinions and recognizing their contributions.
> ➤ They inspire their followers by being enthused about their vision and plans and making them feel they contribute to something important.

We measured to what degree the team leads displayed these behaviors by a set of validated questions. As we assessed the results, one thing immediately jumped out—team leads were seen as less engaging than they thought of themselves. There was evidently room for improvement. We added one more category—task orientation. Were the team leads clear about their expectations? Surprisingly, both employees and team leads gave low scores for this trait. How could our people enjoy their work if they lacked a framework that defined what was expected?

—TRANSFORMATION EXERCISE 16—
The Feedback Fountain

In order to facilitate a constructive collaboration between team leads and their team members, we developed the Feedback Fountain process. This process is designed to make an important contribution to unleashing the motivation of your team. If you dare, you can start using this process today in your organization. Some exciting things are bound to happen within a week's timeframe!

Go to www.paradiseshaper.com and download your free copy of the Feedback Fountain. You will receive a step-by-step process description and the questionnaire to be used. The package includes an interview with the CEO of a high-tech scale-up. He reflects on his experiences and the impact this powerful process had on his leadership and results.

I have used this process for years. In my experience, it only takes five minutes to get such a session going. Then the energy just flows. It's an effective process to build team commitment and a great catalyst to build support for the team lead from all team members.

Basic Psychological Needs

The dust really started to settle when we examined the survey results on basic psychological needs. We measured results on a Likert scale, ranging from 1 (*"I strongly disagree"*) to 5 (*"I strongly agree"*). The ideal organization would score a 4 (*"I agree"*) or above on questions measuring the level of needs satisfaction. Similarly, a score of 2 (*"I disagree"*) or below would be the goal on questions measuring the degree of needs frustration. By subtracting the frustration outcome from the satisfaction result, we obtain a "net satisfaction" score. Logically, we would like this score to be above 2.

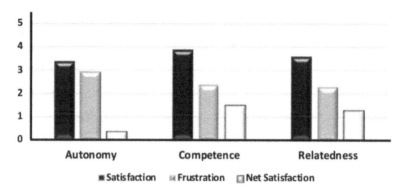

Exhibit 19—Basic psychological needs satisfaction vs. frustration.

Exhibit 19 gave us a wealth of information. None of the satisfaction scores topped the desired score of 4. And all frustration outcomes exceeded the maximum level of 2. It was the net autonomy satisfaction score that made my heart sink. Our people had sent a clear message. Our efforts to grant them freedom to make choices in their daily activities were below par. And all the good that was done with one hand was taken away by the other. This was expressed by the high level of autonomy frustration.

I remember staring at the numbers for quite some time. Then it suddenly dawned on me—the three basic psychological needs were directly linked to our multiple brains!

Autonomy is rooted in our gut brain. It is all about identity, influence, and setting boundaries. Relatedness pertains to our heart brain. It denotes our passion and ability to truly connect with others. Competence is to a large extent a faculty of our head brain. We want to be good at something. We look for opportunities to grow. When all three are well developed and fully in sync, we will experience our highest expression. We enter a state of flow. We transcend our individuality. We perform beyond our wildest imagination.

This is exactly what happens in an organization at large. A company is the sum of many people. As such, it is itself a living organism. Measuring basic psychological needs had a fundamental impact. We had found the barometer to directly measure the level of coherence between the company's multiple brains. It is the ultimate tool for assessing the organization's ability to reach its highest expression.

What people in all organizations around the world are really saying is this:

Give me some space.
Let me meaningfully connect with others.
Let us do something we are good at.
And, together, make a valuable
contribution to society.

It is a marvelous expression of the inside-out nature of our human experience. In the core of our being—our gut brain—we find the depth of who we really are. Once we fully realize our power, we long to ignite our passion—our heart brain—to team up with others and synergize. Our power and passion magnificently expand our cognition—our head brain—to manifest our competences in boundless ways.

The Customer Fulfillment Center was far from reaching this state. And the root cause was likely to be found in the essence of its being—its collective gut brain. We had to drastically change the leadership style in the organization. People needed a culture that fostered autonomy. All other efforts to improve the situation would be futile. The freedom to organize work is key to shaping a company's core identity. Autonomy satisfaction precedes both relatedness and competence. Needless to say, our intervention program would revolve around this key psychological need.[65]

Work Motivation Scale

Self-Determination Theory distinguishes between controlled and autonomous motivation. Controlled motivation always involves a form of external regulation. The employee is triggered by the foresight of a specific reward or aims to avoid punishment. Autonomous motivation implies the behavior is self-determined, and therefore intrinsically regulated. Employees have a choice in selecting the relevant activities in their job. As a result, they are more inclined to do the work and experience improved well-being.

The work motivation scale is an insightful model to demonstrate the dynamics of motivating employees.[66] As shown in exhibit 20, the scale runs from "a-motivation" through three levels of controlled motivation to two levels of autonomous motivation.

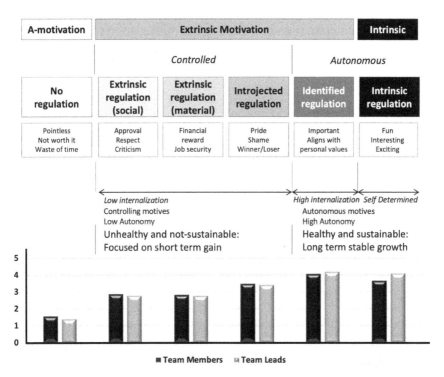

Exhibit 20—Work motivation scale.

A-motivation is a complete lack of motivation. *No regulation* whatsoever can entice the employee to become active. The task is considered pointless and a waste of time.

Controlled motivation is subdivided into three different levels. *Social extrinsic regulation* implies the employee is motivated by the approval of others. These may be superiors, colleagues, or even family members. Fear of criticism from these individuals could also be a driver for action. If the expected remuneration is of a financial nature, we speak of *material extrinsic regulation*. Examples are higher income, bonuses, or stock awards.

The third level of controlled motivation is called *introjected regulation*. An employee exhibits certain behaviors to feel proud, or to avoid embarrassment or guilt. "If I work all weekend and send the report on Sunday, I am a winner" could be the underlying thought. The employee has developed an internal yardstick by which behavior is assessed. It is a very tricky thought pattern. I have often witnessed it as a prelude to stress and ultimately burnout symptoms. Do you see the underlying premise—"my self-worth depends on what I do"—is false? It is a complex form of outside-in thinking. And it is bound to cause trouble.

Autonomous motivation comprises two levels—identified and intrinsic regulation. *Identified regulation* strikes a fine balance. It aligns the employee's personal values with the values the company represents. The employee believes in the company's mission. It has personal significance for the employee to do this work. The ultimate level of motivation is *intrinsic regulation*. The employee comes to work simply because it is fun. The job content is interesting. It is a pleasure to collaborate with colleagues. And it's exciting to have an impact together.

A section of the survey among employees of the Customer Fulfillment Center was devoted to work motivation. We measured their score at each of the six levels in the scale. Employee motivation is considered healthy if autonomous motivation scores a 4 ("*I agree*") or above. Furthermore, low levels of controlled motivation strongly contribute to motivating staff.[67]

The results as shown in exhibit 20 presented an insightful picture. Across the board, our employees experienced a reasonably high level of autonomous motivation. The level of intrinsic regulation— "my work is fun!"—still had room for improvement. Yet, the score was encouraging. On the other end of the spectrum we found low a-motivation scores. Both employees and team leads appeared to be "in the zone."

I became particularly concerned with the high score on introjected regulation—just below 3.5. A vast number of colleagues continuously assessed themselves against their own benchmarks. This indicated a significant risk of stress and absenteeism. I also raised my eyebrows about the controlled motivation scores. Both social and material extrinsic motivation results hovered around 2.8. This was clearly on the high side and potentially unhealthy and unsustainable.[68]

Free the Motivation

"Let's start out with some very good news," Lars said with a hopeful look on his face as he began to summarize the results. I had called for another get-together with my team to assess the situation and agree on our next steps. "The results of the survey proved to be a powerful psychological barometer for the organization. Our hypothesis was correct. We found statistical evidence that Engaging Leadership behaviors by the direct manager indeed are a driver of employee motivation. Even better, we also found the ideal path to amplify this impact. Direct managers play a crucial role in satisfying basic psychological needs. They set the conditions for employees to make their own choices, to connect, and grow their impact. Their behavior will be increasingly driven by their personal values. And by the sheer fun they experience at work."

"Great to hear this, Lars," one of my team members commented. "I'm a man of action. What is it precisely that we should do?"

"Ah!" Lars replied, "that's the beauty of this outcome. It is actually quite straightforward what kind of intervention program we should design to boost motivation and business results. Let's revisit the survey results and directly translate them to concrete steps!"

As we assembled the key findings we were slowly adding more pixels to the picture. It was evident the team leads were key in our transformation. They tended to be overly positive about their own

Engaging Leadership style. Interestingly, they themselves felt they could be more explicit in communicating task arrangements.

At this point in our discussion, my team got really confused. Wasn't this contradicting our other findings on how employee motivation is boosted? If our team leads would grant employees the autonomy to make their own choices, wouldn't they be even less clear about tasks? And how about motivating people? What exact leadership style should the team leads exhibit to be more inspiring and engaging?

At the height of the commotion, Lars perfectly injected an additional input. He had added a few open questions at the end of the survey. The answers to two simple questions in particular provided powerful insights. They dramatically impacted our perspective on motivation and leadership.

The first question was, "What is most motivating in your work?"

Now take a moment to let this question sink in for yourself. How would you answer it? Take a mental note or write it on a piece of paper.

I certainly would have mentioned things like an inspirational vision, a culture of teamwork, challenging customers, or an engaging boss. The answer most given by our employees was much more down-to-earth. It simply was … the work itself. Lars was smiling as we reviewed the answers.

"Ask people in any organization this very question and you'll always get the same answer," he clarified. "Ask an engineer and he will talk about technique and solving problems. Speak with a teacher and she will elaborate on educating children. Pose the question to a group of nurses, and they will emphasize the interaction with patients. It's the work itself that motivates people the most."

The second question that triggered an insightful answer was, "What is still missing in your work?"

Interestingly, nearly all answers to this question pointed to leadership—the lack of a clear direction, common goals, and rules of engagement. Room to disagree or to suggest new ideas. Frustrations about not being heard or involved. Shifting priorities and too much pressure. Having to follow up on instructions that lacked clarity. Do you recognize this picture in your organization?

"As a leader you don't have to motivate your people," Lars concluded. "They already are motivated. The work itself is the very reason they come to work. It is your task to set a clear and solid framework. It provides your employees the freedom to do their work."[69]

To be a leader means you own the process to liberate the motivation of your employees. You don't do this by directive. Nor is there a need to enforce your will and chase people. On the other hand, an organization won't fare well without some structure. Leadership is the art of involving your employees in a co-creation process. It defines the path and sets the boundaries. It provides a framework that grants them freedom (autonomy) and structures their involvement (relatedness). This creates a powerful basis for keeping your employees to their own commitments. Not by pushing, but rather by coaching them on how to find their own answers. In this way you develop their talents and grow their impact (competence). And your business? It is bound to thrive!

TOP THREE TAKEAWAYS

1) Self-Determination Theory is based on the notion that all human beings share three basic psychological needs—the need for autonomy, relatedness, and competence. They strikingly correspond with our gut, heart, and head brains.

2) We can measure the basic psychological needs. Thus, we gauge the coherence between the company's multiple brains. It is the ultimate tool to assess an organization's ability to reach its highest expression.

3) As leaders, we don't have to motivate our people. The work itself is what motivates people the most. It is our task to co-create a clear and solid framework. It will set our employees free to do their work.

SHAPE YOUR PARADISE *ONLINE*

What sets engaging leaders apart from their colleagues? How do you attune your team values to individual values? Which actions can you take to satisfy the basic psychological needs of your team members? How do you liberate the motivation of your people? These questions are central to week 2 of the online module "Paradise Shaper Leadership." Apply your insights directly to your team!

15

FRAME YOUR GAME

*"You don't have to be a genius or a visionary
or even a college graduate to be successful. You
just need a framework and a dream."*
—Michael Dell

Straight to the Point

"If we are to spend the next eight days together, I suggest we start out by agreeing on our rules of engagement," Peter said as he looked around the audience with an inviting smile on his face.

The executive leadership program I had signed up for had started—eight days of long hours, intensive teamwork, and lots of new concepts to absorb in record time. My thirty-nine fellow participants and I agreed that Peter's overture was only fair.

"Who would like to propose a first rule?" Peter asked while he continued to make eye contact with all of us.

After a few uncomfortable seconds of silence, one participant raised her voice. "I think it'd be only practical if we all start on time at every session," she said.

"Thank you, that's a great suggestion. Does everyone agree?" Peter asked, attentively checking for any objections. As there weren't any, he took a marker and wrote on a blank flip chart: "Be on time."

"Marvelous. What other rules can we set ourselves?" he inquired.

"Well, how about we listen when another person speaks?" a colleague asked.

"Sounds awesome to me," Peter responded. "Any issue with this proposal?"

As all appeared in favor, Peter noted on the flip chart: "Listen to each other."

Peter pursued this process for another five minutes until the flip chart was filled with encouraging intentions.

"I think we have a nice list here." he concluded. "Since you've defined these rules yourselves, I am sure they will be easy to live by. Let's take a fifteen-minute coffee break. Will that be enough time for everyone?"

We all nodded. Some of us were already getting up to walk out.

"Perfect, we will resume at 10 a.m. sharp on the clock behind me."

We were well into the coffee break as the clock was approaching the hour. Only a few people were making attempts to finish their conversation and get back to the room. It surprised me. Hadn't we just agreed on being on time at every session? For a second it occurred to me I could activate the team and ensure we started on time. But then again, was it my responsibility to do so? Well, maybe Peter would take it easy this first day. I slowly returned to the room and was just in time. I counted only twelve participants in the room. Peter was patient and entertained a few people with small talk.

When it was five past the hour, another nine people had entered the room. Mabel, a fellow student, got nervous and asked Peter if we shouldn't start.

"I'm here for you guys," he noted. "Once we are all back, I'll be happy to continue."

After three more minutes, Mabel walked out to collect the others. At twelve minutes past 10 o'clock, we had thirty-nine participants present. As the fortieth person walked in carrying a coffee in his hand, Peter addressed him in a pleasant voice.

"Welcome back, Brent. Would you do me a favor and tell me what time it is?" Peter asked.

Brent's body language unveiled a mixture of both surprise and guilt.

"I'm sorry, Peter," he responded, "I had forgotten to visit the bathroom."

"What time had we agreed to be here?" Peter teased in a strikingly friendly way.

"Uh, you said 10 a.m. sharp," Brent mumbled as he stared at the floor.

"And did you consent with that agreement?"

"Yeah, we all did, didn't we?"

Brent was helplessly looking for an escape.

"Indeed," Peter affirmed. "Now who's responsible to be back in time?"

"I am, Peter," Brent admitted. "It won't happen again, I promise!"

With an open palm, Peter cordially invited Brent to take his seat. Now he looked around and shifted his attention to all of us. "At 10 a.m., I counted twelve of you at your seats," he continued. "Who of you had not made it here yet?"

People raised their hands hesitantly. I was wondering where he was leading us.

"I'm just curious, why is it so difficult to keep a commitment you made only fifteen minutes before?" Peter prodded.

Helen, one of our colleagues, spoke up.

"I think we get the point, Peter," she said, looking across the conference room. "Let me speak for myself. I have simply not taken ownership. I was looking at the others. I was having a fun conversation and when the majority didn't appear to move, I also decided to take it easy. My apologies."

"Thank you, Helen, I appreciate your honesty and self-reflection," Peter replied. "And there's another person I would like to commend, and that's Mabel. She is the person who finally got up to fetch the others. That is most appreciated.

"I have one more question for the other eleven of you who were on time," he added. "What thoughts crossed your mind when the majority extended their coffee break?"

My heart started pounding as Peter's eyes caught mine. I felt prompted to respond.

"For a second I thought I should get the others, but then I told myself it wasn't my responsibility," I acknowledged. "I now realize I actually could have warned them."

"That's great, Paul," he confirmed.

Peter had us right where he wanted us. "I'm not trying to impose anything on you guys. I'm only reminding you of your own commitments. I really want all of us to get the most out of these eight days. It will only work if we all take responsibility for ourselves and for each other. Now let's move on, we have lots of work to do!"

The Art of Contracting

It was only after the training course that I realized the full impact of what Peter had done. The setting was a common one we come across every day—the start of a meeting. Yet in essence he gave us the ultimate demonstration of what leadership is all about. In an engaged and consistent way, he first managed the process of co-creating a framework. And right after the break he ensured it was complied with. We all bought into the process as he maintained a basic attitude of "I'm okay, you're okay."

Did you notice Peter did not once tell us what to do? All he did was ask the right questions. He used the power of the group to mold our team spirit. At the end, he conveniently summarized our own conclusions.

Peter applied a technique called "contracting." Everyone enters a meeting with a different set of personal values and expectations. It is crucial you always take a moment to align on the rules of engagement. Right from the beginning, the boundaries must be set. It is this framework that provides clarity and focus. It is a magical paradox that such a voluntary curtailment grants all participants freedom (gut brain!). It fosters teamwork (heart brain!) and acts as a catalyst for creativity and manifestation (head brain!).

As a leader, you coach people how to live their best intentions. The way they behave originates in the framework you have established with their support. If there is unrest in an organization, it is evident that the boundaries aren't clear to everyone. Contracting is a process that's always ongoing. It requires friendly reinforcement during every meeting. At the end of a session, it is important to close with a transparent summary, action points, and owners. If there is something to celebrate, this is a golden opportunity to underscore that our agreed behavior generated results.

It won't surprise you that all our subsequent sessions started on time. During the sessions, Peter ensured the contract was constantly kept alive. If we interrupted a colleague to promote our point of view, he would immediately ask, "Excuse me, what just happened here?"

By the third day, he only needed to point to the flip chart, which he had placed in the middle of the room, for people to correct their behavior. This experience at the start of the program had a remarkable bonding effect. It instilled a leadership culture in us, which we all took with us to our respective organizations.

Powerful Principles

The intensive training opened my eyes. It made me think how a process focus can be effectively combined with a people-oriented approach. Leadership, I learned, is all about channeling team energy. The rules of engagement have to be crystal clear for any game—including business—to be fun. The role of the leader is to orchestrate a team process where boundaries are set and maintained. In this way, all energy is effectively directed towards achieving the team's *raison d'être*.

We don't need to go far to attain some powerful lessons. Just watch the way nature organizes itself. Everything is in constant motion as energy wants to flow. Evolution is constantly improving structures and processes to channel the energy of life. Once this energy is blocked, the structure becomes irresilient and is bound to disintegrate. In companies, this is visible in all kinds of dynamics—missed deadlines, absenteeism, or disturbed relationships between teams.

We will only solve these issues if we work from the inside-out. As leaders we want to foster a culture of value creation, and translate this into a system that effectively delivers on our ambition. We strike a perfect balance between the lower quadrants in the Four Quadrants model (exhibit 15, see introduction to Part III). By providing clarity, we remove existing blockages. The energy will flow freely again. Nature's powerful lessons to frame our game can be summed up in five principles as depicted in exhibit 21.

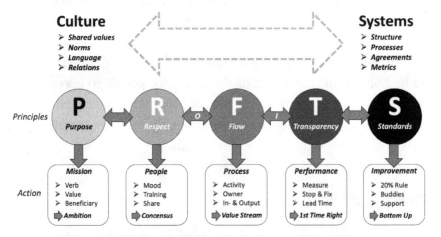

Exhibit 21—The PRoFiTS principles to frame our game.

1) Purpose—align decisions for value creation.
2) Respect—put people at the center of all activity.
3) Flow—continuously move from input to output.
4) Transparency—expose problems to solve them.
5) Standards—improve work by stable processes.

You will have noticed that the first letters are the consonants in the acronym PRoFiTS. This perfectly outlines the paradox of performance. By shifting our focus from results to value creation, we generate even more profits—real profits for the entire system of which we're part. Let's touch upon each of these axioms.

Purpose—Align Decisions for Value Creation

A purpose is all about the creation of value, which I described in Chapter 8 as "providing our customers with pure and inclusive solutions. In this way, we will be enriching humanity—and the planet we live on—with innovations that are in sync with nature and the purpose of our existence." A purpose provides the reason why the organization exists—a sincere commitment to making a positive impact on the world.

To instill a sense of purpose, we put the customer first. The customer is the direct beneficiary of the value we create. This may sound logical. Still you might be surprised how many companies are more concerned with their quarterly results or internal power games. Purpose implies integrity. Therefore every decision we make is judged against this yardstick—are we really living our purpose? We don't compromise on this innate quality when we're tempted by short-term opportunities to earn a quick buck. In the long run, our dedication will pay off.

It is fruitful to translate your company's purpose into a vision for your team. A vision is your desired future. An inspiring vision cannot be defined by leadership alone. It is not even invented. It is bestowed upon the team based on its talents and the environment it serves. Our team leads at the Customer Fulfillment Center guided their teams through a similar process. Every employee in each of the twelve order-desk teams was invited to participate. Their versatile inputs yielded an appealing picture of our emerging future. One could sense the renewed level of self-esteem and energy when one of the team leads summarized the vision:

"To deliver a smooth customer experience will be the cornerstone of our operation. We will take a proactive approach and no longer feel squeezed between the customer and the factory. We'll take the lead in creating full transparency in the chain. We will set standards in our work and continuously improve on them. We will reach out to our colleagues in sales, product development, and the factory to set a joint framework. A significant reduction of our lead time—from customer order to installation at the hospital—will become our shared objective. This will serve our customers, make us flexible, and boost our productivity."

Armed with this vision, the team continued to create a clear mission statement, which is valuable as mission is purpose in action. The teams continued to sharpen their joint mission until they found an oddly simple yet ambitious one:

Orchestrate the customer value chain.

It was a statement that was as much a desire as an invitation to collaborate. It demonstrated the proactivity the teams needed to take their destiny into their own hands. Expressing the aspiration released unexpected levels of energy and support.[70]

—TRANSFORMATION EXERCISE 17—
On a Mission

What is the joint mission of your team in one sentence? What value do you create for whom? Use the momentum you build up in this endeavor to capture the ambition and vigor. Seek to link it to your company's mission statement!

A powerful frame is Verb and Value (for the Beneficiary). Successful mission statements always follow this frame. Here are some examples:

> ➤ LinkedIn: Connect the world's professionals to make them more productive and successful.
> ➤ Nike: Bring inspiration and innovation to every athlete in the world. (Nike's founder Bill Bowerman: "If you have a body, you are an athlete.")
> ➤ Patagonia: We're in business to save our home planet.
> ➤ Tesla: Accelerate the world's transition to sustainable energy.
> ➤ The most succinct one I know is by TED: Spread ideas.

Respect—Put People at the Center of All Activity

It's the people who do the work. They are the experts. It therefore is obvious our employees play a key role in organizing their activities. We want to create an environment where everyone counts and feels safe. Important decisions are taken slowly and by consensus. Different perspectives are seriously considered. Doesn't that take an awful lot of time? You'll be surprised! You gain even more time during execution. Once taken, decisions will be carried out without further ado.

The role of leaders is not to give instructions. They are the least qualified to do so! Their key objective is to grow their people every single day. To live and breathe the company's purpose. They act as process facilitators. They establish the framework that provides clarity, freedom, and team spirit. As such, they are visible at the work floor. They know the process inside out and are nimble problem solvers. Self-reflection is a favorite part of their daily activities. Thus, they establish a culture of continuous improvement.

At the Customer Fulfillment Center, a succinct team session was introduced at the start of each day. This stand-up meeting proved to be a powerful team accelerator. It gave focus and fostered collaboration. People were invited to share their opinion and ask questions in an open atmosphere.

For many teams, working (partially) from home has become the "new normal," making face-to-face team sessions impossible. However, a virtual daily session can work wonders to keep the team connected and on track. This daily check-in would be the only exception to "meeting-free morning" (see Chapter 7). It is a perfect start to the day.

The teams at the Customer Fulfillment Center created a daily dashboard in the workplace. The first section on this board was called People. It contained a "mood board" (how do people feel?) to immediately draw attention to issues on people's minds. These might also be private matters such as a sick child at home. Perhaps a colleague could take over some of the tasks so this person could go home earlier? Other topics included the planning for the day, training activities and other communication to share. This session is not intended for decision making on tough topics. Yet, it is crucial for a smooth day-to-day operation.

Flow—Continuously Move from Input to Output

"Now, you have opened the order entry screen in SAP and entered the order details. What happens next?" Alexander asked. He was absorbed in the moment while inquiring into the process flow. We recently hired him to help our Customer Fulfillment Center teams align their processes. He was in the midst of a "value stream mapping" exercise with our ultrasound order-desk team. Nine colleagues were focused on the wall. Just this morning, Alexander had pasted twenty feet of brown paper on it. When the team entered the room in amazement at what he posted, he warmly welcomed them wearing jeans and rolled-up sleeves.

"I'm here to support you guys," he professed. "But first I'd like you to teach me how you work today and what the impediments are."

So they started plotting every step of the process. It was arduous as Alexander worked with the team through numerous details, inquiring about an array of issues to attain a comprehensive picture.

"What's the exact activity?" he asked. "What inputs do you need? Who needs to provide it? What do you do if you don't get it? How often does that happen? What's the escalation path? What tools are you using? Who do you communicate with and in what way?"

Alexander listed the functional owners of activities on the left side of the paper. He drew horizontal lines between each name and extended them along the length of the wall—these are called "swimming lanes." Alexander meticulously drew every step of the process in the swimming lane of the corresponding functional owner. He used different colors and symbols to distinguish main activities, supporting tasks, data inputs, and a time indication. On the third day, the mapping was completed. It was an exuberant wall decoration that rivaled Picasso's most expressive work.

Such mapping leads us to consider the question of "value adding." Take a look at your work situation. What percentage of the hours spent by your team would the customer see as adding value? Whenever I ask this question in workshops, the typical answers I get range between 50 to 90 percent. At the end of the workshop, all participants acknowledge that the humble reality is only 3 to 5 percent. Indeed, more than 95 percent of hours worked are not spent on activities for which the customer would be willing to pay—the conversion of input to output.

By mapping the value stream we can critically assess all the steps in our current ways of working. This allows us to look for more intelligent ways to do the work. It is helpful to have a "feet on the table" dialogue on what the ideal process flow would look like. This "future state" will serve as the team's North Star. Now every team member will have a vision of what's possible. And it becomes evident how they can contribute personally.

Transparency—Expose Problems to Solve Them

It is a natural tendency for people not to let their mistakes be known. This is especially true if our corporate culture does not accept human error. We try to push the evidence under the rug. We decide to make up for the loss in the work ahead. Even when failure is allowed, I find that many people spend a lot of time correcting it. Some companies have entire rework factories to avoid the need to scrap expensive parts.

We don't want to fix things downstream. We should solve them as soon as they happen. We want to instill a "First Time Right" mentality! Transparency is the gateway to improvement. In Toyota factories, every employee is empowered to stop the production line in case of a problem. The team lead works with the team to assess and fix the problem. Just realize how much trust is placed in people!

As part of the intervention program at the Customer Fulfillment Center, the team leads made tremendous progress. They learned how to create an environment where people felt safe, even invited, to report concerns. The daily dashboard contained a second section dedicated to performance. It provided four to six metrics indicating how well the team was performing. This was done by means of simple graphs depicting actual performance against the standard. The idea is not to put results—the typical financial metrics— on this overview. Instead, leading indicators are used. These are check points early in the process that highlight where the flow has stalled. Process lead time—for instance, for booking an order—is an example of such a leading indicator. We want to go upstream in our processes and fix things at the source!

Standards—Improve Work by Stable Processes

Nature works with standard blueprints to ensure that each step in its processes is stable. DNA is an evident example. Every time a process is used, it produces the same result. An apple seed is programmed to become an apple tree. And every year, the tree produces the exact same apples. But it doesn't stop there. In exchange with the Field, every organism finds a way to transcend its present form (see Chapter 12). It improves on its standard. This means it includes all the valuable features of its present form. This prevents degeneration to a lower level.

Lean thinking is exactly based on this philosophy. Today, it's often associated with rationalization, procedures, and discipline—a pure left side of the brain activity. It is often believed to kill all creativity, flexibility, and human interaction. In most organizations that implemented Lean, it was done with a result-oriented mindset. Implementation teams went cherry picking. They applied only those concepts that were useful in achieving short-term productivity gains. Processes and instructions developed into rigid systems. Leaders became bureaucratic and employees felt demotivated.

In reality, Lean isn't "mean." It's a highly rewarding adventure for both employees and leaders.[71] Top-down change programs rarely take root. But incremental improvements initiated by employees themselves create lasting transformations. Processes and standards are meant to support people, not enslave them. I'm a strong advocate of simplicity. Just as in nature, we want to reduce complexity to the crux of what we wish to accomplish. But no less! We don't want feeble processes that jeopardize our pursuit of quality. We want to work in a playful, creative way where processes make things easy.

I recall an insightful visit to one of our factories in Massachusetts. The plant manager introduced himself in thirty seconds. He then gave the floor to a group of factory operators. I remember Carole, who wore her blue factory coat. She explained how they had reduced the floor space by 80 percent in just four years. "All of us have these aha moments. We suddenly find an easy way to do the same thing. It often turns out to be nonsense. But if it works, *wow!*" she said.

When I asked her about the role of leadership to make this possible, she said, "Make no mistake, only operators know how to do this. It becomes like a game to always think about simpler ways of doing things. All they have to do is take us seriously."

This is what we did. The current processes became the standard. Each employee was invited to dedicate 20 percent of their working hours (yes, that's a lot!) to work on improvements. In my experience, this is best done in buddy teams. A weekly team session was held in which employees discussed their proposals. Improvement progress was reviewed in the third section of the daily dashboard. If needed, help was offered. An initiative was completed when the new standard had been fully incorporated in the work instructions. Step by step, the order-desk teams found the path to the North Star—to carry out their mission to orchestrate the value chain.

TOP THREE TAKEAWAYS

1) We frame our game by co-creating our boundaries. It is a magical paradox that such voluntary curtailment grants all participants freedom (gut brain!). It fosters teamwork (heart brain!) and acts as a catalyst for creativity and manifestation (head brain!).

2) There are five powerful principles to guide our pursuit of real PRoFiTS—a Purpose to create value, Respect for people, continuous Flow, Transparency of problems, and Standards to continuously improve.

3) Lean is often associated with rationalization, procedures, and discipline. In essence, Lean isn't "mean" but a highly rewarding adventure for both employees and leaders. It's a coherent business methodology that structures work in a natural way by relying on people's ingenuity.

SHAPE YOUR PARADISE *ONLINE*

In week 3 of the online module "Paradise Shaper Leadership," you will practice how to create a functional framework for your team. What's an inspiring way to find our vision and mission? How do you ensure all team members check in to the process? How do you introduce a joyful practice of continuous improvement? Step by step, your team will also reach its North Star.

16

COACH FOR IMPACT

"In a way our expertise is not coaching. Even when we
become master coaches, our expertise is human beings."
—Michael Neill

A Dynamic Environment

One of my clients is a team lead at an insurance company. Her team handles customer complaints. To protect her privacy, I'll call her Sarah. In recent years, the administrative burden for Sarah's team had significantly increased. Due to cost restraints, she could not hire new team members. Sarah longed to connect with the other team leads and was certain significant savings could be made if only they streamlined their operations. However, she felt management wasn't doing much to create a team spirit. Therefore, she took the initiative. But every time she reached out to her colleagues, she received only a lukewarm response. Sarah did not understand. Why weren't her colleagues interested in teaming up?

I set the scene for a different approach to coach Sarah. We started an organizational "constellation"—a technique where clients invite representatives to mirror the environment causing difficulties. I asked Sarah to invite stand-ins for her fellow team leads. She appointed four of them. I then asked where she felt they should be positioned in the room. She put them at equidistance from each other at the other side of the demarcated space. Now I watched her standing in front of her "colleagues." I noticed the lack of interaction between the participants. Sarah was desperate for eye contact.

As soon as she took her third step toward the others, the dynamics became visible. The four team leads split into two groups of two. Each pair was heading in a different direction.

I asked the nearest team lead representative how she felt. "I'm starting to feel agitated," she replied. "She's in my space."

"How do you recognize this situation more often in your life?" I then asked Sarah.

She explained it happened all the time. "It must be a matter of our individualistic society. Every time I try to connect, people only mind their own business. It's super frustrating."

Multiple Systems

Where people interact, so do the systems of which they are part. In the past decade, all of humanity has been connected in one global system (see Chapter 2). The outbreak of the coronavirus clearly demonstrated this. It reached every corner of the world in less than three months.

This ties in with complexity theory, which views systems as living organisms with their own dynamics. We are all part of multiple systems that affect us to different degrees. Some have a natural origin. The most prominent example is the family system into which we were born. Other systems have been conceived by people. These can be our sports team, a group of friends, and, of course, the organization in which we work.

A natural system is like the last sentence in "Hotel California" by the Eagles—"You can check out any time you like, but you can never leave."[72] You may denounce your family, but you are still a member of your family system. In Chapter 9 we discussed our childhood conclusions. They play a major role in triggering our habitual thoughts and emotions. All these patterns find their root in our family system. Our relationship with our parents and siblings, in particular, feeds or depletes our energy level.

Organizational Systems

Compared to family systems, organizational systems have a weakness. This may, paradoxically, be their strength. Membership is always on a mutually agreed basis. We always have the option to check out and leave the organization. Or we may be forced to exit. Our connection to the organizational system may therefore not be that profound. The trend of active job-hopping underscores this notion. Leaders have a task of strengthening the relationship contract with employees. This goes far beyond a superficial financial engagement.

All systems are subject to three systemic laws. The system...

1) is inclusive for all its members
2) sustains a certain order between its members
3) maintains a balance between giving and taking

Organizational systems adhere to a fourth law.[73] The system...

4) wants to achieve its mission

In companies, the hierarchy is often depicted in an organization chart. This official pyramid certainly plays an important role. Yet other invisible lines make or break the effectiveness of an organization. These concealed connections are called organizational dynamics. Teams that fail to meet their targets. Communication issues between departments. Unclear tasks. High levels of absenteeism. They arise if one or more of the basic systemic laws are compromised. They may seem negative at first sight. But from a systemic perspective, these dynamics come with a positive intention. Their sole purpose is to maintain the system.

Systemic Work

"Would you like to take it a level deeper?" I challenged Sarah. She consented.

"Tell us about the family composition in your youth," I requested.

"Well, I'm the fifth and youngest child," she answered. "My four elder siblings and I were quite a few years apart. By the time I went to high school, the eldest two had already left the house."

Now we were on to something!

"What was it like for you to be the youngest in this large family?" I asked. Her answer said it all.

"I felt like I was at a party that had already ended," she replied. "My parents seemed tired of parenting. And my brothers and sister flew out to discover the world."

We released the stand-ins for her fellow team leads from their assignment. Now we switched gears. Sarah was asked to invite representatives for her parents and siblings and she positioned them in the room. Interestingly, she put her parents slightly apart—dad on the left, mom on the right. Her four elder siblings ended up as a pack next to her father. I noticed they were all outward facing, with little chemistry between them. When I asked Sarah to take her place, she hesitated. First she took a step forward. Now she was standing on her mother's right side. As I watched Sarah's body language, I noticed a fixation on her father. Meanwhile, mom turned away from dad and looked at Sarah. The plot began to unfold!

I asked mother how she felt.

"I am aching in my stomach. I sensed a deep consolation when Sarah stepped up to me," she responded.

Then I asked what father experienced. He said, "I find it hard to put into words. There's unrest. I feel like I just don't want to be here. I need to get out and do my own thing."

Sarah's eyes widened. As I switched my attention to her, she explained, "This is exactly how it was. Dad was charismatic. A free bird, always out to meet other people. Mom couldn't stand up to him.

When my brothers and sister left the house, she seemed to languish. I always felt left to my own devices."

The experience provided Sarah with a powerful insight. The pain of a lonely childhood in a large family, with parents unable to harbor a family spirit—it left a deep yearning for inclusion. Early in life, she had developed firm childhood conclusions, a combination of "I'm not welcome. I am not enough. I must take control to survive." Those conclusions prompted her to take the lead and seek partnership. In fact, Sarah's subconscious mind constantly placed her in conditions similar to her upbringing. She sought the "perfect environment" to undo her past. To fill her void with warmth and companionship. If her parents didn't bring the family together, she would. And now that her boss seemed absent, she repeated this exact behavior. However, her colleagues didn't appreciate her taking his responsibility. It just wasn't her job.

We had come to the source of Sarah's pattern. Now I offered her an opportunity to initiate the process of dissolving it. Sarah was invited to stand opposite her parents, facing both. As a child, it was not for her to blame her parents. Nor could she claim they should have behaved differently. Parents give what they're able to give. They carry the subconscious burden of their own childhood conclusions. But Sarah could express what she missed. She was able to relinquish her perceived responsibility to keep the family together. Any marital issues between her parents were theirs. It wasn't her task to compensate for them.

A Moving and Knowing Field

Systemic work was developed by Bert Hellinger. In the 1950s, he was a missionary in South Africa.[74] He witnessed how Zulu tribes conducted certain rituals to heal their local war traumas. Hellinger was impressed by the power of these ceremonies in reconciling former enemies. He decided to leave the Catholic priesthood and went back to his native Germany. There, he studied psychoanalysis and a vast number of therapeutic methods. He started his own practice and worked with clients whose lives were seriously affected by World War II.

Hellinger experientially developed a revolutionary approach—the family constellation. These constellations in a sense are ceremonies. Clients invite participants to represent family members, institutions (like the army, church or school), or even certain emotions. They position these representatives in a demarcated space. In this way, a "moving and knowing field" is created. It's a symbolic representation of the client's inhibitions on a subconscious level. It shows where people are blocked in their connection with the Field of Intelligence. Trauma experienced by ancestors up to seven generations back may have been passed on subconsciously. They keep clients from living the life they desire in harmony with others.

This is not a scientific or psychological method. Constellations are based on what is called phenomenological perception. Participants sense their feelings and follow their tendencies. They display the pathological mistakes in the system. They depict where energy in the system is blocked. The method provides a new perspective—a possibility to restore the balance in the system. It's a powerful way to grant the client relief.

Back to the Organization

"What would be an effective way to connect with the other team leads?" I asked Sarah.

Impressed by her recent experience, she had a remarkable proposal. "Why don't we organize a constellation at the management level above me?" she suggested. "We may learn why they walked away from their responsibility."

Without these managers present, this would be like practicing voodoo. A creative, but not sound idea. In systemic work, we only exhibit the client's inner world in a personal situation.

Then Sarah had a new idea. "Let's invite a representative for my direct manager. A simple one-on-one setting, in which I convey how I feel," she said.

This was a much more fruitful idea. Sarah requested the participant who previously served as her father to now represent her boss. As Sarah looked him straight in the eye, she struggled to find the right tone.

"It has been really tough for our teams to cope with the high workload," Sarah said. "We can help you save if only we work together. We could use some coordination to make this happen."

"I'm sorry Sarah, but I cannot feel your pain," I interjected. "And as a boss I wouldn't feel inclined to take action. Get out of your head. Speak from the heart. There's no need to hold back. He's getting paid to address these problems. You serve no one by downplaying."

"All right," Sarah nodded and tried again.

"We are having a hard time..."

"Not *we*, Sarah, *I*!" I prodded. "Let him know what *you* are dealing with. Pain is personal."

Sarah took a deep breath and resumed. "I am stuck," she said. "For years I have tried to keep people motivated, find smarter ways, and get more stuff done. I can't do it anymore. I'm exhausted. I'm asking you for help. I'm sure there are smarter ways to do the job if the team leads really collaborate. But that doesn't happen. I lack structure and a real team spirit. It's not my job to bring us together. I'm not their boss. You are!"

Bingo! Everyone in the room seemed to be holding their breath. The silence of just a few seconds appeared to last forever.

"I cannot believe I just said that!" Sarah exclaimed with a tremulous voice.

A cautious smile came out, contrasting graciously with her watery eyes. Sarah had changed her energy. She felt liberated.

In the week after our session, she had a meeting with her manager. The conversation went surprisingly well.

"I may not have been as outspoken as during our session, but it worked!" Sarah shared afterward.

Her boss said he had no idea the situation was so difficult for

Sarah. He was under the impression that the team leads solved things among themselves. He knew Sarah to be a dedicated, hard-working team lead. Now that Sarah had drawn a line in the sand, something had to be done. He would soon invite the team leads to a team meeting.

Transformational Coaching

In the Transformation Age, Teal leaders are imbued with the inside-out reality of our experience. I call these wise new leaders Paradise Shapers. They understand their role is to orchestrate a setting where their people realize their full potential. It's not about imposing instructions. It's about becoming a channel for the energy of the Field to manifest. This is how all organisms in nature flourish. And so do people and the organizations they form. Every person is born with a unique gift to enrich the human experience. They don't need to be repaired, corrected, or enhanced. By design they are already perfect.

It's just that most people don't believe this truth yet. Their mindset is stuck at a lower level of consciousness. It prevents them from seeing who they truly are. They have comfortably planted their butt in a brand new Ferrari, yet they are constantly looking for a horse to pull them. Their subconscious patterns block their view and prevent them from seeing the truth. Hence, they operate far below their ability. Paradise Shapers understand that energy wants to flow. They see the potential in their people. They apply powerful techniques that allow people to become aware of their self-created impediments. They see through problems of a chronic nature. These issues always have a deeper system layer in which the entanglement originates.

Paradise Shapers facilitate their employees to experience what it means to be in flow. To trust the intelligence that only emerges in the now. Real impact happens when we forget about ourselves—our wealth, health, and safety. When our psychology doesn't hamper us. When we experience freedom, connection, and fulfillment.

Paradise Shapers are first and foremost transformational coaches. They advance to a different impact zone as compared to other fields of coaching. Exhibit 22 provides a simple overview of how the concepts you have become familiar with relate to each other.

The Field

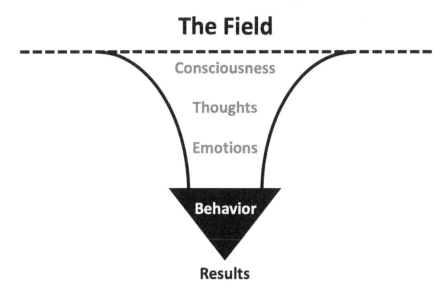

Exhibit 22—The gold is upstream.

In today's Orange society, being "result oriented" has become virtually synonymous with leadership. But if we're pushing for results, we're really at the end of the river. We're about to be pushed into the ocean, yet we're casting about for a different result. We're operating in the world of consequences, the realm of matter.

By shifting our focus to behavior, we are starting to go upstream. Yes, by training our staff certain functional skills, they'll certainly do a better job. This is especially true when dealing with specialized work. After all, it's comforting to realize our dentist has successfully completed a long trajectory of education. Likewise, communication skills can be improved by practicing the desired behavior. But the point is this. No behavioral coaching will have any serious impact if our employees are plagued with their childhood conclusions. They will continue to avoid confrontation, exposure, or loss of control.

When the heat is on, their habitual thinking will sabotage their newly learned skills.

Moving further upstream, we enter the inner world. Emotions are "energy in motion" (see Chapter 9). These feelings lead people to action. They're the driver of behavior. Most people fear their own emotions. They avoid feeling them at all costs. So they seek distraction. They flee in pills or other intoxicants. They go see a shrink. What they don't realize is that their emotions are a barometer of the quality of their thoughts. People aren't really scared, angry, or disappointed. They just *think* they are!

* * *

"If the only thing people learned was not to be afraid of their experience, that alone would change the world."
—Sydney Banks

* * *

Paradise Shapers support their people to see that they *are not* their thoughts. They just happen to *have* thoughts. Any unproductive behavior or outpouring of emotion is completely understandable. We only need to know the limiting thoughts that paint someone's perception of reality. These wise new leaders go to the source of the river, where thoughts originate. They coach their staff by stimulating inner reflection. They offer people experiences that help them see who they really are—a magnificent, creative, and connected human being. The more enhanced their awareness, the more often their genius will be mobilized. They'll be tapping straight from the Field.

Now we're working in the quantum reality. People become resourceful at allowing the future to emerge. The answers and people they need will show up—always in the right place, at the right time.

Transformational coaching paves the way for people to enhance their level of consciousness. In doing so, energy starts to flow. Problems tend to get solved easily. An enhanced awareness does not create them in the first place. It's our natural state. Everything in nature moves without pressure. When the drama disappears, people no longer waste their energy on feeding their fear of survival. The flow naturally moves to fulfill the collective desire—the purpose of the company.

Moving Questions

In any field of coaching, asking the right questions is a key technique in the coach's toolbox. Coachees are encouraged to find their own solutions to the matter at hand. In traditional coaching practice, questions are often of an analytical nature. They aim to dissect the problem by zooming in. The coach delves into the details and tries to discover what is causing the problem. Once the issue is found, an action plan is drawn up to work on the issue. The coach's compelling eyes entice the coachee to execute the plan in subsequent sessions.

A few years ago, I was taught a powerful lesson. As part of my "midlife crisis," I decided to get a motorcycle endorsement to my driver's license. Now, who invented the cone weave at slow speed? I always failed this skill test while practicing. Every time I passed three or four cones, I couldn't keep my balance. I would check the next cone, and as soon as I did, I hit it and the game was over.

After some time, my instructor René made a perfect observation. "Where's your attention?" he probed. "You're focusing on the problem by looking at the cone. Keep your eye on where you want to go!"

He walked twenty feet past the final cone, turned around, and gave me a clear assignment. "Start over and whatever you do, you keep looking right at me. Nowhere else," he chided.

I rode back to the starting line and made eye contact with René. I balanced the clutch and throttle and kept my focus on him throughout the exercise. This time, I perfectly passed all the cones without hitting or skipping any of them.

The insight from this anecdote is not the intervention technique

René applied. After all, he is an instructor, not a coach. But the example does point to the difference in focus of transformational coaching compared to traditional practice. In transformational coaching we don't focus on the problem. We don't want to get sucked into the mud of a razor-sharp analysis of what went wrong in a particular case. Both coachee and coach can easily get entangled in their own psychology and habitual thinking. If our energy is attached to the problem, we'll only amplify it and create even more of it. Instead, we need to zoom out and draw our attention to the world of possibilities.

* * *

"You can't teach anybody anything, only make them realize the answers are already inside them."
—Galileo Galilei

* * *

We're not after what's visible already. We ask questions that take the coachee upstream and broaden their perspective. These "moving questions" are particularly effective when certain issues appear to reoccur.[75] Such issues are often symptoms of invisible, underlying patterns. These blockages are themselves "solutions" to an unconsciously perceived deeper problem of the past.

Moving questions are not result-oriented. They don't come with the intention to change the present situation. The aim is to understand where energy is trapped and then release it. The less we know about the particular case, the more effective we can be. It's not even the answers to our questions that we're interested in. It's the process within the coachee we wish to ignite, to create space and new vistas. Moving questions don't need to be specific. They're never wordy and are often perceived as provocative. We can even use closed questions—an absolute no-go in traditional coaching! When offering our coachee a simple choice, we observe their body language and get a ton of information.

—TRANSFORMATION EXERCISE 18—
Moving Questions

To be effective in transformational coaching, it's crucial you develop your proficiency in generative listening (see Chapter 13). You want to be fully present. Listen deeply with all your senses, including your intuition. You therefore withhold your judgment and don't volunteer your own opinions. This would only color the perspective of the coachee. It's not about you!

Phrasing moving questions is craftsmanship. You'll develop it by practicing a lot. Over time, you will get comfortable being in the moment. You will trust the Field to plant the right questions in your mind. They will help your coachee to see the bigger picture. To get you going, here is some guidance on the type of questions you may want to ask.

Repetition:
➤ When did you first notice this problem?
➤ Have you come across similar situations before? (watch body language!)
➤ If yes, what or who does this situation remind you of?

Blockage:
➤ What is the deeper issue behind this problem?
➤ What part of you has trouble with this issue?
➤ What will you lose if this problem is resolved? What else?

Inclusion:
➤ Who benefits from this problem? In what way?
➤ Who is negatively impacted? In what way?
➤ Who or what is not yet taken into account?

Ownership:
- ➤ What makes you the person to address this problem?
- ➤ Who is the appropriate person to resolve this problem?
- ➤ What can this person accomplish?

Forward:
- ➤ What opportunity presents itself that you have not responded to?
- ➤ Whose approval are you seeking to move forward?
- ➤ Imagine you're free from any impediment. What would you do?

Bonus tip—once you have uncovered where your employee's energy is trapped (convictions, loyalties, fears), you can guide them further downstream by solution-oriented coaching with questions like:

- ➤ What's your next step?
- ➤ Whose support will you seek?
- ➤ Where do you want to be in one year from today?
- ➤ What are the important milestones?

Performance Catalyst

At the Customer Fulfillment Center, a substantial part of the leadership intervention program was devoted to transformational coaching. The high level of absenteeism, declining employee engagement and structural underperformance were all indications that certain organizational dynamics were at play. As discussed, in such cases we first need to identify the underlying breaches of systemic laws. Then the opportunity to restore order and balance within the system presents itself.

The team leads learned to recognize when they were blocked in their own energy flow. By zooming out, they were encouraged to take a broader perspective. A renewed focus on possibilities. They were then trained to take their first steps in transformational coaching themselves. They learned to connect with their teams in a more meaningful way. They went upstream and coached their team members to see the blockages in their path to performance.

The combination of defining a solid framework (see Chapter 15) and transformational coaching proved invaluable. The teams succeeded in curbing the negative performance trend by addressing systemic issues in the "undercurrent." It catalyzed the structural improvements they made by adopting the PRoFiTS principles. And so they released lots of energy in their pursuit of the North Star—to orchestrate the value chain!

TOP THREE TAKEAWAYS

1) We are all part of multiple systems that affect us to different degrees. Constellations are a powerful tool to visualize the undercurrent. They demonstrate where systemic laws are violated. We then have the opportunity to restore the system's order and balance.

2) As leaders, it's our primary duty to orchestrate the process by which our people are encouraged to raise their level of consciousness. This implies we act with complete integrity and coach our people to liberate themselves from their inhibitions.

3) Paradise Shapers are first and foremost transformational coaches. By posing moving questions, they let their employees zoom out. This ignites a process to remove the blockages they have unconsciously created and release the energy.

SHAPE YOUR PARADISE *ONLINE*

This chapter is further explored in week 4 of the online module "Paradise Shaper Leadership." You will practice a number of impactful coaching techniques that you can apply directly in your leadership. Soon you will enjoy the changes in the behavior of your team members as you change yours. Enjoy these sessions and enhance your coaching!

17

THE ART OF CO-CREATION

*"At first, I am giving energy to the creation, but later
the creation seems to be giving energy to me."*
—Robert Fritz

Give me some space.
Let me meaningfully connect with others.
Let us do something we are good at.
And, together, make a valuable
contribution to society.

Nature Shows the Way

The deepest desire of everyone across the world is the same—
to create. Or even better—to *co*-create. It has become a bit of a
buzzword in recent years. There is a burning desire for people to
bring something new into existence. We begin to see this goal is
so much easier if we involve others in the process. Once our ideas
coalesce, we can build on each other. We will manifest things we
couldn't realize just by ourselves.

We all get the high-level concept. But how do we do this in
practice? When do we access the Field to find the source of new
ideas? Isn't that an individual endeavor to begin with? What is the
right time to involve others? How do we unlock the full potential of
the organization?

It is startling how the answers to such contemporary questions are hidden in ancient wisdom. In the Taoist tradition, these mysteries were unraveled by looking at nature. Long before the common era, the Taoists in China studied the cyclicality of the processes that unfolded around them. They noticed how the seasons each exhibit a unique quality in an ever-flowing stream of creation.

➤ At the end of summer, nature is at its highest expression. Trees carry fruit of all tastes and colors. Fields are full of golden grain, corn, and sunflowers. It's the culmination of a full cycle of work, offering abundance for all to enjoy.

➤ Autumn marks the beginning of the energies of nature moving inward. The temperature is dropping. Leaves are changing color and eventually falling from the trees. All flora and fauna let go of their momentous presence and prepare for winter.

➤ In winter, all of nature has withdrawn to the core of its existence to survive the cold. Trees hide their energy in their roots. Animals hibernate in their burrows. Right here, when nature has come to an outward standstill, the very first inward step of a new cycle is born. The animal rejuvenates. The tree prepares for a new expansion with even more *grandeur*. Nothing is visible yet, but the work is done on the inside.

➤ Spring features the outburst of energy. Carried by the rise in temperature, nature is shouting, "Here I am! Look at me!" A palette of the most gorgeous colors demonstrates the joy of life. The blossom is the promise of the fruit. Birds breed their eggs, seeds begin to germinate, and trees start building their infrastructure of new leaves.

➤ In summer, the real work is done. Nature is at full production capacity. Trees and plants are effectively converting oxygen and water to fulfill their destiny—grow fruit, vegetables, grain, nuts, and other food. All of life's energies are in full force working toward their highest expression—the delivery of their produce.

The Spiral of Creation

Since human beings are an integral part of nature, the Taoists logically deduced that this rhythm also applies to us. In fact, nature's impact on us is even more profound. Do you recall the sine graph of a normal breathing pattern? If we look at such a graph from a distance, we can see all seasons pass with every breath we take. This fascinating truth is the basis of every creative process. Our exhalation is like autumn—we let go to make room. Empty lungs correspond to winter when all energies move inward. And then our inhalation brings about a new spring. This culuminates in summer when we're at the peak of our activity. The *breath of life* turns out to be the *breath of creation*.

Exhibit 23 translates the seasons into six practical work areas in natural succession. They form the Spiral of Creation.[76] If we proactively contribute to the specific work required in each phase, our creation is destined to manifest in its highest expression. This process brings together all our transformation work from the past 16 chapters into one natural flow. Let's explore the six work areas that are all equally important.

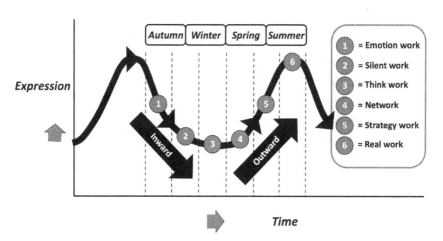

Exhibit 23—The Spiral of Creation.

—Emotion Work—

Any new creation starts in the figurative autumn. We need to fully accept the present situation even though we may not agree with what we see. This acceptance only feeds our desire to create something new. What is needed is "emotion work." We depart on our inward journey. As we have seen, emotions are a direct reflection of the quality of our thoughts. Negative emotions indicate that a pattern is triggered. By getting out of our head and into our body, we release our habitual thinking. We return to our factory settings, which imply we are joyful and open to life's adventures. As a leader, this is the state in which you want to operate. Imagine what happens when you coach your team members to do exactly the same. Transformational coaching (see Chapter 16) is also tremendously powerful for bringing systemic patterns to the surface and allowing them to dissolve. You unleash a magnificent potential if you facilitate your people to enter the Spiral of Creation with emotion work.

—Silent Work—

Just as in winter, it is time to conduct the "silent work." We need to come to an outward standstill in order to take the very first inward step of a new cycle. As human beings, we are destined to realize our true desires. And here's the secret. We do not conceive our desires. They come to us when we're fully receptive. Once we silence our busy minds and let our habitual thinking subside, the perfect idea will appear as a fresh new thought. It's not just a possibility. Our New Tomorrow (see Chapter 11) is a premonition. We have tuned in to the creative force of the Field. And it is strictly personal—each desire perfectly matches what we are capable of accomplishing. It is a promise that has no other option but to manifest as long as we follow the process. Being aware of and really pursuing our desires is the most fulfilling way to live.

Human beings have this awesome talent to create our future

through visualization. Canadian tennis player Bianca Andreescu won the U.S. Open in 2019 against the aforementioned legend Serena Williams. What was her secret? Daily meditation and visualization! For years she had gone through the scenario in her mind's eye. She would "see" in concrete detail how Serena would be her opponent, what majestic points she would score, and what winning would look and feel like. She even wrote herself a winner's check for her victory in the prestigious tournament. Her comment? "I guess these visualizations really, really work!"[77]

—Think Work—

The last part of our inward journey is called "think work." To ensure that our fresh, new ideas get a chance to materialize, we need to truly believe in them. We don't want to get trapped in any doubts our busy mind may concoct as to why we couldn't do it. Instead we would like our mind to become our matchmaker and find ways to make our desire come true.

We sometimes find it hard to move beyond this stage. What is actually blocking us? Remember, we used to live in the wild as hunter-gatherers. In millions of years, our minds developed a quality to always look for danger because doing so increased our chances of survival. Our heart and gut brains cannot distinguish between the actual world we register with our five senses and the imaginary world we visualize in our mind's eye. The "security check" that our mind performs on what we visualize does not really serve us. We therefore want to neutralize the doubts it raises, which prevent us from realizing our desires.

Now is the time to use our mind for what it does best—to be creative in developing all elements of our vision. We need to think it out! Draw it on a piece of paper. Keep a file on our computer and take every spare minute we have to work on our dream. We want to make it so concrete that we are absolutely convinced we will accomplish it. Our subconscious mind will accept it as an instruction. It will do anything to make it happen.

—Network—

Spring is in the air! We are now perfectly equipped to begin our outward journey. We accepted the present situation for what it is, found our true desires, visualized how they will manifest, and firmly believe they are bound to happen. It is time to reach out to others, which is to "network."

It is crucial to pick the right people. Our ideas are precious to us and the verdict of our early listeners may easily hurt our feelings— which would actually demonstrate we got carried away by our outside-in thinking! Expressing our desires to others tremendously accelerates their manifestation. Once people start sensing our devotion to realizing our dream, we become like a magnet. They want to know what we see that is not yet visible to them. If it touches them, they will want to join us. Even if it's not their cup of tea, they love to be instrumental in supporting our mission. Success knows many fathers. If we set the wheel in motion, people just love to help us spin it.

We don't need to know how to realize our dreams. The virtue of this phase is that we will meet the people who do. If we move our attention from our head to our body, we connect with our intuition— the creative potential. As soon as we admit we really don't know how to realize our dream and dare to ask for help, miracles will happen. We are bound to tap into the Field. Our abiding faith in the future will guide us to unexpected introductions and sources of information. If we look back, we will clearly see how exactly the right person crossed our path at exactly the right time. This is called synchronicity, and it is anything but coincidental.

—Strategy Work—

We know what we desire. We are convinced we will get there. We have involved others and been given a picture of the route to be walked. The moment is there to turn possibilities into action. We need to get down to "strategy work." It's exciting to really think things through and to challenge the limits of what seems possible. Yet we need to be realistic. This is about planning our chain of activities that will take us to our future ambition. A solid plan focuses our actions on the right things at the right time.

If there is one thing that Control-Based Leadership has strongly developed, it is planning. But let's not overdo it. A smile comes to my face when I think of the countless management courses I have attended and the business literature I have read. They all preached an astoundingly shortsighted perspective on the process of creation— Plan-Do-Check-Act. As if people get inspired by a plan and correcting their course if they fail to meet their deadlines. A case in point is the great question one of my friends once asked, "Would the civil rights movement in the sixties have been so forceful if Martin Luther King would have proclaimed, 'I have a plan!' instead of 'I have a dream!'?"

Planning is extremely useful to organize work and turn our desires into action. Yet it's a huge mistake to think that planning is effective in and of itself to inspire people to do their job. Our desire is the master, our plan is the servant. Therefore, it is crucial that our inner work of emotion, silence, and thinking, as well as our external networking, precede our strategy work. Intrinsically motivated people won't need a plan to get active. But they will embrace a plan as part of a co-created framework that helps them to realize their desire.

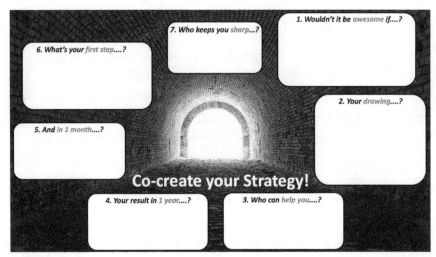

Exhibit 24—Practical planning.[78]

Exhibit 24 is a seven-step self-explanatory process I often use to guide people in converting their intrinsic desire to short term planning of activities. For teams, I have it printed poster size so we can work on it in subteams. Ultimately, we merge the results in a plenary session. It fosters full alignment on the planning. A reference is set for a monthly cadence. Of course, these activities can be further detailed using spreadsheets and charts. The power of this chart is in the process—not imposed, but bottom up. It connects the shared mission and vision with the daily work.

Once the planning is in place, we have arrived at a glorious moment—the "go or no go" decision. Do we really have the guts to pursue our dream? We tend to think that this requires a tremendous commitment on our part. We make lists showing the pros and cons of the investment in time, effort, and money. Decisions become a lot easier when we learn how to use our multiple brains effectively. If our desire originates from the depth of our being, our gut brain will instantly tell us what is right to do. Consulting our head brain to assess the consequences of either scenario would only blur the picture.

—Real Work—

It's summertime, congratulations! We have successfully co-created our path. Our preparations have been completed and all scaffolding has been erected. We're ready for the "real work"—the manifestation of our mission. Summer is the time for most of us to take a break and enjoy the weather. Yet all of nature is performing at its peak. You may be surprised this is only one of the six phases. The actual time consumption can take a considerably larger share in the entire process. As we've defined our standards, all we have to do is to adhere to them to deliver our repetitive work with a built-in quality. Our other, more unique work requires that we maintain a high level of consciousness to perform it as best we can.

One thing we can be sure of—we will face some challenges to complete our voyage. Our habitual thoughts will catch us off guard and tempt us to throw in the towel. These setbacks are merely invitations to reconnect with our initial desire. We fully commit ourselves to delivering on the promise. For when we complete the expedition, there is no greater fulfillment than seeing our dreams come true.

Changing the Game

How was the Spiral of Creation applied at the Customer Fulfillment Center? Of course, we embedded its natural flow into the leadership intervention program. It completely changed the game. The team leads learned to create a caring culture within a shared framework. Taking an inside-out perspective boosted their resilience. They took a proactive stance and carried out their role as process facilitators. They practiced deep listening and held impactful coaching conversations. They learned how to reflect on situations they encountered with their fellow team leads. All was geared to their fast-track growth as "self-determination shamans"—boosting the autonomy, relatedness, and competence of their teams. In only nine months, the twelve teams bent the curve on all three metrics (see exhibit 25):

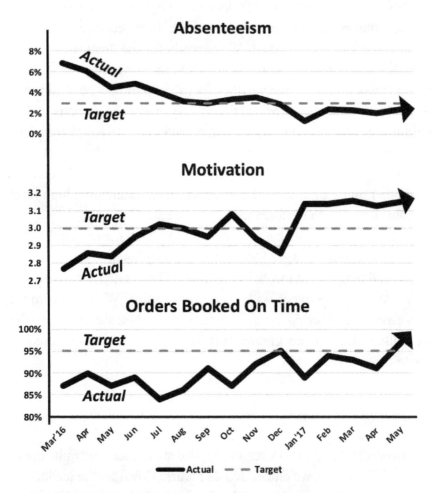

Exhibit 25—Impact of the leadership transformation program.

➢ Absenteeism dropped to a level between 3 and 4 percent in six months' time and structurally oscillated between 2 and 2.5 percent after nine months.

➢ Motivation levels were above target after four months, dropping again at year's end—peak season for order booking. After nine months they remained stable well above target.

> ➤ Since we discontinued our intense focus on the business metric—orders booked within forty-eight hours—performance initially deteriorated. Then the teams' creativity kicked in, with results gradually improving at a "two steps forward, one step back" pace. After nine months the organization hit the target of 95 percent for the first time in history. The teams continued to improve to structurally deliver on this metric.

The determination, passion, and performance of the teams were the ultimate proof. Indeed, the team leads held the key to unlocking the organisation's potential. They gained confidence in engaging their people. And collectively, they found answers to the challenges that once seemed unsolvable.

Celebrate Good Times

I felt it was time to celebrate the successful turnaround. I wanted to invite all employees to a hotel for an uplifting afternoon and evening program with the intention to honor our people. I planned to book some inspiring speakers from the healthcare industry. We would share our plans for the year and host an interactive game. In the evening there would be a walking dinner with food in different themes. And we'd dance to the beat of a DJ.

I talked about this plan with a few order-desk officers at the coffee machine. The downright negative response by a few of them completely derailed my plans.

"Please don't make us sit all afternoon and listen to some egghead" and "I don't like to spend my free Thursday evening at a company party" were some of the comments I picked up. I must admit that I felt somewhat agitated by (what I saw as) their ungrateful attitude. Then I realized I was still susceptible to outside-in thinking.

I ruminated for a few days. One evening, while playing tennis, a question suddenly popped into my head. Was I serious about involving our employees in making decisions? Then why was I organizing an event *for* them? It was obvious what my next move should be. I invited a small group of nine order-desk officers for a brainstorming session. This group comprised both a few critics and their colleagues who had voluntarily offered support.

Nine pairs of eyes were staring at me as I entered the room. They all worked in different functional teams. So they wondered why I had gathered this gang. "I'd like to make you an offer," I said, breaking the ice right after our check-in. "As you know, I'd like to organize an event to thank our employees and kick off the new year. Each one of you has expressed explicit ideas about what such an event should look like. Here's my proposal. Why don't the nine of you take the lead in organizing this event? *You* become our change agents. Develop a few scenarios. Engage the organization to find the preferred setup."

I went on to frame the game. "You'll have a free hand as long as two conditions are met. Firstly, our employees regard this event as recognition. And second, there will be a time slot where I can share our strategy. I am available as a sparring partner on a weekly basis. And last but not least, you own the full twenty-grand budget that we have reserved for this activity."

As my words permeated the room, my colleagues looked at each other to determine the appropriate response. Then Lynne took the lead. "So we can decide on a completely different event?" she asked.

"Certainly, do what excites *you*, not what I had in mind," I clarified.

"What if we don't need all that money, and plan a more down-to-earth version?" Kenny inquired.

"Well, if it meets the two criteria, I'm fine with it. Feel free to organize another activity later in the year," I suggested.

I saw Dragana's eyes light up. She arranged her thoughts and said, "That would be brilliant! With twenty-three different nationalities in the Customer Fulfillment Center, we can really use a cross-cultural training. And how about equipment demos? Some officers book orders for systems they've never seen."

The iEngage Team

The team took up the gauntlet with unexpected energy. The first thing they did was choose a name for themselves—the iEngage team. They even designed their own logo:

大Engage

The iEngage team immediately reached out to the organization. They collected inputs and worked out a rough outline of the event. At our third meeting, the team presented a detailed spreadsheet. It listed four events they would organize this year. And it provided a breakdown of the budget I had allocated. I was impressed with their work and encouraged the team to organize the recognition event first. It was already March when the big day arrived.

It was a very different event than I had imagined. At five minutes' walking distance from the office, we were expected at a "party farm" at noon sharp. There were no seats, so everyone was standing. I was given fifteen minutes to present our outlook for the year. Then they invited a research fellow to give an inspiring glimpse into the innovation kitchen of the company. Next on the program was an interactive "Kahoot-quiz," which we played using our mobile phones. As the energy rose, the official program ended on a high note—the Employee of the Year award ceremony.

The iEngage team had consulted me on the categories of favorable behaviors they wanted to acknowledge. We agreed to link them to the four anchors that the order-desk teams had defined to operationalize our mission:

> ➤ Reliability—we do what we promise
> ➤ Agility—we innovate the value chain
> ➤ Collaboration—we work as one
> ➤ Productivity—we operate by standards

Two weeks prior to the event, all employees were invited to nominate colleagues who embodied one of the anchors. Digital elections among these candidates were held the week before the event. The power of these awards could not be overestimated—they were *for* the employees, *by* the employees. And what an impact they had! Everyone was cheering for the winners, who personified the future organization.

A sandwich and salad buffet opened at 1 o'clock. We all mingled to socialize and took the opportunity to congratulate the award winners. At 2, the program finished, and everyone returned to the office, all in a good mood to resume what they like best—the work itself.

A New Awakening

"Thank you so much for a stellar event. I never thought an extended lunch session in just two hours could be so impactful!" I congratulated the team.

The iEngage team members were glowing with energy.

"You know what?" Dragana asked, challenging me with a mysterious look, "We haven't even spent 10 percent of our overall budget."

"That's outstanding, so what's next?" I responded, curious to know.

Dragana was jumping for joy. "I'm so excited!" she said. "The cross-culture training will be next month. And remember I mentioned the need for equipment demos?"

I sure did.

"It turns out the research department works with our systems in the building next door. They're happy to give us a free tour!"

I left the party farm with a contented smile on my face. It was the perfect moment for a little detour. I exited the High-Tech Campus and crossed a small bridge to the adjacent park. After about half a mile I noticed a bench and took a seat. I placed my feet flat on the ground and exhaled deeply as I reconnected with my three brains.

It had been a year. Yes, we had turned around the organization. We co-created a framework that allowed our people to thrive. Every day, they made their own decisions. They used their talents to passionately carry out their newly found mission. Their unity in diversity entirely changed their game.

But something else happened along the way. I transformed myself. Or rather, I had learned to tune in to the Field to navigate my leadership. As I shifted my awareness from my head to my heart, I began to sense a new awakening. At first it was very subtle, but as I stayed with it, it became almost palpable. I yearned to liberate the motivation of the next generation. To guide talented teams in their discovery of the inside-out reality of our existence. To unleash their tremendous power as they unveil the secret that sets them free. And together, outshine the gremlins of our time.

I let my attention sink further to my stomach. I clearly felt some discomfort.

Will I really have the guts to do this? Leave the company I love? Embark on an exhilarating adventure of entrepreneurship?

I smiled as I recognized the voice of the insecure child in me speaking. I might have been scared, but it wasn't about me. This was an opportunity to move beyond my psychology. I took another deep breath, exhaled through the belly and asked myself a moving question.

Imagine you're free from any impediment. What would you do?

And then I suddenly saw her. A butterfly landed on an early daffodil just six feet in front of me. Or rather, a stunning hummingbird moth. She rolled out her long tongue and reached for the nectar inside the flower.

A new spring had arrived! The dawn of the Transformation Age.

TOP THREE TAKEAWAYS

1) The Spiral of Creation mirrors the process by which nature manifests all creation. In each of the six phases, we are invited to engage in the specific work required. If we do so proactively, our mission is destined to manifest in its highest expression.

2) Business literature often suggests that the process of creation can be reduced to four steps—Plan-Do-Check-Act. It's only part of the story. We first have inner work to do— emotion, silence, and think work. Only then will we know our common desire. It will inspire our people to embrace the strategy and real work.

3) When our creation fully manifests, we reap the fruit of our hard work. We tap directly from life's flow of energy. It fills us with the magic of the moment. Even a recognition event is infinitely more effective when our people organize it themselves.

SHAPE YOUR PARADISE *ONLINE*

How do you implement the Spiral of Creation in a practical way? What kind of events can you organize to lead your team full circle from emotion work to celebrating success? Week 5 of the online module "Paradise Shaper Leadership" guides you through this dynamic process step by step. Complete your inside-out transformation by taking your team along!

ACKNOWLEDGMENTS

*"No man ever steps in the same river twice, for it's
not the same river and he's not the same man."*
—Heraclitus

Writing a book is, in a sense, an impossible endeavor. I try to grab the elusive. To express phenomena that are of a transient nature. That's why a river is such a telling metaphor for life. As fleeting as water, life treats us on a continuous stream of experiences. Everything is constantly moving from potentiality to temporary realization. And once things materialize, they are bound to evaporate into oblivion again.

It is not about you. It's about your journey. There's nothing to hold on to. You will never know the river by viewing it from its shore. The river is patient. It invites us to embark on an adventure. Resistance is pointless. We better learn to build our boat. To become skilled at navigating. One day we'll be brave enough to go upstream to discover its source. From there we just need to stay in the flow. We will be amazed where the river will take us.

This book is a rendition of my boat trip. When I leave for my next expedition, I will certainly gain new insights. Fresh experiences transcend our current perspective and explore new frontiers. And so we evolve! If it contributed even the tiniest bit to your growth in consciousness, this book has already proven its worth.

I would like to extend a first word of gratitude to my loving parents. To my father Johan, who showed me what caring for people truly means. To my mother Margré who taught me at a young age that challenges are merely life's invitations to become more resourceful. Your vitality, harmony and flexibility still inspire me every day.

I feel blessed by the magnificent teachers who masterfully and unselfishly share their wisdom. I would especially like to mention Integral Theory philosopher Ken Wilber, Three Principles supercoach Michael Neill, Isha Foundation yogi Sadhguru, and Tao sifu Reinoud Eleveld. I hope I have done a decent job translating your insights into the leadership requirements of the Transformation Age.

I want to acknowledge all amazing colleagues and clients I have worked with during my twenty-five-year career. All the teams I led, the leaders I worked for, and the partners in crime. Thank you for letting me experiment with leadership. Your openness and feedback encouraged me to develop the Paradise Shaper method. As such, this book is the fruit of our co-creation.

A huge thank you to the wonderful folks at Balboa Press. They gave me the right feedback at the right time. Without realizing it, they instilled a crucial lesson that the creation of this book follows its own spiral.

I am grateful to Eric de Haan for the support in the early stages of this book project. Eric helped me structure my work. This framework allowed my energy to flow in a focused direction. Liesbeth Heenk proved invaluable in the final phase. She made sure the book was corrected for style, grammar, and spelling.

A special word of thanks goes to Willem van Rhenen. Our conversations about self-determination brought me back to academia. I found it highly inspiring to seek ways to bridge the gaps between science, ancient wisdom and business.

I also thoroughly enjoyed my business mentoring sessions with Lianne Ebbinkhuijsen. Thank you, Lianne, for encouraging my perspective that wise new leadership is all about a transformation in consciousness.

I feel carried by a strong network of friends. They played a much bigger role in the writing of this book than they will realize. I would especially like to mention two dear buddies. First, motivation expert Lars van Tuin. Who would have thought our leadership intervention program would be this impactful? It is the greatest honor that you have asked me to play a ceremonial role in your official PhD defense. Then, my business partner Walter van Kuijen. For the past sixteen years you have been a role model to me of what it means to be a Paradise Shaper. I feel blessed by your guidance and friendship.

This book aims to contribute to an improved workplace for both employees and leaders. We owe it to the next generation to establish optimal conditions for them to thrive. Roger, Donna, Joshua and Benjamin—thank you for personifying the impeccable potential of the next generation. The grace of fatherhood fills me every minute I spend with you.

And finally, to Dorine—twenty-seven years ago I had the guts to ask you out for a romantic dinner. Our conversation has only grown richer since that wonderful evening. I thoroughly enjoy your versatile coaching, which helps me convert my wild ideas into pragmatic concepts. This book is dedicated to you. Thank you for being the love of my life.

May I look into your eyes
and recognize your divine nature.
May we drop our limiting beliefs
and let our hearts merge.

Namasté,
Paul

ENDNOTES

Introduction

1   Simon Sinek on Millennials in the Workplace. Interview with Tom Bilyeu, episode of Inside Request on YouTube.
2   Transamerica Center for Health Studies, *Millennial Survey: Young Adults' Healthcare Reality*, 2016. This self-administered online survey was held among 1,171 U.S. millennial adults.

—Prelude—

Chapter 1

3   David Enard, et al., "Viruses are a dominant driver of protein adaptation in mammals," eLife, 2016, e12469.
4   James Lovelock, *Gaia: A New Look at Life on Earth*, (Oxford, UK: Oxford University Press, 1979). Lovelock named his hypothesis after the goddess in Greek mythology who personifies Earth.

Chapter 2

5   Lance H. Gunderson and C. S. Holding, *Panarchy: Understanding Transformations in Human and Natural Systems*, (Washington, DC: Island Press, 2002). Gunderson and Holling coined the term "adaptive cycle" for the insightful framework. Their magnificent work applies not only to the field of biology. It laid an important foundation for studying how systems formed by complex networks of people really operate.
6   Adapted from *Panarchy* edited by Lance H. Gunderson and C. S. Holding, Figure 2-1, page 34. Copyright © 2002 Island Press. Reproduced by permission of Island Press, Washington, DC.

7   Robb Smith, *The Great Release*, (e-book, integrallife.com, 2017). Smith builds on the work of Giovanni Arrighi, a former professor of sociology at Johns Hopkins University. Arrighi studied the economic cycles in the past eight hundred years of capitalist history.

8   Adapted from *The Great Release* by Robb Smith, page 40. Reproduced by permission of the author.

9   Ingo Piepers, *2020—WARning. Social Integration and Expansion in Anarchistic Systems: How Connectivity and Our Urge to Survive Determine and Shape the War Dynamics and Development of the System*, (Amsterdam, The Netherlands: IP-Publications, 2017). The book can be downloaded for free at social4cast.org.

—Part I—

10 Nuernberger wrote an enlightening book in which he translated yoga wisdom and exercises into a western setting. Phil Nuernberger, *Strong and Fearless: The Quest for Personal Power*, (Saint Paul, MN: Yes International Publishers, 1996).

Chapter 3

11 Grant Soosalu and Marvin Oka, *mBraining: Using Your Multiple Brains to Do Cool Stuff*, (mBIT International Pty Ltd, 2012). Soosalu and Oka combined neuroscientific and behavioral research, the results of which they describe in this fascinating book. When our three brains are fully aligned, each operates in its optimized state. Soosalu and Oka call this state the "highest expression." It is courage for the gut brain, compassion for the heart brain, and creativity for the head brain.

12 HeartMath Institute, *Science of the Heart*, (e-book, heartmath.org). In the past three decades this nonprofit institute has made tremendous contributions in bridging science and ancient wisdom.

13 Image by Gerd Altmann from Pixabay.

14 Franziska Hoche et al., "The cerebellar cognitive affective/Schmahmann syndrome scale," Brain—*A Journal of Neurology* 141 (2018): 248–270.

15 Mikkel Hofstee, *Primal Human 2.0: How Your Ancestral Genes Affect Your Behavior Today*, (Hilversum, The Netherlands: Uitgeverij Water, 2019). In this captivating book, Hofstee points out how most of our hormonal responses and behavior can be traced back to our evolutionary background as primeval humans.

16 Yuval Noah Harari, *Sapiens: A Brief History of Humankind*, (London, UK: Penguin Random House UK, 2011). This *magnum opus* provides a fascinating

overview of the evolutionary journey of humanoids. From the bottom of the food chain to global rule, Homo sapiens' cerebral development enabled a staggering progression.

Chapter 4

17 The measure of frequency is hertz (Hz), which indicates the number of vibrations per second.

18 Doc Childre and Howard Martin with Donna Beech, *The HearthMath Solution: The Institute of HearthMath's Revolutionary Program for Engaging the Power of the Hearth's Intelligence*, (New York, NY: HarperCollins Publishers, 1999). HeartMath provides research-based evidence for powerful breathing and meditation techniques that enhance health and performance.

19 Rollin McCraty et al., "The Global Coherence Initiative: Creating a Coherent Planetary Standing Wave," *Global Advances in Health and Medicine* 1, no. 1 (2012): 64–77. The Global Coherence Initiative (GCI) conducts scientific research into the Earth and sun's magnetic fields and the connection with human and animal life. The GCI has established magnetometers in different locations across the globe to observe changes in the Earth's magnetic field. The effects of emotions caused by major global events, as well as their relationship to solar storms, are continuously monitored.

Chapter 5

20 Christopher S. Kilham, *The Five Tibetans: Five Dynamic Exercises for Health, Energy, and Personal Power*, (Rochester, VT: Healing Arts Press, 2011). Kilham provides an in-depth overview of the wide range of benefits associated with each of the Five Tibetan Rites.

Chapter 6

21 Bert W. Herring, M.D., *The Fast-5 Diet and the Fast-5 Lifestyle: A Little Book about Making Big Mistakes*, (e-book, bertherring.com, 2006).

22 Wim Hof and Koen de Jong, *The Way of the Iceman: How the Wim Hof Method Creates Radiant, Longterm Health Using the Science and Secrets of Breath Control, Cold-Training and Commitment*, (Dragon Door Publications, 2017). This book offers fascinating insights into Hof's journey, supported by academic research data.

Chapter 7

23 Ronald C. Kessler, et al., "Insomnia and the Performance of US Workers: Results from the America Insomnia Survey," SLEEP 34, no. 9 (2011): 1161–71. A national sample of more than seven thousand employed health-plan subscribers was included in this insomnia survey.

24 Maurice M. Ohayon, "Epidemiological Overview of Sleep Disorders in the General Population," *Sleep Medicine Research* 2, no. 1 (2011): 1–9.

25 William van der Klaauw, *Perfect Slapen in 7 Stappen*, (e-book, slaapwijzer. net, 2015), in Dutch.

26 Nick Littlehales, *Sleep: The Myth of 8 Hours, the Power of Naps, and the New Plan to Recharge Your Body and Mind*, (Penguin Random House UK, 2016). Littlehales provides practical tips on how to structure your day in accordance with the circadian rhythm.

—Part II—

27 I'm referring to Bob Dylan's timeless song (1963) about the civil rights protest. It also heralded a shift in perspective.

28 Gallup Report, *State of the Global Workplace*, (New York, NY: Gallup Press, 2017). The World Poll covers the labor market situation and workplace conditions in 155 countries.

Chapter 8

29 For example, Stephen R. Covey, *The 7 Habits of Highly Effective People: Powerful Lessons in Personal Change*, (London, UK: Simon & Schuster, 1989) and Anthony Robbins, *Awaken The Giant Within: How to Take Immediate Control of Your Mental, Emotional, Physical and Financial Destiny!*, (London, UK: Simon & Schuster, 1991).

30 "Inner Engineering" is the flagship program of Isha Yoga foundation. Isha was founded by Indian mystic Sadhguru. He is a master in imparting authentic yogic science to millions of people.

31 I highly recommend Michael Neill's *The Inside Out Revolution: The Only Thing You Need to Know to Change Your Life Forever*, (Carlsbad, CA: Hay House, 2013) and *The Space Within: Finding Your Way Back Home*, (Carlsbad, CA: Hay House, 2016). Neill explains esoteric wisdom in powerful contemporary metaphors.

32 C. Otto Scharmer and Katrin Kaufer, *Leading from the Emerging Future: From Ego-System to Eco-System Economies*, (Oakland, CA: Berrett-Koehler Publishers, 2013).

Chapter 9

33 Bruce H. Lipton and Steve Bhaerman, *Spontaneous Evolutions: Our Positive Future (and a Way to Get There from Here)*, (Carlsbad, CA: Hay House, 2009). A magnificent book that combines the scientific evidence from the field of biology with deep insights into the power of our mind.

34 Lisette Schuitemaker, *The Childhood Conclusions Fix: Turning Negative Self-Talk Around* (Kaminn Media, 2017). Schuitemaker coined the term "childhood conclusions" as a gentler term for Reich's "character defense structures." Her book is a practical guide to gaining a better understanding of our ongoing inner dialogues and the steps we can take to discover the innate treasures behind them. On her website, lisetteschuitemaker.com, you can test your own childhood conclusions!

35 Alan S. Cowen and Dacher Keltner, "Self-Report Captures 27 Distinct Categories of Emotion Bridged by Continuous Gradients," *Proceedings of the National Academy of Sciences*, September 5, 2017, E7900–E7909.

36 Philip A. Kragel and Kevin S. LaBar, "Multivariate Neural Biomarkers of Emotional States Are Categorically Distinct," *Social Cognitive and Affective Neuroscience* 10 (2015): 1437–48.

Chapter 10

37 Ken Wilber, *A Brief History of Everything*, (Boulder, CO: Shambhala Publications, 1996). Wilber has been referred to as "the Einstein of consciousness." His Integral Theory encompasses both Eastern esoteric wisdom and Western psychological models. It aims to integrate the polarities of existence into a natural development path. Every person holds a colorful artist's palette displaying different "lines of development," such as cognitive, emotional, moral, or values. Each of these lines progresses through the stages separately. Consequently, organizations (and society as a whole) are a kaleidoscope of mixed levels of consciousness.

38 Frederic Laloux, *Reinventing Organizations: A Guide to Creating Organizations Inspired by the Next Stage of Human Consciousness*, (Brussels, Belgium: Nelson Parker, 2014). Frederic Laloux provides a summary overview

of these stages. I merely present the highlights. More about his impressive research later in this chapter.

39   Robert Kegan calls it the "impulsive order." Kegan is a Harvard professor emeritus and an authority in the field of human development. Robert Kegan, *In Over Our Heads: The Mental Demands of Modern Life*, (Boston, MA: Harvard University Press, 1994).

40   Kegan aptly labels it the "imperial order."

41   In Kegan's work this is referred to as the "interpersonal order."

42   Kegan calls this stage the "institutional order," as people become the authors of their own standards.

43   Kegan integrates the results of a large number of studies to report a percentage range of adults functioning at each of the developmental stages (that he calls "orders"). Moreover, in his introduction to Laloux' book, Wilber also gives an indication of the percentage of the Western population at each stage. As can be expected, these percentages are (about 10 points) higher for Orange and Green as compared to the global picture.

44   Kegan refers to this stage as the "interindividual order."

45   Laloux, *Reinventing Organizations*. This book really is a pioneering masterpiece. Even though the twelve organizations Laloux studied don't know each other, they share three common breakthroughs. These are self-management, wholeness, and evolutionary purpose.
       ➤   Self-management implies all work is organized by peer relationships.
       ➤   Wholeness means people are invited to reclaim their emotional and intuitive parts.
       ➤   Evolutionary purpose entails the organization has a sense of direction of its own.

Chapter 11

46   Image by https://imgbin.com.

47   Terahertz = 10^{12} Hz or one trillion (1,000,000,000,000) vibrations per second.

48   Eckhart Tolle, *The Power of NOW: A Guide to Spiritual Enlightenment*, (Novato, CA: New World Library, 1999). This fascinating mind shift is from the introduction to his world-renowned book.

49   Joe Dispenza, *Breaking the Habit of Being Yourself: How to Lose Your Mind and Create a New One*, (Carlsbad, CA: Hay House, 2012). Dispenza has taught thousands of people how to overcome their habitual thinking and create "a new mind" by meditation. He measured the coherence of their brain while they were in deep states of meditation and found phenomenal

results. Participants had completely changed their energy as they elevated their thoughts and emotions to the "quantum state."

Chapter 12

50 Authentic Kabbalah is taught by the Bnei Baruch Education & Research Institute. The institute was established by Michael Laitman in 1991. It has become an international movement to bring about the unity of all people.

51 For inspiration, I highly recommend Elizabeth Gilbert's TED Talk called "Your Elusive Creative Genius."

52 Lynne McTaggart's comprehensive treatise, *The Field*, extensively describes the breathtaking research conducted across the globe. Lynne McTaggart, *The Field: The Quest for the Secret Force of the Universe*, (New York, NY: HarperCollins Publishers, 2008).

53 Systems theorist Ervin Laszlo calls it the Akashic Field. The Sanskrit concept of Akasha represents the field of potential in which all possible manifestations already exist. It's the womb that creates our physical world, and to which everything eventually returns. Ervin Laszlo, *Science and the Akashic Field: In Integral Theory of Everything*, (Rochester, VT: Inner Traditions, 2007).

54 David Bohm, *Wholeness and the Implicate Order*, (New York, NY: Routledge, 1980).

55 In 2016, theoretical physicist Erik Verlinde published a cutting-edge article on a major unresolved question in physics—what explains the 96 percent missing energy, also called "dark energy," which causes the universe to expand at an accelerated pace? One would expect the gravitational pull between solar systems to slow down this expansion. Verlinde theorized that we should look at gravitation very differently. It's an emergent force, the result of a deeper layer that's not of a physical nature. That layer he also calls "information." It is the Mind of the universe, the energy field that shapes our physical reality. Erik Verlinde, "Emergent Gravity and the Dark Universe," *SciPost Physics* 2, number 16 (2017): 1–41.

56 Laszlo, *Science and the Akashic Field*.

57 Wilber, *A Brief History of Everything*.

58 Image by Clker-Free-Vector-Images from Pixabay.

—Part III—

Chapter 13

59 Effective listening is at the heart of Covey's fifth habit: "Seek first to understand, then to be understood." Stephen R. Covey, *The 7 Habits of Highly Effective People: Powerful Lessons in Personal Change*, (London, UK: Simon & Schuster, 1989). Covey distinguishes five levels of listening in order of increasing effectiveness—from "ignoring" all the way to "empathic listening." In his eye-opening Theory U, Otto Scharmer describes the process of profound innovation and change. C. Otto Scharmer, *Theory U: Core Principles and Applications*, (Oakland, CA: Berrett-Koehler Publishers, 2009). Scharmer refers to empathic listening as the third of four levels of listening. He adds a next level, called "generative" listening. I overlaid both scales of Covey and Scharmer and added two additional levels—absent (level one) and transcendent (level eight) listening.

Chapter 14

60 Marcus Buckingham and Curt Coffman, *First, Break all the Rules: What the World's Greatest Managers Do Differently*, (New York, NY: Simon & Schuster, 1999). This brilliant book shares an important insight based on Gallup data from over 105,000 employees, "We had discovered that the manager—not pay, benefits, perks, or a charismatic corporate leader—was the critical player in building a strong workplace. The manager was the key."

61 Van Rhenen is professor of Engagement & Productivity at Nyenrode Business University in the Netherlands. Van Rhenen translates theoretical concepts into a pragmatic approach to reduce stress and increase engagement in organizations.

62 Richard M. Ryan and Edward L. Deci, *Self-Determination Theory: Basic Psychological Needs in Motivation, Development, and Wellness*, (New York, NY: Guildford Press, 2017). This comprehensive volume is an overview of the magnificent work they, and other authors, have dedicated to exploring this field of research.

63 We put together a list of around one hundred validated questions. It would take the order-desk employees about fifteen minutes to complete this survey in Likert scale format, a five-point range from *"I strongly disagree"* to *"I strongly agree."*

64 Wilmar B. Schaufeli, "Engaging Leadership in the Job Demands-Resources Model," *Career Development International* 20, no. 5 (2015): 446–63. Schaufeli is a professor emeritus at Utrecht University (Netherlands) and an

authority in engaging leadership. Lars van Tuin's dissertation saw the light under Schaufeli's and van Rhenen's guidance.

65 Lars van Tuin has published a series of academic articles based on the research he conducted in my organization. The first article explains the leadership intervention program. Van Tuin concludes the study "showed that a leadership development program focusing on engaging leadership and psychological well-being led to significant positive business results and lower absenteeism." Lars van Tuin, Wilmar B. Shaufeli, Willem van Rhenen, and Rebecca M. Kuiper, "Business Results and Well-Being: An Engaging Leadership Intervention Study," *International Journal of Environmental Research and Public Health* 17, no. 12 (2000): 4515, http://doi.org/10.3390/ijerph17124515.

66 Marylène Gagné et al., "The Multidimensional Work Motivation Scale— Validation Evidence in Seven Languages and Nine Countries," *European Journal of Work and Organizational Psychology* 24, no. 2 (2015): 178–96. This is a multidimensional scale that was tested in seven languages across nine countries.

67 Anja Van den Broeck et al., "Unraveling the Importance of the Quantity and the Quality of Workers' Motivation for Well-Being—A Person-Centered Perspective," *Journal of Vocational Behavior* 82, no. 1 (2013): 6978.

68 Ilona van Beek et al., "For Fun, Love or Money—What Drives Workaholic, Engaged and Burnt-Out Employees at Work?" *Applied Psychology* 61, no. 1, (2011): 30–55.

69 In his second academic article, Van Tuin demonstrates how needs satisfaction plays a crucial role in employee motivation. He describes the implications for leadership as follows: "A leader who recognizes the essential aspect of autonomy may very well promote a person's freedom and engagement while simultaneously offering a clear work context through, for example, presenting a compelling vision an employee can identify with and support or, more fundamentally, is invited to co-create." Lars van Tuin, Wilmar B. Schaufeli, and Willem van Rhenen, "The Satisfaction and Frustration of Basic Psychological Needs in Engaging Leadership, *Journal of Leadership Studies* 14, no. 2) (2020): 6–23, http://doi.org/10.1002/jls.21695.

Chapter 15

70 Van Tuin's third article addressed the fact that the relationship between a corporate purpose and employee engagement has hardly been studied empirically. The survey conducted at my organization did include questions to assess this connection: "The results highlight that employees who report

being inspired by their organization's higher purpose assert they are positively contributing to its realization. They also state they are striving to make the world a better place and are more engaged than others for whom the corporate purpose is less inspirational." Lars van Tuin, Wilmar B. Schaufeli, W.B., Anja Van den Broeck, and Willem van Rhenen, "A Corporate Purpose as an Antecedent to Employee Motivation and Work Engagement," Frontiers in Psychology, 11 (2020): 393, http://doi.org/10.3389/fpsyg.2020.572343.

71 The powerful impact of Lean Thinking on a company's performance has been recorded by Womack and Jones. They offer a complete menu of all the elements involved, illustrated by a wealth of real business examples. James P. Womack and Daniel T. Jones, *Lean Thinking: Banish Waste and Create Wealth in Your Corporation*, (London, UK: Simon & Schuster, 2003).

Chapter 16

72 I loved this analogy used by systemic trainer Peter Dalmeijer. Peter is a great music lover and a bass guitarist. He has written several thought-provoking books (in Dutch) on systemic coaching and NLP, including on the metaphorical theme of "sensitive strings."

73 Jan Jacob Stam, *Wings for Change: Systemic Organizational Development*, (Het Noorderlicht, 2016). Stam provides a deep insight into the systemic way of looking at organizational dynamics. There are lots of examples from all over the world.

74 Dan Booth Cohen, "'Family Constellations'—An Innovative Systemic Phenomenological Group Process from Germany," *Family Journal* 14, no. 3 (2006): 226–33.

75 Siets Bakker coined the term "moving questions" in her book with the same title. It's a practical guide of how systemic work can be applied to a one-on-one coaching relationship. Siets Bakker, *Moving Questions: How to Let Questions Work for You*, (Independently Published, 2019).

Chapter 17

76 The originator of the Spiral of Creation is Marinus Knoope. He defined these six work areas while exploring the natural flow in the creative process. Marinus Knoope, *De Creatie Spiraal*, (Nijmegen, the Netherlands: KIC, 1998), in Dutch.

77 Christopher Clarey, "Bianca Andreescu wins the U.S. Open, Defeating Serena Williams," *New York Times*, September 7, 2019.

78 Image by Peter H from Pixabay.

INDEX OF TRANSFORMATION
EXERCISES

ABOUT THE AUTHOR

Paul Smilde holds master's degrees in business economics and law. He studied in Oregon, Spain and the Netherlands, where he lives with his wife and four children. His postgraduate training increasingly focused on an in-depth understanding of ancient wisdom traditions and our human design.

In his twenty-five-year business career, Paul has built a strong reputation as a business innovator. He has led global organizations spanning six continents through existential transformations. His unique approach to leadership is a game changer—customer satisfaction and business growth are strongly boosted while costs are significantly reduced.

Paul has captured the secret to his success in the Paradise Shaper method. He founded Paradise Shaper Academy to guide leaders and their teams to thrive from the inside-out. As wise new leaders, they transform their existing fear-based systems into sparkling communities of trust. And consequently, they dramatically improve their results.

Paul's international keynote speeches are praised for igniting the spark of transformation in any audience. His coaching sessions, courses, expeditions and boot camps pave the way for leaders and their teams alike. They experience the miracle of delivering stellar results, while enjoying their work to the fullest.

CPSIA information can be obtained
at www.ICGtesting.com
Printed in the USA
LVHW090606040521
686437LV00001B/5